A BRIEF GUIDE
TO WRITING
FROM READINGS

Seventh Edition

A Brief Guide to Writing from Readings

Stephen Wilhoit
The University of Dayton

PEARSON

Boston   Columbus   Hoboken   Indianapolis   New York   San Francisco
Amsterdam   Cape Town   Dubai   London   Madrid   Milan   Munich   Paris   Montréal   Toronto
Delhi   Mexico City   São Paulo   Sydney   Hong Kong   Seoul   Singapore   Taipei   Tokyo

Senior Acquisitions Editor: Brad Potthoff
Program Manager: Eric Jorgensen
Product Marketer: Ali Arnold
Field Marketer: Mark Robinson
Executive Digital Producer: Stefanie Snajder
Content Specialist: Erin Jenkins
Project Manager: Rebecca Gilpin
Text Design and Project Coordination:
    MPS North America LLC
Electronic Page Makeup: Laserwords Private Ltd

Associate Director of Design: Andrea Nix
Design Lead: Beth Paquin
Cover Designer: Studio Montage
Cover Photo: Doyeol Ahn for Getty Images
Senior Manufacturing Buyer:
    Roy L. Pickering, Jr.
Printer/Binder: RR Donnelley/
    Harrisonburg North
Cover Printer: Lehigh-Phoenix Color/
    Hagerstown

Acknowledgments of third-party content appear on pages 293–294, which constitute an extension of this copyright page.

PEARSON, ALWAYS LEARNING, and MYWRITINGLAB are exclusive trademarks in the United States and/or other countries owned by Pearson Education, Inc., or its affiliates.

Unless otherwise indicated herein, any third-party trademarks that may appear in this work are the property of their respective owners and any references to third-party trademarks, logos, or other trade dress are for demonstrative or descriptive purposes only. Such references are not intended to imply any sponsorship, endorsement, authorization, or promotion of Pearson's products by the owners of such marks, or any relationship between the owner and Pearson Education, Inc., or its affiliates, authors, licensees, or distributors.

Library of Congress Cataloging-in-Publication Data

Wilhoit, Stephen, author.
  A brief guide to writing from readings / Stephen Wilhoit, The University of Dayton.
— Seventh Edition.
      p. cm.
  Includes bibliographical references and index.
  ISBN 978-0-13-380033-3
1. English language—Rhetoric—Handbooks, manuals, etc.   2. Academic writing—Handbooks, manuals, etc.   3. Interdisciplinary approach in education.   4. College readers.   I. Title.
  PE1408.W586 2015
  808'.042—dc23

                                                      2014026627

10 9 8 7 6 5 4 3 2 —DOH—17 16 15

                                              www.pearsonhighered.com
                      Student Edition ISBN 10:   0-13-380033-4
                      Student Edition ISBN 13: 978-0-13-380033-3
                          A la Carte ISBN 10:   0-13-380042-3
                          A la Carte ISBN 13: 978-0-13-380042-5

PEARSON

CONTENTS

Chapter 4   SUMMARY   *61*

Chapter 5   ANALYSIS   *81*

Chapter 6   RESPONSE ESSAYS   *97*

Chapter 7   CRITIQUE   *111*

Chapter 8   RHETORICAL ANALYSIS OF WRITTEN TEXTS   *139*

Chapter 9 RHETORICAL ANALYSIS OF
VISUAL TEXTS   *161*

Chapter 10   INFORMATIVE SYNTHESIS   *183*

Chapter 11   ARGUMENTATIVE SYNTHESIS   *213*

Chapter 12   PLAGIARISM   *249*

PREFACE

In the seventh edition of *A Brief Guide to Writing from Readings*, my goal remains unchanged from the earlier editions: to help students master one of the most common academic genres—writing from readings. Toward this end, and based on responses from students and faculty using the book, I have made several significant changes to the seventh edition. The changes include the following:

- a new chapter on analyzing readings and composing analytical essays
- new coverage of literary analysis and the inclusion of a short story
- eight new academic readings: two on controversies surrounding academic freedom, three on the ethics of human genetic enhancement, and three on leadership
- readings drawn from a wider range of academic sources than in previous editions
- four new sample essays
- expanded coverage of how to include electronic sources of information on APA reference lists and MLA works cited lists

To accommodate these changes, I have dropped the appendix, which offered instruction on peer review of writing, but which reviewers indicated was not widely used.

With these changes to the seventh edition, *A Brief Guide* extends its coverage of source-based writing, most notably through the inclusion of a new chapter with instruction on analyzing texts, the addition of a short story (Kate Chopin's "The Story of an Hour"), and an examination of how to write literary analysis essays. This new chapter compliments the instruction on analyzing arguments already included in the chapter on writing critiques and the chapter on analyzing visual texts. However, much remains the same in this new edition. Faculty and students have long noted the collegial tone of the book and the utility of the summary charts located at the end of most chapters, in addition to the revision checklists. These features have all been retained. From the first edition, I have tried to maintain a clear, process-oriented approach to writing instruction, laying out for writers a series of steps they can follow or modify as needed when composing commonly assigned source-based essays.

As in previous editions of the textbook, the sample readings are drawn from a range of disciplines with an emphasis on academic sources. Readings vary in length and in difficulty, but all are intended to pique student interest and serve as prompts for class discussion. Each sample student essay I include in the text can serve as a model for students to follow in terms of its thesis, organization, and use of sources, but none of them is perfect. Students should be encouraged to read the sample essays in this textbook as critically as they read any other material in college. They may identify several ways each essay can be improved. In fact, instructors might consider asking their students to do just that: to use the instruction offered in *A Brief Guide* to critique and revise these sample essays.

In the end, my hope, as always, is that the instruction offered in this textbook will help students develop the skills they need to successfully complete source-based college writing assignments, to read texts honestly and critically, and to explore connections they find between the material they read and their own knowledge, experience, and beliefs.

SUPPLEMENTS

MYWRITINGLAB: NOW AVAILABLE FOR COMPOSITION

MyWritingLab is an online homework, tutorial, and assessment program that provides engaging experiences to today's instructors and students. By incorporating rubrics into the writing assignments, faculty can create meaningful assignments, grade them based on their desired criteria, and analyze class performance through advanced reporting. For students who enter the course under-prepared, MyWritingLab offers a diagnostic test and personalized remediation so that students see improved results and instructors spend less time in class reviewing the basics. Rich multimedia resources, including a text-specific ebook in many courses, are built in to engage students and support faculty throughout the course. Visit www.mywritinglab.com for more information.

INSTRUCTOR'S MANUAL

An Instructor's Manual is available for *A Brief Guide to Writing from Readings*. The Instructor's Manual includes a brief introduction to each chapter, an examination of problems students commonly face when writing each type of source-based essay, and a series of exercises and assignments designed to help students improve their writing.

ACKNOWLEDGMENTS

I would like to thank the following reviewers for their helpful suggestions as I prepared each new edition of *A Brief Guide to Writing from Readings:* Curtis R. Burdette, Central Michigan University; Jennifer Campbell, University of Denver; Jacqueline E. Cason, University of Alaska, Anchorage; Tim Catalano, Marietta College; Jane Creighton, University of Houston–Downtown; Sally Ebest, University of Missouri, St. Louis; Daniel P. Galvin, Clemson University; Karen Gardiner, University of Alabama; Monica E. Hogan, Johnson County Community College; Wesley Jones, University of Mary; David D. Knapp,

Front Range Community College; Greg Luthi, Johnson County Community College; Raj Mohan, Cleveland State University; Anne Pici, University of Dayton; Kathy Overhulse Smith, Indiana University–Bloomington; and Mary Trachsel, University of Iowa. Reviewers of the seventh edition include Nathan A. Breen, College of Lake County; Sarah K. Cantrell, University of Alabama; David M. Higgins, Inver Hills Community College; Brooke Parks, University of West Georgia; Kari Vara, Cleveland State University; and Carmaletta M. Williams, Johnson County Community College.

Stephen Wilhoit

A Brief Guide to Writing from Readings

Chapter 1

....

CRITICAL READING

In this chapter you will learn how to

1. Read closely and critically
2. Highlight and annotate readings
3. Take notes while you read

DEFINITION AND PURPOSE

Most successful college writers are also sophisticated, critical readers. They assume a skeptical attitude toward texts: instead of believing whatever they read, they critically examine the author's ideas and their own responses to the reading. They are active, reflective readers who ask questions about the words on the page, mark passages, take notes, and draw connections between the author's ideas and their own experiences and knowledge. They are open to new ideas, but do not accept them without serious, reflective consideration. Unreflective readers, however, tend to accept unquestioningly what they see in print. In their view, if something has been published, it must be accurate. Instead of asking questions about what they read, they tend to accept the author's words at face value.

A major difference, then, between reflective and unreflective readers is the way they try to learn from what they read. Unreflective readers usually believe that the meaning of a text can be found in the words on the page: to understand a text, all a reader has to do is understand the meaning of the author's words. For them, reading is a rather simple, straightforward process: they read through a text, look up any words they do not know, isolate the author's main ideas, perhaps take some notes, and then move on to the next reading. They also tend to believe that because the meaning of a text resides in the author's words, students reading the same material ought to come away with the same information; the text should mean roughly the same thing to any competent reader who studies it.

Reflective, critical readers, however, tend to adopt a different view of reading. They believe that the meaning of a text resides in the *interaction* between the reader and the words on the page: to understand a text, readers must be aware of how their own knowledge, feelings, and experience influence their *interpretation* of the words on the page. For them, reading is a rather dynamic, fluid process: they read through a text skeptically, assess the author's words and ideas in light of their own knowledge and experience, jot down some notes that capture their questions and responses, reread the text after they have had some time to consider what the author had to say, and then move on.

Viewing reading as an interactive process can help you better understand the complex nature of writing from sources and the need to be an active, critical reader. For example, it helps you understand why a story you read during your first year in high school means something different to you when you read it again in your first year in college. The words on the page have not changed—you have, and because you have changed, the "meaning" of the story has changed for you as well. This interactive view of reading also helps explain how twenty students in an introductory philosophy class can read the same meditation by Descartes and come away with twenty slightly different interpretations of the piece. Active, critical readers understand that for any given person, the meaning of a text results from the interaction between the words on the page and that reader's knowledge, feelings, and expertise; reading involves more than a simple transfer of information from the words on the page to the mind of the reader.

Does this mean that all interpretations of a reading are equally valid? No. Although every person forms his or her own understanding of a reading, people can and often do misread texts: they may not read carefully, they may not understand certain terms or ideas, or they may lack the knowledge and experience they need to form an adequate interpretation of the text. As a safeguard against misinterpretation, critical readers discuss the material with others who have read it. Comparing their own reading of a text with a teacher's or a peer's reading can help clarify the material and prevent misunderstanding.

In addition, the author of the piece plays an important role in reading. Good writers try to influence their readers' understanding of and response to a text. When writing, authors manipulate the language, structure, and content of their prose to achieve a certain effect on their audience. Success is never guaranteed, but good writers know that they can at least influence how readers might respond to their work through the choices they make while composing. Critical readers take this into account when approaching a text—they try to be aware not only of what they bring to the reading, but also of the choices the writer has made to achieve a certain goal.

Learning to read material actively and critically can be difficult. However, critical readers tend to understand course material more fully, prepare for class more efficiently, and write from readings more effectively. Following are a number of suggestions aimed at helping you become a more active, critical reader. Central to this process is the ability and willingness to ask good questions about your reading of a text and to keep a written record of your responses. Critical readers refuse to sit back passively while they read; they actively question and respond to texts in light of their own knowledge, feelings, and experience.

ASKING QUESTIONS ABOUT WHAT YOU READ

Instead of passively accepting the ideas an author presents, a critical reader attempts to engage in a dialogue with the text, posing and working out answers to tough questions concerning the material's purpose, audience, language, and content.

The most productive critical questions center on the connections that exist between a text's author and his or her audience, subject, and language. Everything you read has been written by someone for someone about something using certain words on a page. Learning how to identify and question the relationship between these various aspects of a reading can help you understand the material more fully and determine its meaning and importance.

Typical questions you should ask of a reading include:

- Who is the author of the piece?
- What is her stand on the issue she is addressing?
- What are her interests, qualifications, or possible biases?
- What was her intent when writing this piece?
- Who is the intended audience?
- How does the author support her contentions?
- What language has she used to convey her ideas on this topic to this audience for this purpose?
- Based on my own knowledge and experience, what do I think about her ideas, intent, language, and support?
- How well does the author achieve her goal?

When you are confronted with conflicting sources of information on a topic (as is frequently the case in college), asking questions such as these is a particularly important way to sort out the authors' different positions, evaluate the worth of each source, and decide who presents the clearer, more convincing case.

Forming a full, critical understanding of a reading requires asking the right kinds of questions about the author, subject, audience, and language of the piece. Following you will find a series of questions to ask before, during, and after your reading. However, these questions are merely suggestive, not exhaustive; they indicate only starting points for your critical assessment of a text. Your teacher and peers may suggest other questions to ask as well. Finally, it is a good idea to write out your answers to these questions. Do not rely on your memory alone to keep track of your responses.

QUESTIONS TO ASK BEFORE YOU BEGIN A CLOSE READING OF A TEXT

Whether you are assigned to read material in history or art, biology or sociology, before you begin you need to ask yourself a series of questions concerning the author and publication in which the piece appeared as well as your own knowledge of and attitude toward the topic. Answering these questions may help you determine any biases present in the reading and ensure that you remain open to any new perspectives or information the author has to offer.

Questions Concerning the Author

- Who is the author?
- What are his credentials?
- What else has he written on the topic?
- What possible biases might have influenced his work?

Before you begin to read a text, try to assess the credibility and expertise of the person who wrote the piece. Who is the author, and what are his or her qualifications for writing on this topic? If, for instance, you are writing a paper about global warming for your English class and find an article you want to use in your essay, note whether you are reading a research report produced by a scientist who conducted her own studies on the topic, an informative article composed by a reporter who interviewed that scientist, or an opinion piece written by a television star who has no particular expertise in climatology. The first author is probably well qualified to offer expert opinion; the second author, while less qualified than the first, may still be a legitimate source of information. However, approach the third author skeptically: good actors are rarely good scientists. If you plan to use any of these readings to support a position of your own in an essay, understand that academic readers will tend to believe authors with solid, professional credentials and demonstrated expertise in the topic.

Also determine, as best you can, any biases operating in the authors' work. Note who the writers work for, who supported their research, and who publishes their results. Writers are never completely objective; all writers bring to their work certain biases or preferences, whether political, religious, or methodological. These biases may influence the type of study authors conduct, the type of evidence they use to support their contentions, the language they employ, and the conclusions they draw. When researching a paper on abortion, for instance, it would be important to note whether the author of a piece is a member of the National Abortion Rights Action League or Operation Life, even if the writer claims to be presenting the results of an objective study. In college you will often read expert testimony that presents conflicting views and interpretations of the same topic, data, or event. Often your job as a *writer* is to examine these different perspectives, compare their quality or worth, and use them to form and defend a position of your own. However, recognizing potential authorial bias in a reading does not disqualify it as a legitimate source of information: it simply puts you in a better position to read the work skeptically and to ask better, more critical questions.

Most academic journals include brief biographical entries on the authors at the beginning or end of each article or in a separate section of the journal typically labeled "Contributor Notes" or "Contributors." Many popular magazines also include some information on the author of each article they publish. (If you cannot find this information, see a reference librarian for help locating biographical dictionaries. Later, including in your essay the credentials of the authors whose work you are quoting or paraphrasing can help increase the credibility of your assertions.)

Questions Concerning the Publication

- In what regard is the publication held by professionals in the field?
- Toward what type of readership is the publication aimed?
- How long ago was the piece published?
- What, generally, is the editorial stance of the publication?

When assessing the quality of a publication, your first questions ought to address its credibility and audience. Do members of the profession or the academy consider this a reputable journal? Does it publish scholarly work or general interest features? What type of reader is this publication trying to reach: scholars or the general public? Answering these questions can help you determine whether work published in this journal or magazine is appropriate for inclusion in an essay of your own.

To answer these questions about the publication, first consult your teacher. He or she can probably tell you in what regard a particular journal is held by professionals in the field. Also, if you want to consult only scholarly sources of information, you may want to limit your research to specialized scholarly indexes and databases—drawing information from *The Applied Science and Technology Index* rather than from *Academic Search Complete*. Again, your teacher or a reference librarian can help you identify scholarly reference works.

Just as individual authors have certain biases or preferences that may influence their writing, publications have certain editorial slants that may influence what they print. Some publications will have definite political or ideological agendas. For example, *The New Republic* and *The National Review* are not likely to publish the same article on gun control. Other publications may exhibit certain methodological biases: they prefer to publish only historical studies or empirical studies or Marxist studies of a topic. Determining the editorial or methodological slant of a publication can be difficult: if you have not read widely in a field, you may not know a great deal about its principal publications. Often, your best recourse in gathering this type of information is to scan the titles and abstracts of other articles in the journal to determine its political or methodological preferences or, if you are reading newspaper or magazine articles, to read the editorials.

However, a particular periodical's political or methodological slant does not necessarily make it any more or less valid a source of information. Recognizing these preferences, though, should help you read material more skeptically. A publication's biases may affect the content of the articles it publishes, its authors' interpretations of statistics, even the nature of the graphics and illustrations accompanying the text. When you are thoroughly researching a topic, gathering information from several different sources is one way to guard against one-sided, unbalanced treatments of a topic.

Questions Concerning Your Own Views of the Topic

- What are my beliefs about the issue addressed in the reading?
- How open am I to new ideas on this topic?

Just as every author and publication presents material from a particular perspective, readers, too, bring their own prejudices and preferences to a text. Though absolute objectivity may be impossible for readers and writers to attain, knowing your own predispositions toward the topic an author addresses can help you guard against unfairly judging someone else's arguments or shutting yourself off from potentially helpful ideas.

Author Peter Elbow suggests two frames of mind students ought to assume when reading material. First, he advises students to play the "believing game"—that is, to assume that what the writer has to say is correct. If the author of the piece is right in what he says, how do his ideas influence your current views on the topic? What are the implications of the author's ideas? Can you draw any connections between what the author has to say and what you already know? Next, Elbow suggests that students play the "doubting game"—that is, assume a more critical stance toward the author's ideas. What are the weaknesses in the writer's arguments? What are the limitations of his ideas? In what ways are the author's ideas incompatible with what you already know about the topic?

Being aware of your own stance on an issue *before* you begin to read something for the first time can help you play the believing and doubting games more effectively. First, reading with your own beliefs firmly in mind can help you recognize which ideas are hard for you to accept or even to consider fairly. We all resist ideas that run counter to our beliefs: giving them legitimacy forces us to question our own positions. However, being a critical reader means you are willing to do just that, to consider ideas that you might otherwise ignore or reject. When you dismiss an idea in a source text, consider why: if it is only because that idea runs counter to your views, try playing the believing game before moving on.

Second, reading with your beliefs firmly in mind can help you recognize which ideas are hard for you to question and criticize. We all like to read material that confirms our present positions, because such reinforcement is comforting and reassuring. However, as a critical reader you must be willing to question authors who voice opinions you endorse, to criticize fairly and thoroughly ideas you are predisposed to accept unquestioningly. If you accept information without question, consider why: if it is only because you agree with the author, try playing the doubting game before moving on.

QUESTIONS TO ASK WHILE YOU READ AND REREAD MATERIAL

After you have read material with these questions in mind, reread it. If necessary, read it a third or fourth time—very few of us truly understand a text the first time we read it. When rereading material, though, you should consider another set of questions that focus your attention on the audience, purpose, content, and organization of the piece, along with your response to the author's ideas.

Questions about the Audience of the Piece

- What audience does the author seem to be trying to reach?
- What type of reader would be attracted to the author's writing, and what type would be alienated by it?
- How does your sense of the text's audience influence your reading of the piece?

Audience is one of the most important concepts in writing: an author's sense of audience will greatly affect, among other things, the language she uses, the material she includes, and the organizational strategy she employs. However, *audience* can be a difficult term to define. In one sense, it refers to actual people a writer may know. When composing a letter to a friend, for instance, a writer can make fairly accurate predictions about the way her reader will react to what she says or the language she uses.

In another sense, though, *audience* can have very little to do with specific people the author has in mind as he writes a text. Much of what you read in college, for example, was written by people who possessed a much more nebulous sense of audience as they wrote. They knew the *type* of reader they were trying to address (for example, a first-year student taking an introductory geology course) or perhaps the *type* of reader they wanted to interest (for example, people curious about feminist interpretations of literature). When writing, they did not have in mind as their audience a specific, individual reader. Instead, they were trying to produce prose that would attract or interest a particular type of reader.

Therefore, as you read and reread material, try to determine the audience the author is trying to address: how is she attempting to interest or appeal to that type of reader? How successful is she in achieving that goal? Pay attention to the language, content, and organization of the piece as you try to answer questions such as these:

- Was the author trying to reach a general reader, an educated reader, or a specialist?
- What language does the author use to try to reach this audience? What examples? What graphics?
- What type of reader would actually find the work helpful, informative, valuable, or difficult?
- Would any readers be alienated by the material in the piece? Why?

Answering these questions will help you better understand how the text you are reading came to assume its present form. When writing, authors choose language, examples, and a structure they believe will help them achieve their desired effect on an audience. Part of reading a text critically is determining in your mind how successful each writer has been in making these choices.

Realize, too, that when you read something, you become a member of that writer's audience. *Your* response to what you read is extremely important to note as you try to understand what the author has to say. Is the writer communicating his ideas effectively to you? Do you find the material in the piece interesting or boring, helpful or irrelevant, engaging, or alienating? What choices has the writer made that led to these responses? What knowledge or experience do you bring to the text that contributes to your reaction? Understanding the complex relationship between the audience and the writer of a piece can help you become a more sensitive, critical reader.

Questions about Purpose

- What was the author's purpose in writing the piece?
- What is the author's thesis?
- Does the author successfully achieve his or her goals?

Generally, when writing a text, an author will have one of three aims: to entertain, to inform, or to persuade his readers. Many times a work will serve multiple purposes—it will both entertain and inform, or inform and persuade. However, as a critical reader, you ought to identify the primary purpose of the piece you are reading. To criticize an article for failing to present an effective argument on a topic would be unproductive and unfair if all the author intended was to write an informative essay.

However, determining an author's purpose or goal can be difficult. In social science and natural science journals, look for the author's stated purpose in his abstract or thesis ("The purpose of this article is . . ." and "The authors seek to prove that . . ."). The conventions of most humanities journals, however, require authors to be less straightforward or declaratory in stating their purpose, but again thesis statements and abstracts are good places to start your search. Even if the author states his or her goal somewhere in the paper or abstract, be wary. When you finish rereading the piece, ask yourself, "Given the content, language, and structure of this piece, what do *I* believe to be the writer's primary goal or purpose?"

Questions about Content

- What are the author's major assertions or findings?
- How does the author support these assertions or findings?

When examining the content of any reading, try first to locate the author's thesis and paraphrase it. A thesis statement will be either stated or implied. If it is stated, you will be able to point to a sentence or two in the reading that serves as the thesis. If it is implied, a general idea or argument unites and guides the writing, but the author never explicitly puts it into words. When you paraphrase or recognize this general idea or argument, you have identified the thesis. In either case, as a first step in analyzing a reading's content, state the author's thesis in your own words to form a clear idea of what the author is trying to accomplish in the piece.

Next, note how the author supports her thesis—identify her primary ideas, arguments, or findings and the evidence, reasons, or examples she offers to support them. As you reread the piece, ask yourself what empirical, philosophical, theoretical, or other type of evidence or reasoning the author has provided to support her thesis and achieve her goal.

Finally, be sure to examine what you already know about the topic—what you have learned in the past and what you are learning now by reading *this* piece. Has the author left out any important information or arguments? Has she neglected certain interpretations of evidence others have offered? If so, why do you think that is? How can the reading's content be explained by its author, audience, or purpose?

Questions about Organization

- How is the material organized?
- What headings and subheadings does the author provide?
- What does the organization of the essay tell you about the author's view of the material?
- What gets stressed as a result of the organization?

As a writer composes his piece, he has to make a series of decisions about organization: he needs to determine the order in which he will present his findings, ideas, or arguments. Good writers organize their material purposefully—to make their article clear, to make their book more persuasive, or to make their findings more accessible. Through the order in which they present their material and through their use of paragraph breaks, headings, and subheadings, they try to help the reader understand or accept their views.

As you read a source text, think critically about its organization. First, form at least a rough idea of how the writer has organized his ideas. What are the major sections of the text? In what order are the ideas, arguments, or findings presented? You might want to produce a scratch outline or list that captures the reading's organization. Also, use the headings and subheadings the author provides to get a better understanding of how he views his material and how he sets priorities among his findings. For example, what ideas, arguments, or findings get emphasized through the author's selection of headings? How do the headings and subheadings guide you through the piece? Are there any instances in which you think a heading or subheading is misleading or poorly stated? Why?

Questions about the Author's Sources

- How does the author use other people's ideas or findings?
- How credible are the sources the author uses to support his ideas or findings?

As you analyze the content of a reading, examine the sources the author relied on when writing. What is documented? Flip back to the works cited list or bibliography at the end of the piece. Where does the author's information come from? Is the paper based on library research, primary research, or interviews? If much of the text's material comes from previously published work, how credible are the sources the author used to support her claims? For example, is the author relying on scholarly sources of information? Is there any apparent bias in the author's use of source material: is most of her material taken from journals that share similar editorial stances, or has the writer tried to draw information from sources representing a variety of political, theoretical, or methodological perspectives? Answering questions such as these can help you determine the credibility and utility of the author's ideas, arguments, or findings.

Questions about Graphics

- How clear are the charts, graphs, tables, or illustrations the author provides?
- How well does the author explain the graphics?
- How well do the graphics support or explain what the author has to say?

Graphics include charts, tables, graphs, drawings, and pictures. Although authors may add graphics to entertain readers, most include them to support arguments, summarize findings, or illustrate ideas. As you read a text, try to determine how the author is using graphics in her work and how clear, helpful, or informative you find them.

Questions about Your Reactions and Responses

- How do I feel about the topic, issues, or findings addressed in the reading?
- What is convincing? What is unclear?
- What ideas in the piece contradict my understanding of the topic?
- What ideas in the piece are new to me? Which ones do I accept and which ones do I reject?

People's beliefs and knowledge influence how they read material—what they take note of, what they understand the author to be saying, what they remember after they read the piece. Understanding your response to the material you read can help you become a more critical reader and a more effective writer in several ways. First, honestly assessing your response can help you be balanced and fair. As a skeptical reader you need to be both critical of ideas you at first enthusiastically support and open to ideas you at first strongly reject.

Second, examining your response to what you read can help you decide on and develop effective paper topics—your responses may help you identify an interest or question you can later pursue more thoroughly in an essay. Especially consider what you learn from a reading. What information is new? How do the author's ideas or findings confirm or contradict what you have come to think? Examining your answers to questions such as these can result in some interesting essays.

MARKING TEXTS

Look at the books of active, critical readers and you will see pages filled with underlined passages, marginal comments, questions, and reactions. Because they have recognized the close link between reading and writing, they rarely read without a pencil in hand. They underline the reading's thesis statement and any important passages they find. As they question the material they are reading, they annotate the text and write down the answers to the questions they ask so that when they return to the material later, they can recall the author's purpose and findings, remember how they responded to the author's ideas, and locate the information they want to use in their papers.

The two most common ways of marking texts are highlighting and annotating. Highlighting typically involves underlining, circling, bracketing, or color coding passages, while annotating involves writing comments or questions in the margin or at the end of the text.

HIGHLIGHTING TEXTS

Highlighting involves underlining, color coding, or in some other way marking important passages in a reading. Most students tend to highlight too little or too much. Some never make a mark in their books. Perhaps they were trained in high school not to mark up readings, or maybe they are concerned about the resale value of their books. Whatever their reason, these students rarely, if ever, highlight material they read. Other students highlight too many passages in a reading—practically every sentence is underlined, and almost every paragraph is shaded yellow or pink. You have to be selective in what you highlight: you mark up a reading in order to understand it more clearly and to identify important passages you may return to later when you write your paper.

In order to highlight a reading effectively, you need to develop your own marking system, a kind of code that helps you locate certain types of information in a text. Good writers usually develop unique ways of highlighting readings: they underline certain kinds of passages, place brackets around specific types of information, and circle other parts of the text. Later, when they return to the reading to write their paper, they can easily find the information they need. Following are some suggestions about what to mark in a text:

1. Mark an author's thesis, primary assertions, and supporting evidence.
2. Mark the names of authors, dates of studies, locations of research projects, and other important facts mentioned in the reading.
3. Mark key passages you might want to reread, quote, or paraphrase later as you write your paper.
4. Mark words or terms you do not know so you can look up their definitions.

Establish your own way of highlighting a text: circle authors' names, bracket dates, use a yellow highlighting pen to mark any passages you may want to quote and blue ink to indicate questionable statements, or whatever variations make sense to you. When you establish your own highlighting system, writing from readings will become much easier for you.

ANNOTATING TEXTS

While you are highlighting a reading, you should also annotate it—that is, *write out* your responses, questions, observations, or conclusions. Generally, there are two types of annotations you will use: marginal and end comments. Marginal annotations are notes that you make to yourself in the top, bottom, or side margins of the page; end annotations are notes that you make at the end of the text.

Marginal Annotations

Marginal annotations are typically short and in many cases may make sense only to the person who wrote them. Generally, they can be divided into content notes, organization notes, connection notes, questions, and responses.

Content notes typically identify the meaning or purpose of the marked passage. For example, after bracketing an author's first argument—that eliminating a particular government program may have negative consequences on the poor, for instance—you may write in the margin, "Argument 1—consequences for poor." When you review a reading to find material you want to use in your paper, content notes help you easily locate what you need, which is particularly important if you are completing a research project involving multiple readings.

Organization notes identify the major sections of a source text. After underlining an article's thesis, you may write *thesis* in the margin in order to find it more easily later, then bracket the first few paragraphs and write *introduction* in the margin. You might draw a line down the margin beside the next few paragraphs and write *first argument* in the margin, then highlight the next section and write *refutation of first argument*. Organization notes help you understand how the author has structured the piece and may help you locate particular sections of the text you would like to review.

Connection notes identify the links you see between an author's ideas and those offered by other writers or between ideas an author develops in different sections of a reading: "this idea echoes Weber's argument," "illustrates first point," or "contradicts teacher's position." As you read an article, you should note how the author's ideas confirm or refute ideas developed by other writers. Note the connections in the margin of the essay you are reading in case you want to examine the link more closely later: do not rely on your memory. If you are reading multiple sources on the same topic, distinctions between the texts can quickly blur; you may have a difficult time remembering who wrote what if you do not write good connection notes. Also, use connection notes to trace the development of each writer's thesis. Note in the margin of the reading the link between the various ideas, arguments, or findings the writer offers and his or her thesis.

Questions can serve several purposes. First, they can identify passages you find confusing: in a question, try to capture *precisely* what you find confusing in a passage, especially if you will have a chance to discuss the reading in class. Second, questions can help you identify in a reading the material you want to dispute. Try to capture in a critical question or two why you disagree with what the author has written. Finally, questions can identify where the author has failed to consider important information or arguments. These are typically "what about" questions: "What about the theory proposed by Smith?" "What about people who can't afford day care?" Your goal is to indicate with a question possible limitations to an author's ideas or arguments.

Response notes record your reactions to what you read. These notes may indicate which ideas you accept, which ones you reject, and which ones you doubt. They can range from a simple "yes!" or "huh?" to more elaborate and detailed reactions that allow you to explore your response in some detail.

Remember to keep your marginal notes brief. Their purpose is to help you read the text more critically and recall your responses and questions when you reread the material.

End Annotations

End annotations typically make some type of comment on the source as a whole and can assume different forms, including summaries, responses, and questions.

Summaries offer brief, objective overviews of a reading. You may want to write a one- or two-sentence summary at the end of a reading, especially if you are reading several source texts for your paper. The purpose of these summaries is to jog your memory about the reading's content or thesis so you don't have to reread the entire text. These summaries are especially helpful if you have to read several texts with similar titles: it is easy to confuse these readings, and the summaries can often help you find the particular text you need.

Responses capture your reaction to the work as a whole. Try to capture in your note your response to the author's ideas, argument, writing style, or any other aspect of the reading that strikes you as important. These responses can help you form comments to offer in class when you discuss the piece and often they serve as a good starting point for developing a topic for a paper: you may want to investigate and develop your response more thoroughly and formally in an essay.

Questions written at the end of a reading typically address the source's clarity, purpose, or effectiveness. Your questions might address the reading's claims, evidence, or reasoning; its syntax, tone, or structure. Other questions might address the reading's relationship to what you already know about the topic or what you have already read. These questions help you draw connections between the readings and your own knowledge and experience. Still other questions might indicate specific aspects of a topic you still need to investigate ("I wonder how his ideas might have an impact on part two of my paper—need to reconsider?") or links between two or more authors' claims that need further consideration ("Do her arguments refute the textbook's claims?").

You will usually jot down several different types of endnotes when you finish reading a text. You may write out a brief one- or two-sentence summary, a few questions, and a response. These endnotes can prove very helpful when you return to the material later: they indicate your assessment of the source text's content, strengths, weaknesses, and worth.

Together, highlighting and annotating can help you fully understand a reading and determine the best way to use it in your own writing. A word of warning, though: do not be blinded by your own annotations and highlights. When you review a source text you have already marked and annotated and are now planning to use in your paper, be critical of your *own* highlighting and annotations. Be sure to question whether your highlighting and annotations *really* capture the source's key points. As you review your comments and marked passages, ask yourself whether you feel the same way now about the reading. If you have been engaged in researching a topic, are you now in a better position to assess the value and meaning of the reading before you? Have your views changed? Also, try to answer the questions you asked in the margins or at the end of the article. Reassess your original reactions.

SAMPLE ANNOTATED READING

Review the following sample annotated reading. Your system for marking a reading will likely be different from the system used here. Note, though, how the reader used highlighting and annotations to gain a better understanding of the author's content, structure, language, and purpose.

Hard Choices

Patrick Moore, Ph.D.

founded Greenpeace

Check bio. notes — who is this person?

More than 20 years ago, I was one of a dozen or so activists who founded Greenpeace in the basement of the Unitarian Church in Vancouver, British Columbia. The Vietnam War was raging and nuclear holocaust seemed closer every day. We linked peace, ecology and a talent for media communications and went on to build the world's largest environmental activist organization. By 1986, Greenpeace was established in 26 countries and had an annual income of more than $100 million.

open w/ personal information

In its early years, the environmental movement specialized in confronting polluters and others who were damaging public lands and resources. Groups such as Greenpeace played a valuable role by ringing an ecological fire alarm, wakening mass consciousness to the true dimensions of our global predicament.

Brief history of environ movement

ecological movement wins?

By the 1980s, the battle for public opinion had been won. Virtually everyone inside and outside politics and industry expressed a commitment to environmental protection and good stewardship. Environmentalists were invited to the table in boardrooms and caucuses around the world to help design solutions to pressing ecological problems.

Are companies environ friendly now?

Rather than accept this invitation to be part of the solution, many environmentalists chose instead to radicalize their message. They demanded restrictions on human activity and the uses of natural resources that

Thesis?

too "radical"

anti-science ?

not build on earlier successes

far exceed any scientific justification. That tactical decision created an atmosphere in which many environmentalists today must rely on sensational rhetoric and misinformation rather than good science. Programs have gone forward without input from more knowledgeable environmentalists and other experts; the public debate has been needlessly polarized as a result of the movement's unwillingness to collaborate with others less radical.

environ not work w/others ?

In addition to choosing a dubious tactic, the environmental movement also changed its philosophy along the way. It once prided itself on subscribing to a philosophy that was "transpolitical, transideological, and transnational" in character. Non-violent direct action and peaceful disobedience were the hallmarks of the movement. Truth mattered and science was respected for the knowledge it brought to the debate.

says current movement rejects truth & science

Thesis →

That tradition was abandoned by many environmental groups during the 1990s. A new brand of environmental extremism has emerged that rejects science, diversity of opinion, and even democracy. These eco-extremists tend to be:

note headings

*Anti-technology and anti-science. Eco-extremists entirely reject machinery and industry; they invoke science as a means of justifying the adoption of beliefs that have no basis in science to begin with.

anti-science

*Anti-free enterprise. Although communism and state socialism have failed to protect the environment, eco-extremists are basically anti-business. They have not put forward an alternative system of organization that would meet the material needs of society.

anti-business

point not developed well

*Anti-democratic. Eco-extremists do not tolerate dissent and do not respect the opinions and beliefs of the general public. In the name of "speaking for the trees and other species," we are faced with a movement that would usher in an era of eco-fascism.

anti-democratic

The international debate over clearcutting offers a case study of eco-extremism in action. Groups such as Greenpeace and the Sierra Club have mounted major

example of clearcutting

need clearcutting

campaigns against clearcutting, claiming that it is responsible for "deforestation" on a massive scale in
Canada and elsewhere. In fact, no such deforestation is
taking place in Canada or the United States, and a ban
on clearcutting could do more harm than good.

It is an (ecological fact) that many types of forest
ecosystems thrive most successfully when they are pe-
riodically cleared and allowed to regenerate. Fire, vol-
canic eruptions, windstorms, insect attacks, disease and
climate change (ice ages) destroy massive areas of
forests, part of a natural cycle of forest destruction and
renewal that has existed since long before modern humans arrived on the scene.

ignores diversity— usually replanted w/only one type of tree

The use of (hype and myths) by Greenpeace and the
Sierra Club is symptomatic of the larger problems facing the modern environmental movement. Confrontation
too often is preferred over collaboration, and (eco-extremism) has shoved aside the earlier spirit of tolerance
and concern for the fate of humanity. The results
have been harmful to the movement as well as to the
environment we seek to protect.

hype and myths of Green & Sierra

As an environmentalist in the political center, I
now find myself branded a traitor and a sellout by this
new breed of saviors. My name appears in Greenpeace's
"Guide to Anti-Environmental Organizations." But surely
the shoe belongs on the other foot: The eco-extremists
who have taken control of the nation's leading environmental organizations must shoulder the blame for the
anti-environmental backlash now taking place in the
United States and elsewhere. Unless they change their
philosophy and tactics, the prospects for a protected environment will remain dim.

he is in political center— how defined?

founder now an enemy?

why a backlash?

Patrick Moore earned a Ph.D. in ecology from the
University of British Columbia in 1972. He was a
founding member of Greenpeace and for seven years
served as director of Greenpeace International.

credentials but who does he work for?

Summary— "Eco-extremists" reject science, truth, alternative views →why lose pop. support?

NOTE TAKING

Especially when working on an extended writing project, you may want to take notes on a source text after carefully reading and annotating it. If you are working on a research paper for a class, check with your instructor about any requirements he or she might have concerning your notes. Some teachers, for example, require their students to take notes on index cards following rather specific guidelines. Other teachers set no guidelines concerning notes. It is always a good idea to check with your instructor concerning his or her requirements.

If you take notes on index cards, be sure you indicate somewhere on each card the title and/or author of the work you are reading. If your cards get out of order, you need some way of identifying the source of the information on each card. If you are more comfortable taking notes on paper, try to use only one side of each sheet. Using your notes to write your essay is easier if you are not constantly flipping over sheets of paper to find the information you need.

Some writers like their notes to consist only of quotes; others mix quoted, paraphrased, and summarized material. Some write notes in complete sentences; some use a combination of sentences, sentence fragments, and even single words or diagrams. As with annotations, you will need to work out your own system for taking notes, one that helps you sort out and organize the useful material you find in the sources you read.

Keep in mind the guidelines that follow as you take your notes. Following them can help you avoid problems later as you use your notes to write your paper.

Before Jotting Down Any Notes, Always Write Down the Source Text's Full Bibliographic Information

Whenever you take notes on a reading, be sure to write down the author's full name, the exact title of the piece, the full title of the publication, all the publication information, and the inclusive page numbers. Often students will be completing a paper the night before it is due and realize they used material that needs to be documented. Without having the full bibliographic information with their notes, they have to make a frantic last-minute dash back to the library. If you are careful to write down this information before you take your notes, you can avoid some problems later.

In Your Notes, Carefully Distinguish between Material You Quote and Material You Paraphrase

One of the major sources of unintentional plagiarism is faulty note taking. This problem occurs when you copy down a passage word for word from a source text into your notes but fail to enclose that passage in quotation marks. If you then copy that material directly from your notes into your paper—thinking you originally paraphrased the passage—and fail to place quotation marks around it in your essay, you will be guilty of plagiarism. You can avoid this problem if you carefully indicate with quotation marks which passages in your notes are exact quotations and which are paraphrases of an author's ideas.

CAREFULLY LIST PAGE NUMBERS

In your notes, be sure to indicate the exact page number of the source text that contains the material you are quoting, paraphrasing, or summarizing. You will need this information later for proper documentation.

PAY ATTENTION TO THE PUNCTUATION IN THE SOURCE TEXT

If you are quoting material in your notes, reproduce the original punctuation exactly as it appears on the page. Many times students misquote material because they incorrectly copied the original punctuation into their notes.

IN YOUR NOTES, CLEARLY DIFFERENTIATE BETWEEN THE AUTHOR'S IDEAS AND YOUR OWN

Again, failing to differentiate between what an author says about a topic and what you have to say is a major source of unintentional plagiarism. As you take your notes, you may want to jot down some observations or ideas of your own—reading other people's ideas will often lead you to new insights of your own. However, if you do not make the distinction clear in your notes—if, when reviewing your notes, you cannot tell which ideas were yours and which were the other writer's—you might attribute ideas to authors who never suggested them or take credit for ideas that were originally developed by someone else. To make this distinction clear in your notes, perhaps you could place your ideas and reflections in brackets.

BE CONSISTENT WITH YOUR NOTE-TAKING SYSTEM

Whether you use a notebook, looseleaf paper, index cards, or a personal computer for taking notes, be consistent in how and where you note bibliographic information, page numbers, and your responses to the material. Adhering to a system will make it easier for you to find material in your notes and will help you avoid making mistakes.

Additional Reading

Getting Serious about Eradicating Binge Drinking

Henry Wechsler

Henry Wechsler *directs the College Alcohol Studies program at Harvard's School of Public Health.*

Most of us are aware that binge drinking is a major problem on many college campuses. Since the Harvard School of Public Health's first College Alcohol Study used that term, in 1994, to describe the drinking pattern of significant numbers of American college students, the problem has drawn media attention across the nation. Despite this, the problem has not declined over the past four years. In fact, our latest research findings, released in September, showed little change in the proportion of college students who binge. Among more than 14,500 students surveyed at 116 institutions, 43 percent reported that they had binged at least once in the preceding two weeks, compared with 44 percent in the earlier study.

Although the number of students who abstain from alcohol grew to 19 percent this year from 15.6 percent in the first study, among students who drink we found an increase in drunkenness, in drinking deliberately to get drunk, and in alcohol-related problems—including injuries, drunk driving, violence, and academic difficulties. For example, among students who drink, 52 percent said a major motivation was "to get drunk," compared with 39 percent in the first study. Thus, despite a spate of widely publicized student deaths in alcohol-related incidents, the binge goes on.

Why isn't this behavior decreasing? For one thing, binge drinking has been so deeply entrenched for so long at colleges that it can't be expected to disappear overnight. However, the more important reason that change eludes us is that some colleges have relied too much on one approach to solve the problem—trying to get the binge drinkers themselves to stop, rather than focusing equal attention on factors that make it easy for students to drink too much.

Of course, some campuses use multiple approaches to attack the problem, but many focus most of their energies on educational efforts directed at drinkers, particularly during events such as the recent Alcohol

Awareness Week. Such educational efforts are an important way to teach some students the facts about alcohol abuse. But those efforts overlook the environment around binge drinkers that condones and supports and often even encourages their behavior.

So what are the factors that promote binge drinking at colleges? One is that students who binge tend to think they represent the norm; they argue that they're just doing what most of their peers do. Most binge drinkers don't think they have a problem. They think they are only having fun, and most consider themselves to be moderate drinkers. Doing research into actual behavior and then informing students about how many students actually binge—generally fewer than binge drinkers believe—can help to reduce the behavior.

Another approach to changing student norms is to focus on the disruptive behavior of binge drinkers. Colleges are civic communities, and all too frequently they are disrupted by the behavior of students who drink excessively. Rather than search for contraband alcohol, a college would be wise to engage student leaders in helping administrators work out a clearly worded code of conduct that penalizes drunken behavior—and then to enforce it consistently.

Students who become drunk and disorderly should be made to take responsibility for the messes that they have created: They should have to clean up vomit in the bathrooms made unusable on weekends, help care for drunken students at the college health center, repair damage from vandalism, and pick up litter. The punishment should fit the crime.

But with repeat offenders, colleges need to consider enforcing a "three strikes and you're out" policy for alcohol-related violations of the student conduct code.

At the center of binge drinking on many campuses are fraternities and sororities. While they attract only a small percentage of students nationally, they continue to play a prominent role in campus life at many institutions. Our data shows that in fraternity houses, four of five residents binge, and more than half are frequent binge drinkers. And fraternity parties are attended by many more students than just members. They attract even some high-school seniors—future college students who are introduced to binge drinking as a social norm. Not surprisingly, most of the alcohol-related deaths of college students recently reported in the media involved fraternity parties.

While some colleges have begun to address the drinking culture created by fraternities, many administrators are still hesitant to move strongly against fraternities, for fear of angering alumni donors who fondly remember their own college years of partying. But administrators have a responsibility to protect all of their students against alcohol-related disruptions and injuries, and should not wait for tragedy to strike before they revoke official recognition of fraternities that consistently cause problems. Colleges also can require all first-year students who live on campus to reside in dormitories, and not in fraternity or sorority houses. Of course, then those colleges must work to create interesting alcohol-free activities centered in the residence halls, to show students that out-of-control drinking need not be the focus of social life.

A third impetus for binge drinking on college campuses—one rarely mentioned publicly—involves alumni at tailgate parties during homecoming activities and sporting events. Any alcohol-control measures adopted for students must also apply to visiting alumni. Banning alcohol at home sporting events for everyone except alumni who contribute more than $50, as one college did recently, is not a good way to win students' support for new alcohol-control policies. I would hope that most alumni, if informed that an institution is trying to cope with a serious problem, would cooperate. Colleges that base their decision making on fund-raising concerns must ask themselves: What will cost the college more money—alumni who might decrease their contributions if they're cut off from alcohol at sporting events, or a few large jury awards of damages to families of injured or deceased students?

Another center of college binge drinking is found in athletics programs. Athletes binge more than other students, according to our data. In fact, involvement in athletics—compared with time spent in other activities— increases rather than decreases a student's propensity for binge drinking. Students involved in athletics are one and a half times as likely to be binge drinkers as are other students. This tradition is kept alive through the beer-advertising blitz that surrounds sports. After all, Mark McGwire's 70th home run was hit at Busch Stadium.

As a first step, college athletics officials should stay clear of alcohol-industry promotions and advertising. Further, although coaches at some colleges require team members to abstain from alcohol during the competitive season, relatively few coaches are involved in campus-wide programs to reduce alcohol abuse. Colleges should make it a priority to enlist their coaches and athletics directors in programs designed to reach all students with the message that binge drinking interferes with performance in every area of their lives. The National Collegiate Athletic Association should encourage this. Colleges also should press coaches to stress the institution's commitment to preventing alcohol abuse when they recruit high-school athletes.

Another important point of intervention is at the high-school level. Half of college binge drinkers start in high school. Colleges should begin to address this problem at high schools that send a large number of freshmen to their campuses, by sending college students from those high schools back to talk to the younger students about alcohol and other substance abuse. The volunteers should stress that one in five college students nationally abstains from alcohol, and that another two in five drink, but not to excess.

High-school students are more likely to believe the messages of college students than those of teachers and other adults. Let future freshmen get their first view of college life from these volunteers, rather than from attending fraternity parties or tailgate events. Once freshmen have unpacked and settled in, it may be too late to tell them about college rules on alcohol use. That message should be sent before they even apply.

Colleges also need to focus more attention a block or two away from the campus—on the ring of bars and liquor stores that encircles many institutions. Colleges need to map the density of those establishments; many institutions have more than 50 such alcohol outlets surrounding them. These are formidable competitors for students' attention, and cannot be coped with by the college alone; community leaders must be enlisted to help, particularly in barring the low-price specials that the outlets use to compete with each other: two-for-one offers, cut-rate drinks and free food during happy hours, and free drinks for women on certain nights. Some states and communities already have laws that ban those types of sales. Remember, the problem is not alcohol itself; it is the availability of a large volume of alcohol at a low price, usually to be consumed in a short period of time.

All of the problem areas that I've cited cannot be attacked by every college at once. Some issues may be more pressing than others on particular campuses, and the solutions must be fashioned to fit local circumstances.

Some important actions are being taken by colleges and universities across the country. Many are trying to sever the connection between alcohol and sports by banning advertising in the programs for sporting events and prohibiting alcohol at college stadiums. Some colleges are discontinuing the practice of not holding classes or exams on Fridays, and are no longer allowing local bars to advertise drink specials in campus publications. And some colleges are experimenting with new student-housing arrangements, such as living–learning centers that take faculty members and classes into the dorms, to try to completely change the environments there.

Institutions also are trying to give students more alcohol-free entertainment options. Some are working with neighborhood groups, as well as community and state officials, to find legal and other means of controlling students' behavior off campus. Other colleges are imposing stricter sanctions on students who break the rules—notifying parents after a certain number of infractions, and suspending or expelling repeat offenders.

What institutions need to avoid are one-dimensional programs that focus on particular students but ignore the ways in which colleges help enable some students to continue binging for four years. Not holding classes or exams on Fridays, for example, enables students to binge from Thursday to Sunday without interruption. Making new rules, but not enforcing even the old ones—for example, banning alcohol in the dormitories, but allowing it to be carried in unmarked cups—tells students that the college is not serious about eradicating the problem.

To anyone who thinks that binge drinking is behavior that cannot be changed, I offer the following challenge. At the next meeting you attend, look around and count how many people are smoking. Not many years ago, the room would have been filled with smoke. Today, because of the wide recognition that smoking hurts both the smoker and people nearby, through secondhand effects, the air is clear. Binge drinking can become equally unacceptable on college campuses.

Summary Chart

CRITICAL READING: ASKING QUESTIONS

---

1. Questions to Ask Before You Begin a Close Reading of a Text

Questions concerning the author:
- *Who is the author?*
- *What are her credentials?*
- *What else has she written on the topic?*
- *What possible biases might have influenced her work?*

Questions concerning the publication:
- *In what regard is the publication held by professionals in the field?*
- *Toward what type of readership is the publication aimed?*
- *How long ago was the piece published?*
- *What, generally, is the editorial stance of the publication?*

Questions concerning your own views of the topic:
- *What are my beliefs about the issue addressed in the reading?*
- *How open am I to new ideas on this topic?*

---

2. Questions to Ask While You Read and Reread Material

Questions concerning the audience of the piece:
- *What audience does the author seem to be trying to reach?*
- *What type of reader would be attracted to the author's writing, and what type would be alienated by it?*
- *How does your sense of the text's audience influence your reading of the piece?*

Questions concerning the purpose of the piece:
- *What was the author's purpose in writing the piece?*
- *What is the author's thesis?*
- *Does the author successfully achieve his or her goals?*

Questions concerning the content of the piece:
- *What are the author's major assertions or findings?*
- *How does the author support these assertions or findings?*

Questions concerning the organization of the piece:
- *How is the material organized?*
- *What headings and subheadings does the author provide?*

- *What does the organization of the essay tell you about the author's view of the material?*
- *What gets stressed as a result of the organization?*

Questions concerning the author's sources:
- *How does the author use other people's ideas or findings?*
- *How credible are the sources the author uses to support his ideas or findings?*

Questions concerning graphics in the piece:
- *How clear are the charts, graphs, tables, or illustrations the author provides?*
- *How well does the author explain the graphics?*
- *How well do the graphics support or explain what the author has to say?*

Questions concerning your reactions and responses to the piece:
- *How do I feel about the topic, issues, or findings addressed in the reading?*
- *What is convincing? What is unclear?*
- *What ideas in the piece contradict my understanding of the topic?*
- *What ideas in the piece are new to me? Which ones do I accept and which ones do I reject?*

Summary Chart

CRITICAL READING: MARKING TEXTS

1. Highlighting Texts

Highlight the text's thesis, primary assertions, and supporting evidence.

Highlight the names of authors, specific dates mentioned, and principal sources cited.

Highlight key passages you may want to reread, quote, or paraphrase later.

Highlight terms you do not understand or want to discuss in class.

2. Annotating Texts

Marginal annotations

- *Content notes: identify the meaning or purpose of the marked passages.*
- *Organization notes: identify the major sections of the text.*
- *Connection notes: identify links between readings and within a reading.*
- *Questions: identify confusing, controversial, or questionable passages.*
- *Response notes: identify your reactions to the reading.*

End annotations

- *Summaries: convey a brief overview of the reading.*
- *Responses: convey your overall reaction to the piece.*
- *Questions: convey your assessment of the reading's clarity, purpose, or effectiveness.*

Summary Chart

CRITICAL READING: NOTE TAKING

1. Before jotting down any notes, always write down the source text's full bibliographic information.
2. In your notes, carefully distinguish between material you quote and material you paraphrase.
3. Carefully list page numbers in your notes.
4. Pay attention to the punctuation in the source text.
5. In your notes, clearly differentiate between the author's ideas and your own.
6. Be consistent with your note-taking system.

Chapter 2

QUOTATION

In this chapter you will learn how to

1. Quote material properly

2. Integrate quoted material into your own writing

3. Avoid misquoting material

4. Document quoted material

DEFINITION AND PURPOSE

When you use someone else's words in your paper, you have to place them in quotation marks and supply proper documentation. Quoting and documenting material tells your readers where they can find that *exact* language in the source text. If you make any significant changes in a passage you are quoting, you need to indicate the alterations in your text with ellipses, brackets, or an explanation.

Generally, if you take more than three words in a row from a source text and incorporate them word for word in your essay, you need to place quotation marks around the passage. However, there are several exceptions to this general guideline. For example, if you repeat in your paper someone's official title as it appears in the source text (e.g., president of the school board), you do not need to quote the title, even if it is longer than three words. Also, if you use in your paper a *single* word or term from a source text that is significant or unusual, you *may* need to quote it. Learning what to quote and when to quote takes some time, practice, and thought. Making good decisions about quoting can be easier, though, if you keep in mind one of the main reasons for quoting material: you want to acknowledge an author's distinctive language.

When employed properly and judiciously, quotations can add color and credibility to your writing; they can help make your papers clearer, more entertaining, and more persuasive. If used improperly, quotations can give the impression that you cannot think through a topic for yourself or cannot articulate ideas in your own words. Therefore, knowing how to quote material properly is an extremely important part of writing from readings.

GUIDELINES ON WHEN TO QUOTE MATERIAL

You ought to have a good reason for quoting material in your paper. Do not quote material just to fill up space or to avoid thinking about your topic. Instead, consider how quoting material will help you support your thesis or explain important ideas to your reader. The following guidelines will help you decide when to quote a word or passage and offer suggestions on how to use that material in your paper. As you plan and draft a source-based paper, consider ways to integrate *a few* carefully selected quotations with your own writing to present your ideas as clearly and effectively as possible.

QUOTE PASSAGES WHEN THE AUTHOR HAS WRITTEN SOMETHING IN A DISTINCTIVE OR ESPECIALLY INSIGHTFUL OR INTERESTING WAY

Often an author will express an idea so well it is difficult or impossible for you to express it better by paraphrasing it. The author may have expressed the idea succinctly, employed especially effective adjectives or metaphors, or supplied an especially interesting example. In such cases, quote the word or passage—it may help make your paper more entertaining or persuasive.

QUOTE MATERIAL THAT LENDS SUPPORT TO A POSITION YOU ARE TRYING TO MAKE IN YOUR PAPER

Letting your readers see for themselves that an expert agrees with a position you are advocating can help persuade them to accept your argument or can help them better understand your position. You must be sure, though, that in your effort to find support for your position, you do not misrepresent an author's thoughts or findings. By leaving words out of a quotation or by adding language to it, you should not misrepresent what the author actually had to say. For example, several years ago a student of mine quoted an editorial writer as saying, "President Reagan's proposed budget cuts will . . . double the number of people living in poverty." I checked the original editorial; the actual sentence read, "President Reagan's proposed budget cuts will not double the number of people living in poverty." By leaving out the word *not,* this student clearly misrepresented the author's intended meaning. Such changes to a quotation are unethical.

Also, in an effort to find support for your thesis, do not limit your research to those authors who agree with the position you are advancing. For several reasons, this strategy is a mistake. First, in doing research, you should learn about a topic by studying many different views. Quite often writers change their position as they write and rewrite their papers; sifting through the material they have read frequently leads them to rethink and restate their thesis.

Second, you may want to quote authors who present ideas that challenge your thesis: doing so can increase your credibility in the eyes of many readers. Finally, by seeking out alternative perspectives and learning more about the topic, you place yourself in a better position to defend your assertions, improving the likelihood that your readers will value what you have to say on the topic because of your expertise. Therefore, do not neglect opposing viewpoints when searching for material to quote in your paper.

When you use expert testimony to support a position in your paper, it is a good idea to mention the person's credentials in your paper:

> According to Helen Carter, former president of the First National Bank, ". . . "
> Milton Friedman, noted economist and winner of the Nobel Prize, contends that ". . ."

Citing the credentials of the experts you quote may help convince your readers to accept or at least seriously consider what they have to say. Again, you do not need to cite the credentials of every author every time you quote from his or her work. You also do not want to cite so many credentials that the sentence is hard to read. Variety is the key to using quotations well—cite the credentials when you think they are significant, and do so in a way that fits the overall tone of your paper.

Quote Authorities Who Disagree with a Position You Are Advocating or Who Offer Alternative Explanations or Contradictory Data

Often it is a good idea to quote authors who offer views or data that call into question the position you are advocating in your paper. Many beginning authors balk at this idea. They believe that introducing opposing views will only weaken the impact of their thesis. However, when you include in your paper a variety of perspectives, your readers are more likely to perceive you to be fair and thorough in your treatment of the subject: these quotations demonstrate that you recognize and understand alternative points of view. Second, such quotations allow you the opportunity to examine critically the other person's position, acknowledging its worth or value when needed and criticizing it when appropriate.

If you decide to quote authors who challenge your thesis, you must somehow address their ideas or findings, usually in one of four ways. You need to explain in your own words:

- how that author's ideas do not seriously damage your thesis,
- how that author's ideas or findings may actually support your contentions,
- how your thesis may be altered slightly to accommodate the author's ideas, or
- how that author's ideas are incorrect or at least questionable.

If you do not somehow address the opposing ideas you quote in your paper, your reader will likely be confused, wondering how that material fits your paper's thesis.

GUIDELINES ON WHEN NOT TO QUOTE MATERIAL

When writing from sources, students often rely too heavily on quoted material: their essays are a string of quotations. These papers more accurately represent the ideas and language of the source texts than they do the ideas and language of the student. To avoid producing a paper like this, consider these guidelines outlining when you should *not* quote material. Use quotations *selectively;* they should never make up the bulk of your paper.

DO NOT QUOTE PASSAGES MERELY TO FILL SPACE

Too often when writing from sources, students try to pad their essays with extensive quotations, and their final papers end up being a patchwork of quoted material. This is especially true when students are writing to meet a length requirement. If a teacher wants a paper eight to ten pages long, some students think the easiest way to reach that length is to keep piling on quotations. However, in college your readers will usually want to know what *you* think about your subject, what conclusions *you* have reached through your research, and how *you* understand material. Do not substitute other people's views and voices for your own; use theirs to *support* your own.

DO NOT QUOTE PASSAGES AS A SUBSTITUTE FOR THINKING

In addition to using quotations to fill space, too often students rely on quotations alone to clarify, defend, or substantiate a finding or position. They may introduce an idea in a topic sentence, then string together two or three quotations to substantiate the point they want to make. Instead of presenting their own ideas in their own language, they rely on quoted material to present and defend their case.

The better course to follow is to integrate selected quotations into your essay carefully: their purpose is to advance your argument or support your conclusions or findings. Do not expect a quotation alone to convince your readers to accept some contention you want to make. As you work through a writing assignment, find language that reflects and communicates the conclusions you have drawn and the assertions you want to make. When appropriate, support or illustrate your position with quoted material. Also remember that when you do quote material, in most cases you will need to comment on it, explaining in your own words the quotation's meaning, relevance, or importance.

DO NOT QUOTE PASSAGES BECAUSE YOU DO NOT UNDERSTAND THE AUTHOR'S IDEAS WELL ENOUGH TO PARAPHRASE THEM

As you read material in college, you will often run into words you do not know, ideas that seem strange, arguments that are hard to follow, and research methodologies and discussions of findings that seem to be written in a language of their own. If you have to write papers based on these readings, do not rely on quotations as a way to avoid thought. You need to understand the material you quote. As a general guideline, if you cannot paraphrase the material, do not quote it. That is, if you cannot convey that information in your own words, quoting it is probably a bad idea.

INTEGRATING QUOTATIONS INTO YOUR WRITING

There are several ways to place quoted material in your papers. You should study and practice several of these techniques because varying the way you integrate quotations into your writing can make your papers more interesting.

One of the real difficulties in learning to write from readings in college is the fact that different disciplines follow different rules concerning the proper way to document and punctuate quotations. Two primary style manuals used in your college courses are those published by the Modern Language Association (MLA), primarily used in humanities classes such as English and history, and by the American Psychological Association (APA), primarily used in social science classes such as psychology and sociology. Because each of these manuals offers its own set of rules concerning the proper punctuation and documentation of quotations, when you receive an assignment, always ask your instructor which style manual he or she expects you to follow. (See Chapters 13 and 14 for a complete discussion of the documentation guidelines suggested by each.)

TWO BASIC TYPES OF QUOTATIONS

When you quote material, you will either set it off in a block quotation or integrate it into the body of your essay. Your choice depends on length: longer passages must be block quoted, while shorter quotations should be integrated.

Properly punctuating quotations can be tricky: again, the rules you follow depend on the academic stylebook your teacher wants you to follow. Although the two major style manuals generally agree on how to punctuate integrated quotations, they offer different guidelines for formatting, punctuating, and documenting block quotations. Pay close attention to how the following sample quotations are punctuated. All of the sample quotations will draw on passages from the following essay published in *America*.

Generation Text

The Dark Digital Ages: 13 to 17

Mark Bauerlein

Mark Bauerlein *is a professor of English at Emory University and author of*
The Dumbest Generation: How the Digital Age Stupefies Young Americans and
Jeopardizes Our Future.

Children between the ages of 13 and 17 who have a mobile phone average
1,742 text messages each month, according to a report by the Nielsen
Company in September 2008. That comes to nearly 60 per day. They also
make 231 voice calls each month, close to eight per day. They play games on
the device as well, and browse the Web, take pictures and log hours of social
networking.

No wonder so many of them consider the cellphone (for some it is a
BlackBerry or an iPhone) an essential part of their lives. Half of all young
people between the ages of 8 and 12 own one such device, according to a
Harris Interactive poll conducted in July 2008. The rate rises to around four
out of five for teenagers; that's a 36 percent increase over the previous three
years, which means that these tools have swept into young people's lives
with the dispatch and coerciveness of a youth fad (like Pokemon and Harry
Potter). The devices are more than just consumer goods. They are signs and
instruments of status.

The age-old force of peer pressure bears down hard. Indeed, 45 percent
of the teens that sport one agree that "Having a cellphone is the key to my
social life"—not just helpful or useful, but "the key." If you don't own a
cellphone, if you can't text, game, network and chat, then you are out of the
loop. It is like not being picked to play kickball back in the primitive days of
neighborhood sandlot gatherings. If a 16-year-old runs up 3,000 text
messages in one month (and does not have a flat payment plan), mom and
dad take the phone away. It's just a silly, expensive toy, they think. But the
16-year-old thinks, "You have destroyed my life!" And for them, this seems
true. Digital tools are the primary means of social contact. When they lose
them, kids feel excluded and unpopular, and nothing hits a 16-year-old harder
than the disregard of other 16-year-olds. They do not care what 40-year-olds
think, and they do not worry about what happened at Thermopylae or what

Pope John Paul II said about the "splendor of truth." They care about what other students in biology class think, what happened last week at the party and what so-and-so said about them.

It is an impulse long preceding the advent of the microchip, but digital devices have empowered that impulse as never before. Think about the life stage of adolescence. Teenagers stand at a precarious threshold, no longer children and not yet adults, eager to be independent but lacking the equipment and composure. They have begun to leave the home and shed the influence of parents, but they don't know where they are headed, and most of them find meager materials beyond the home out of which to build their characters. So they look to one another, emulating dress and speech, forming groups of insiders and outsiders, finding comfort in boyfriends and girlfriends, and deflecting more or less tenuously the ever-present risk of embarrassment.

Everyone passes through this phase, but this generation's experience marks a crucial change in the process. In the past, social life proceeded intermittently, all day at school and for a few hours after school. Kids hung out for an afternoon over the weekend and enjoyed a movie or party on Friday or Saturday night. Other than that, social life pretty much ended. They went home for dinner and entered a private space with only a "landline" as a means of contact (which appears to young people today a restricted connection—show them a rotary phone and watch them scowl). Teenage social life and peer-to-peer contact had a limit.

Teenagers did not like it. I certainly didn't want to listen to my parents when I turned 16. But the limit was healthy and effectual. Adolescents needed then and need now a reprieve from the tribal customs and peer fixations of middle school and high school. Wounds from lunchroom gossip and bullying, as well as the blandishments of popularity and various niche-crowd memberships, disable the maturing process. These form a horizon of adolescent triumphs and set the knowledge of history, civics, religion, fine art and foreign affairs beyond the pale of useful and relevant acquisitions. If a sophomore sat down on a bus with the gang and said, "Hey, did you see the editorial on school funding in *The Times* this morning?" the rest would scrunch up their faces as if an alien being sat among them.

Youthful mores screen out such things, which is all the more reason for parents to offer an alternative. A home and leisure life separate from teen stuff exposes youths to heroes and villains that surpass the idols of the senior class, to places beyond the food court and Apple Store, to times well before the glorious day they got their driver's license. It acquaints them with adult duties, distant facts and values and truths they will not fully comprehend until much later. They don't like them and rarely find them meaningful, but in pre-digital times teens had nowhere else to go after they entered the front door. They had to sit at the dining table and listen to parents talk about grocery shopping, vacation plans, Nixon, gas prices and the news.

No longer. In 1980, when an angry parent commanded, "Go to your room—you're grounded!" the next few hours meant isolation for the teen. Today, the bedroom is not a private space. It's a social hub. For many kids, the bedroom at midnight provides a rich social life that makes daytime face-to-face conversations seem tame and slow. Amid the pillows with laptop or BlackBerry, they chat with buddies in 11th grade and in another state. Photos fly back and forth while classmates sleep, revelations spill forth in tweets ("OMG, Billy just called Betty his ———"), and Facebook pages gain flashier graphics.

In this dynamic 24/7 network, teen activity accrues more and more significance. The events of the day carry greater weight as they are recorded and circulated. The temptation for teens to be self-absorbed and self-project, to consider the details of their lives eminently memorable and share-able, grows and grows. As they give in online, teenagers' peer consciousness expands while their historical understanding, civic awareness and taste go dormant before they have even had much chance to develop. This is the hallmark of what I have called the Dumbest Generation. These kids have just as much intelligence and ambition as any previous cohort, but they exercise them too much on one another. They are building youth culture into a ubiquitous universe, and as ever, youth culture is a drag on maturity. This time it has a whole new arsenal.

THE BLOCK QUOTATION

The APA and MLA style manuals both agree that longer quotations must be set off from the rest of the text, but they differ in how they define "longer":

- APA states that quotations of forty words or more must be block quoted.
- MLA says to block quote passages that would be more than four typed lines in your paper.

Regardless of the style manual you follow, you should introduce a block quotation with a colon. You do not add quotation marks at the beginning or end of the passage, and all the punctuation in the source text stays the same in the block quotation.

APA Guidelines

According to the APA style manual, you should start a block quotation on a new line in your paper, setting the left margin of the quotation one-half inch in from the original left margin. Subsequent lines of the quotation align on that indent. (If you are quoting additional paragraphs in the source text, indent the first line of each an additional half inch.) The right margin stays the same, and the whole passage is double-spaced.

Example 1

In "Generation Text," Mark Bauerlein (2009) describes how the nature of "being grounded" has changed due to advances in technology:

> In 1980, when an angry parent commanded, "Go to your room—you're grounded!" the next few hours meant isolation for the teen. Today, the bedroom is not a private space. It's a social hub. For many kids, the bedroom at midnight provides a rich social life that makes daytime face-to-face conversations seem tame and slow. Amid the pillows with laptop or BlackBerry, they chat with buddies in 11th grade and in another state. Photos fly back and forth while classmates sleep, revelations spill forth in tweets ("OMG, Billy just called Betty his ——"), and Facebook pages gain flashier graphics. (p. 36)

Kids sent to their bedroom today do not face isolation. Thanks to modern technology, they can stay in constant contact with their friends.

Analysis

Notice that the period at the end of the quotation precedes the parenthetical citation. (If the quotation runs longer than one page in the source text, use "pp." to introduce the inclusive page numbers.) There are no quotation marks added at the beginning or end of the block quote. The words "Go to your room—you're grounded!" are quoted because they have quotation marks around them in the source text. If any words are italicized in the source text, they remain italicized in your block quote. Note also that the left-hand margin of the block quotation is indented a half inch.

MLA Guidelines

MLA says to begin a block quotation on a new line, indent the left margin one inch (and a quarter inch more for new paragraphs within the block quote), leave the right margin unchanged, and double-space the block quotation.

Example 2

In "Generation Text," Mark Bauerlein describes how the nature of "being grounded" has changed due to advances in technology:

> In 1980, when an angry parent commanded, "Go to your room—you're grounded!" the next few hours meant isolation for the teen. Today, the bedroom is not a private space. It's a social hub. For many kids, the bedroom at midnight provides a rich social life that makes daytime face-to-face conversations seem tame and slow. Amid the pillows with laptop or BlackBerry, they chat with buddies in 11th grade and in another state. Photos fly back and forth while classmates sleep, revelations spill forth in tweets ("OMG, Billy just called Betty his ——"), and Facebook pages gain flashier graphics. (36)

> Kids sent to their bedroom today do not face isolation. Thanks to modern technology, they can stay in constant contacts with their friends.

Analysis

Note how the parenthetical documentation follows the period at the end of the quotation. No quotation marks are added to the block quote. The words quoted from the original passage retain their punctuation. There is a new left margin, but the right margin remains unchanged.

Example 3

> Bauerlein introduces "Generation Text" by citing some interesting, and perhaps startling, statistics concerning children's use of technology:
>
>> Children between the ages of 13 and 17 who have a mobile phone average 1,742 text messages each month, according to a report by the Nielsen Company in September 2008. That comes to nearly 60 per day. They also make 231 voice calls each month, close to eight per day. They play games on the device as well, and browse the Web, take pictures and log hours of social networking.
>>
>> No wonder so many of them consider the cellphone (for some it is a BlackBerry or an iPhone) an essential part of their lives. Half of all young people between the ages of 8 and 12 own one such device, according to a Harris Interactive poll conducted in July 2008. The rate rises to around four out of five for teenagers; that's a 36 percent increase over the previous three years, which means that these tools have swept into young people's lives with the dispatch and coerciveness of a youth fad (like Pokemon and Harry Potter). (34)
>
> According to Bauerlein, this technology has spread quickly in the culture like so many other fads.

Analysis

Since this block quotation runs longer than one paragraph, note how the first line of the second paragraph is indented an additional quarter inch.

THE INTEGRATED QUOTATION

Short quotations should be integrated in the body of your essay rather than set off in a block quotation. As you will see, you have several ways to integrate quoted material into your paper. Try to use several of these techniques when writing an essay—such variety can help make your paper more interesting to read.

The APA and MLA style manuals generally agree on where to place quotation marks, how to use single and double quotation marks, and how to otherwise punctuate integrated quotations. Remember that all quotations must be documented. Again, see Chapter 13 for a detailed discussion on how to document quotations. In the following samples, I alternate between APA and MLA documentation conventions.

Introduce a Quotation with a Verb

Probably the most common way of introducing a quotation is to give the author's name, perhaps his or her credentials, maybe even the title of the work, followed by an appropriate verb—*says, notes, comments, contends, asserts,* and so on. Place a comma after the verb of saying.

Example 4 (MLA Documentation)

> Bauerlein, believing that owning a cellphone is a sign of social status and inclusion, writes, "Indeed, 45 percent of the teens that sport one agree that 'Having a cell-phone is the key to my social life'—not just helpful or useful, but 'the key'" (34).

When you integrate material from a source text that already contains quotation marks, the regular quotation marks in the original (" ") are changed to single quotation marks (' ') in your paper.

Note the punctuation at the end of the sentence; the final period follows the parenthetical citation. If the last sentence of the quotation ends with an exclamation point or a question mark, include it before the closing quotation mark and place a period after the parenthetical citation. This punctuation guideline holds true for the APA and MLA style manuals.

Example 5 (APA Documentation)

> Bauerlein (2009) states that this generation of students, unlike others, expect to use only modern technology to communicate. In the past, he writes, children ". . . went home for dinner and entered a private space with only a 'landline' as a means of contact (which appears to young people today a restricted connection—show them a rotary phone and watch them scowl) (p. 35).

Again, note how a comma follows the verb (in this case, "writes"), how the material quoted in the source text is placed in single quotation marks, how the ellipsis indicates part of the passage was left out of the quote, and how the final period follows the documentation.

Example 6 (MLA Documentation)

> Bauerlein claims, "Children between the ages of 13 and 17 who have a mobile phone average 1,742 text messages each month . . . " (34).

Introduce a Quotation without a Verb

A more formal way of integrating a quotation into your paper is to introduce it with a colon. Commonly, quotations used as illustrations or elaborations of a point you have just made are introduced this way. Make sure that the colon comes at the end of a complete sentence; leave one space between the colon and the opening quotation mark.

Example 7 (APA Documentation)

> Toward the end of his essay, Bauerlein (2009) assumes a darker tone: "This is the hallmark of what I have called the Dumbest Generation. These kids have just as much intelligence and ambition as any previous cohort, but they exercise them too much on one another" (p. 36).

Example 8 (MLA Documentation)

> In generations past, teens needed a place to escape their peers: "Adolescents needed then and need now a reprieve from the tribal customs and peer fixations of middle school and high school" (Bauerlein 35).

Note that in this last example, because I did not use Bauerlein's name in the passage, I had to include it in the citation.

Run Your Sentence and the Quotation Together

This particular technique can be hard to master. Instead of separating your words from the quoted passage with a comma or colon, you run the two together seamlessly, relying on the quotation marks to let your reader know when you begin using someone else's language. Integrating quotations in this way, while sophisticated stylistically, can also lead you to misquote material if you are not careful. As students first learn to run their sentence and the quotation together, they tend to alter the quotation to fit the sentence they are writing rather than to alter their sentence to fit the quotation. As you practice this method of quoting material, try to craft your sentence so it runs smoothly into the quotation. If you have to change the quoted passage in any substantive way, you must indicate the changes (see the section on "Altering Quoted Material and Avoiding Misquotations," which follows).

When you employ this technique properly and read your essay aloud, a listener would not be able to tell where the quotation started and ended. Note that you do not need to place a comma before the quoted material or insert an ellipsis if you are picking up the quotation in midsentence.

Example 9 (APA Documentation)

> Bauerlein (2009) believes that "the age-old force of peer pressure bears down hard" (p. 34).

In this example, note that the capital *T* in *The* can be changed to lowercase without the addition of brackets. Also, when using this approach, you do not need to include an ellipsis if you begin a quotation in midsentence.

Example 10 (MLA Documentation)

> Changes in education and technology have "set the knowledge of history, civics, religion, fine art and foreign affairs beyond the pale of useful and relevant acquisitions" (Bauerlein 35).

Pick Out Only Certain Words to Quote in Your Sentence

You do not always have to quote entire passages or sentences in your paper. Often you want to quote only a few key words or phrases. Be sure, though, to include proper documentation even if you quote only one word.

Example 11 (MLA Documentation)

> Bauerlein believes teens "stand at a precarious threshold" and that they are "eager to be independent" (35).

This particular example needs only one parenthetical citation because all the quoted material comes from the same page in the source text. If it came from different pages in the source text, parenthetical citations would follow each quoted word or phrase.

Example 12 (APA Documentation)

> According to Bauerlein (2009), because "peer pressure bears down hard" (p. 34), the children's use of social technologies "accrues more and more significance" (p. 36).

ALTERING QUOTED MATERIAL AND AVOIDING MISQUOTATIONS

When you place quotation marks around material in your essay and document that passage, you are telling your readers that if they turn to that page of that source text, they will find that passage as it appears in your paper: the words and punctuation have not been changed. If that is not the case—if you have made any substantive changes to material you are quoting—then you need to acknowledge those alterations. Especially important is learning how to indicate that you left words out of a quotation, added words to a quotation, or changed the emphasis given words in a quotation.

LEAVING WORDS OUT OF A QUOTATION

Use an ellipsis (. . .) to indicate that you left material out of a quotation. Add a fourth dot to act as a period if you omit the end of a sentence or leave out an entire sentence when block quoting. When you introduce a quotation with a colon, include an ellipsis if you pick up a quotation in the middle of a sentence in the source text.

Example 13 (MLA Documentation)

> Bauerlein observes, "No wonder so many of them consider the cellphone. . . an essential part of their lives" (34).

Example 14 (APA Documentation)

> Escaping the detrimental effects of social technologies, students will better learn adult behaviors: ". . . adult duties, distant facts and values and truths they will not fully comprehend until much later" (Bauerlein, 2009, p. 35).

ADDING WORDS TO A QUOTATION

When you add words to a quotation, use square brackets, not parentheses, around the words. Add material to quotations sparingly. Do it only when absolutely necessary to avoid confusing your readers.

Example 15 (MLA Documentation)

> Home life is devalued, "So they [teenagers] look to one another, emulating dress and speech. . . " (Bauerlein 35).

NOTING EMPHASIS ADDED TO A QUOTATION

If you want to emphasize a word or passage in a quotation, put it in italics. The stylebooks offer different guidelines on how to indicate the addition of emphasis to a quotation:

- APA style: immediately after the emphasized words, place in square brackets the words "emphasis added."
- MLA style: after the quotation itself, place in parentheses the words "emphasis added," after the page number (if any). Or place "emphasis added" in square brackets immediately after the emphasized words.

If you do not indicate otherwise, readers will assume any words italicized in a quotation appear in italics in the source text.

Example 16 (APA Documentation)

> Bauerlein (2009) notes that "everyone passes through this phase, but this generation's experience marks a *crucial change* [emphasis added] in the process" (p. 35)

Example 17 (MLA Documentation)

> English Professor Mark Bauerlein observes that "everyone passes through this phase, but this generation's experience marks a *crucial change* in the process" (35, emphasis added).

Summary Chart

GUIDELINES ON QUOTATIONS

1. **When to Quote Material**

   Quote passages when the author has said something in a distinctive or especially insightful or interesting way.

   Quote material that supports the assertions you make in your paper.

   Quote authorities who disagree with a position you are advocating or who offer alternative explanations or contradictory data.

2. **When Not to Quote Material**

   Do not quote passages merely to fill in space.

   Do not quote passages as a substitute for thinking.

   Do not quote passages because you do not understand the author's ideas well enough to paraphrase them.

Summary Chart

INTEGRATING QUOTATIONS INTO YOUR WRITING

1. **Block Quotations**

   Employ this method with longer quotations.

   Follow guidelines established by the style manual your instructor requires.

2. **Integrated Quotations**

   Introduce the quotation with an appropriate verb.
   - *precede with a comma*
   - *employ a verb of saying that fits the overall tone of your essay, such as:*

says	holds
states	maintains
asserts	contends
claims	explains

   Introduce the quotation without a verb.
   - *a more formal way of introducing the quotation*
   - *precede with a colon*

   Run your sentence and the quotation together.
   - *edit your sentence so it fits the tone and syntax of the quoted passage*

   Pick out only certain words to quote.
   - *quote interesting uses of language such as coined or controversial terms*
   - *quote terms to draw attention to them*

QUOTATION REVISION CHECKLIST

	Yes	No
1. Did you check your quoted passages against the original to make sure the wording is accurate?	_____	_____
2. Is the capitalization of words in the quotation proper and accurate?	_____	_____
3. Is the punctuation in the quotation proper and accurate?	_____	_____
4. Do you need to add italics, underline certain words, or use single quotation marks in the quotation?	_____	_____
5. Did you check the punctuation you employed to introduce the quotation?	_____	_____
6. Did you check the format of your block quotations?	_____	_____
7. If you added words to or deleted words from the source passage, did you confirm that you have not misrepresented the author?	_____	_____
8. Is the format of your documentation at the end of the quotation in the correct style?	_____	_____
9. Did you list the right page number or numbers in your documentation?	_____	_____

Chapter 3

PARAPHRASE

In this chapter you will learn how to

1. Paraphrase material accurately and effectively

2. Vary the way you paraphrase material

3. Integrate paraphrased material into your own writing

4. Document paraphrased material

DEFINITION AND PURPOSE

When you paraphrase a passage, you express an author's arguments, findings, or ideas in your own words. Much of the writing you do in college will require you to paraphrase material. Some of these assignments will simply ask you to gather and convey information. To write this type of paper, you study the work of various authors, then paraphrase what they have written, trying to convey to your readers as clearly and accurately as possible what each has to say about the topic.

In other assignments you will rely on paraphrased material to help you develop and defend an argument. Paraphrasing the work of experts who agree with your position in a paper can be quite persuasive. Even paraphrasing the work of authors who *disagree* with a position you have assumed in your essay can be helpful: after you objectively present that opposing view, you can examine its strengths and weaknesses and adjust your position to accommodate ideas you can neither discredit nor dismiss. However, when paraphrasing information as a part of an argument you are advancing, you must fairly represent an author's views. It is always tempting to misrepresent what people say, especially when you disagree with them, either by oversimplifying their position or by employing misleading language. Try to resist these temptations; always try to be fair to an author when you paraphrase his or her work.

Finally, paraphrasing allows you to convey your unique understanding of a reading. Paraphrases of the same material written by different students are not likely to be exactly the same because writing a paraphrase involves a series of choices: each writer decides what information to include, what language to use, and what organization to employ. Though you should attempt to be objective in your paraphrase of a reading, the details you choose to include and the language you choose to substitute for the author's will be communicating your unique view of the passage.

QUALITIES OF A GOOD PARAPHRASE

Generally, a good paraphrase of a passage exhibits four characteristics. It is thorough, accurate, fair, and objective:

- *Thorough*—it will include all of the author's primary ideas or findings.
- *Accurate*—it will reflect what the author actually wrote.
- *Fair*—your choice of language will be as evenhanded as possible.
- *Objective*—you will avoid voicing your own opinion on the topic or on the quality of the source text.

THOROUGH

A paraphrase of a passage differs from a summary of a passage in its comprehensiveness. In a summary, you try to reduce the source material to its most essential message; in a paraphrase, you try to capture the entire content of the passage. Because you change words and sentence structure when paraphrasing material, your paraphrase of a passage may actually be longer than the original text. Summaries, however, will always be shorter than the original passage. Even though your goal is to be thorough, writing a paraphrase involves making some choices concerning content: you may leave out what you believe to be insignificant details, examples, or explanations found in the source text. Guiding these decisions, though, should be your desire to produce as complete a paraphrase as possible.

ACCURATE

Because you are not quoting authors when you paraphrase their work—because you are substituting your words for theirs—you must take care to be accurate in what you write. Your paraphrase should offer your reader a precise restatement of what the author wrote: though the language is different, your paraphrase should convey the same information or arguments found in the source text. However, accuracy can be hard to achieve. Even slight changes in language can drastically alter the meaning of a passage. Therefore, when writing and revising a paraphrase, check your work against your understanding of the source text. Have you at all misrepresented the *content* of the other writer's piece? Would the author read your paraphrase and agree that you have indeed captured what he or she wrote?

FAIR

Being fair in your paraphrase is related to being accurate. Writing a paraphrase involves putting into your own words someone else's ideas, arguments, or findings. When doing so, first you want to be fair to the author whose work you are paraphrasing. In exchanging your words for his or hers, you want to be as evenhanded as possible. Avoid language, for example, that implies a judgment on your part or makes an author's work appear more sophisticated or more simplistic than it actually is. Second, you want to be fair to your readers. When people read your paraphrase of an author's work, they expect you to give them a fair and accurate understanding of that material. They do not expect you to censure or praise the source text—that's the function of a critique, not a paraphrase.

For a number of reasons, paraphrases are often inaccurate or unfair. First, students often *misread source texts* and make flatly incorrect assertions about the author's work. This type of problem can be avoided through a careful, critical reading of the source text before you try to paraphrase it and by discussing the reading with others. Second, students often *paraphrase material out of context*. Their paraphrase of a passage is misleading because in the larger context of the work the passage has an entirely different meaning from the one reflected in the student's essay. This type of error frequently occurs if the author of the source text is summarizing opposing views in his work. Students who paraphrase this material out of context will frequently misrepresent the author's views, making it appear the author actually agrees with his critics. When you paraphrase someone else's ideas, be sensitive to the relationship between the passage you are working with and the meaning of source text as a whole. Finally, students often produce unfair paraphrases of a source text by *relying on emotionally charged or heavily connotative language*. If an article talks about "presidential aides" and you substitute "presidential cronies," "presidential lackeys," or "presidential co-conspirators," you probably are not being entirely fair in your paraphrase.

OBJECTIVE

A good paraphrase does not take sides. Students often fail to be objective in one of three ways. First, as discussed above, they may employ language that clearly editorializes. In writing a paraphrase, try to use language that fairly and accurately captures the meaning and intent of the source text, not language that reflects your views of the topic or the quality of the source text itself. Second, in writing a paraphrase, sometimes students want to comment directly on the topic the author is addressing. When paraphrasing an author's views on abortion rights, for instance, they may want to articulate their stand on the issue. That material does not belong in a paraphrase, where your goal is to communicate someone else's views. Finally, students sometimes want to include in their paraphrase comments on the quality of the author's work—that they found the argument convincing or faulty, that the author's style was cumbersome or flowing, that the article was "good" or "bad." These types of comments are appropriate for a critique, not for a paraphrase. Your goal in a paraphrase is to be as objective in your content and language as possible.

Before you try to paraphrase someone else's ideas, though, be sure you understand what he or she has written. Again, one of the most common causes of inadequate paraphrasing is failing to grasp the meaning of the source text. Therefore, whether you are paraphrasing a sentence, paragraph, chapter, or essay, you need to understand fully what the author has written before you attempt to put that person's ideas into your own words. Your paraphrase of that person's ideas or findings must be complete, accurate, fair, and objective. It cannot meet these standards if you are confused or at all uncertain about what the author has written.

However, paraphrasing a passage can also be an effective way of determining its meaning. If you are not sure what a passage means, try paraphrasing it. Putting someone else's ideas into your own words is often the best way for you to understand what the author has written. Always reread your paraphrase and the source text to be sure you have been thorough and fair, especially if the paraphrased material is going to be a part of a paper you are turning in.

HOW TO PARAPHRASE MATERIAL

Generally, you paraphrase material by changing words, changing sentence structures, or changing the order of ideas in a passage. More often than not, you will make all three types of changes each time you paraphrase someone's ideas.

CHANGING WORDS

One way to paraphrase a passage is to substitute your words for the author's. However, finding appropriate synonyms for words in the source text can often be challenging. Many students are tempted to turn immediately to a thesaurus for a list of possible replacement words. However, it is usually better to try to come up with appropriate synonyms on your own. Remember, writing a paraphrase involves putting someone else's ideas into *your* own words. If you can come up with replacement words that are fair, accurate, and appropriate for the tone of your paper, use them. If you cannot come up with a new word on your own, then turn to a thesaurus. However, after you look up a possible substitute word in the thesaurus, check its definition in a dictionary to see if the word accurately reflects the meaning you want to convey. The words you find in a thesaurus are not always interchangeable; there are often subtle differences in meaning that you can determine by checking the definition of each term in a good dictionary.

Whether you rely on your own resources or on a thesaurus, using synonyms in a paraphrase raises similar concerns:

- Does the new word convey the author's original idea accurately and objectively?
- Does the new word fit the overall tone of the rest of your essay? Is it too formal or informal? Too technical or too general?

Often, it may be impossible to find an adequate substitute for a word or phrase in a passage: perhaps the author coined a phrase or used an unusual or shocking term. In such cases, it is appropriate for you to quote the language found in the source text (see Chapter 2 for guidelines on quoting material). When paraphrasing material, however, try to keep the number of quotations to a minimum. Also, remember that *all* paraphrased passages you include in your papers must be documented—even though you change the language of the source text when you paraphrase, you need to acknowledge through your documentation the source of the *ideas* you are discussing.

Below are examples of passages paraphrased primarily through word substitution. You will find the original passage, a rough-draft paraphrase, and a final paraphrase. The original passages in all of the following examples are drawn from the readings included in Chapters 1 and 2.

Example 1

A. Original

"Teenagers stand at a precarious threshold, no longer children and not yet adults, eager to be independent but lacking the equipment and composure."

B. Rough-Draft Paraphrase

Teenagers stand at a dangerous moment in their lives, between childhood and adulthood, wanting to be independent but not possessing the ability and maturity to do so.

C. Final Paraphrase (APA Documentation)

Teens face a dangerous time in their lives, between childhood and adulthood, wanting desperately to live on their own but not possessing the skills and maturity they need to enter the next phase of their lives (Bauerlein, 2009, p. 35).

Discussion: In my rough draft, I changed a few words: "precarious threshold" became "dangerous moment in their lives," "no longer children and not yet adults" became "between childhood and adulthood," and "lacking the equipment and composure" became "not possessing the ability and maturity to do so." In places, my first attempt was still too close to the wording in the original passage, and I wasn't sure I captured the connotative meaning of several words. I liked "between childhood and adulthood," but I retained the word "independent" (which I thought I needed to change), "ability" did not seem like the right word to replace "equipment," "moment" wasn't the right word to replace "threshold," and I did not think the end of my paraphrase captured what the author meant in the context of the original. So in my next draft, I changed "moment in their lives" to "time in their lives," changed "ability" to "skills" (which I think comes closer to the author's word—"equipment"), and added the last part of the sentence to clarify what I think the author meant in the original. The basic sentence structure has remained the same; I've only tried to change some of the words.

Example 2

A. Original

"For many kids, the bedroom at midnight provides a rich social life that makes daytime face-to-face conversations seem tame and slow."

B. Rough-Draft Paraphrase

Many kids, even in their bedrooms in the middle of the night, have a richer social life electronically than they do talking one-on-one to their friends during the day.

C. Final Paraphrase (MLA Documentation)

Thanks to technology, many kids have a more exciting life electronically with friends overnight in their bedrooms than they have talking with them one-on-one during the day (Bauerlein 36).

Discussion: This was a difficult text to paraphrase out of context. In the original work, the author is clearly discussing the impact of technology on teenagers' social lives, but that word, "technology," does not appear in the passage. In my rough draft, I added the word "electronically" after "social life" to capture this meaning. The word "midnight" became "middle of the night," and "daytime face-to-face conversations" became "talking one-on-one to their friends during the day." I switched "rich social life" for "richer social life," which clearly needed to be changed or quoted. In my final draft, I opened the sentence with "Thanks to technology" to place the passage in context, changed "richer social life" to "more exciting life electronically." Again, I'm still not entirely happy with this paraphrase because I've only substituted words—it would be a better paraphrase if I also employed the techniques described below.

CHANGING SENTENCE STRUCTURE

Besides changing words, when composing a good paraphrase of material, you may also need to alter the sentence structure employed in the source text. Often such changes involve rearranging the order of ideas in a sentence or altering the order of dependent and independent clauses.

Example 3

A. Original

"Although communism and state socialism have failed to protect the environment, eco-extremists are basically anti-business."

B. *Rough-Draft Paraphrase*

"Eco-extremists" oppose business interests even though communism and state socialism have failed to protect the environment.

C. *Final Paraphrase (MLA Documentation)*

"Eco-extremists" oppose business even though communist and socialist governments have permitted environmental degradation (Moore 16).

Discussion: In my rough draft, I first changed the order of the ideas in the sentence. I could not think of an appropriate substitution for "eco-extremist" so I quoted it and changed "anti-business" to "oppose business." In my final draft, I had to find a better way of addressing the second half of my paraphrase. I started by changing "communism and state socialism" to "communist and socialist governments" and reworded the idea about failing to protect the environment to "have permitted environmental degradation." Looking at it now, I think "degradation" may not be the best word—some additional changes might be needed.

COMBINING SENTENCES

When you paraphrase longer passages, you will often have to "combine" sentences in the source text to paraphrase the material adequately. After you read the entire passage, you may feel that you can condense the information into fewer sentences while still being thorough and fair in your paraphrase. By changing words, altering sentence structures, and combining information found in two or more source sentences into one sentence of your own, you can often achieve a smooth, effective paraphrase of material.

Example 4

A. *Original*

"In addition to choosing a dubious tactic, the environmental movement also changed its philosophy along the way. It once prided itself on subscribing to a philosophy that was 'transpolitical, transideological, and transnational' in character. Non-violent direct action and peaceful disobedience were the hallmarks of the movement. Truth mattered and science was respected for the knowledge it brought to the debate."

B. *Rough-Draft Paraphrase*

In recent years the environmental movement has adopted a new philosophy. It once believed its philosophy cut across political, ideological, and national lines. While its adherents believed in direct action and peaceful disobedience, truth also mattered, as did science, which brought knowledge to the debate.

C. Final Paraphrase (APA Documentation)

According to Patrick Moore (1995), the environmental movement has changed its guiding philosophy. They used to believe their ideas cut across political, ideological, and national lines. They also believed in peaceful protests, respected the truth, and valued science for the information it brought them.

Discussion: In my rough draft, I condensed the four sentences found in the source text into three sentences in my paraphrase. I was especially interested in combining the last two sentences. At the same time, I was trying to change some of the words. For example, I altered "transpolitical, transideological, and transnational" but let stand much of the language in those last two sentences. To begin my final draft, I added the author's name and dropped "in recent years," which I had added in the rough draft. In the next two sentences I tried to echo the term "philosophy" with the word "believed" and achieve parallel structure by using "They" twice. I continued to change some of the terms, substituting "peaceful" for "non-violent" and again tried to achieve some sense of parallel structure in my last sentence (which combines two sentences in the source text).

"UNPACKING" SENTENCES

Sometimes a sentence in a reading may be so densely written, so full of ideas, that in your paraphrase you may need two or three sentences to convey the same information. When "unpacking" a sentence like this, your goal remains to convey the author's ideas fairly and thoroughly in your own language. Be sure first, however, that you fully understand the source passage—densely written material is often hard to read.

Example 5

A. Original

"So they look to one another, emulating dress and speech, forming groups of insiders and outsiders, finding comfort in boyfriends and girlfriends, and deflecting more or less tenuously the ever-present risk of embarrassment."

B. Rough-Draft Paraphrase

Because many teenagers are still trying to define themselves, they look to each other for support. They end up dressing alike. They define who their friends are. They look to boyfriends or girlfriends. All the time, though, they are trying not to embarrass themselves.

C. Final Paraphrase (MLA Documentation)

Many teenagers look beyond their home and parents to define themselves. Instead, they look to each other for support. Ironically, in an effort to define their individuality, they end up dressing like their peers, forming cliques, and devoting themselves to girlfriends or boyfriends. All the time, though, they try, more or less successfully, to keep from embarrassing themselves (Bauerlein 35).

Discussion: This was a difficult passage to paraphrase. First, the original sentence makes little sense out of context, so in my rough draft, I paraphrased the sentence that leads up to this one in the source text: "Because many teenagers are still trying to define themselves." I then broke up the original sentence into five sentences, each covering one of the main ideas in the source text. This passage, however, was choppy and repetitive; I needed to combine them for better coherence. The final version has four sentences, and in the third sentence I added "Ironically" to capture the tone and intent of the original sentence as I interpreted it. Even at this stage, though, I think the first two sentences could be combined to make the paraphrase even more concise—perhaps going back to the syntax I used in the rough draft.

COMBINING STRATEGIES: PARAPHRASING LONGER PASSAGES IN SOURCE TEXTS

There may be times when you have to paraphrase passages from a source text that are several sentences or even several paragraphs long. When this is the case, you will likely need to employ all of the strategies discussed in this chapter.

Example 6

A. *Original*

"At the center of binge drinking on many campuses are fraternities and sororities. While they attract only a small percentage of students nationally, they continue to play a prominent role in campus life at many institutions. Our data shows that in fraternity houses, four of five residents binge, and more than half are frequent binge drinkers. And, fraternity parties are attended by many more students than just members. They attract even some high-school seniors—future college students who are introduced to binge drinking as a social norm. Not surprisingly, most of the alcohol-related deaths of college students recently reported in the media involved fraternity parties.

"While some colleges have begun to address the drinking culture created by fraternities, many administrators are still hesitant to move strongly against fraternities, for fear of angering alumni donors who fondly remember their own college years of partying. But administrators have a responsibility to protect all of their students against alcohol-related disruptions and injuries, and should not wait for tragedy to strike before they revoke official recognition of fraternities that consistently cause problems. Colleges also can require all first-year students who live on campus to reside in dormitories, and not in fraternity or sorority houses. Of course, then those colleges must work to create interesting alcohol-free activities centered in the residence halls, to show students that out-of-control drinking need not be the focus of social life."

B. Rough-Draft Paraphrase

Even though only a small number of students join fraternities and sororities in college, they are responsible for much of the binge drinking on U.S. campuses. In fact, one study showed that four of five fraternity and sorority members binge drink, more than half, frequently. In addition, high-school students sometimes attend Greek parties, introducing them to binge drinking even before they enroll in college. Recently, several students have even died after becoming drunk at fraternity parties.

Although they know fraternities are often the site of binge drinking, college administrators are often reluctant to crack down on them because they are afraid of angering alumni donors who themselves were Greeks. However, in doing so, administrators fail to uphold their responsibility to protect all students. One way to attack the problem would be to require all freshmen to live in dorms, but schools would then also have to provide alcohol-free recreational opportunities to demonstrate that students do not have to get drunk to have fun.

C. Final Paraphrase (MLA Documentation)

In the United States, while only a small number of students join fraternities and sororities in college, they are responsible for much of the binge drinking. One study showed that four out of five fraternity and sorority members binge drink (over 50 percent, frequently) and often introduce binge drinking to high-school students who attend their parties. Although administrators know that fraternities are often the site of binge drinking (and that some students have died after getting drunk at fraternity parties), they are reluctant to crack down on them—many potential alumni donors were Greeks and may object to such action. To address the problem, administrators could prohibit freshmen from living in Greek housing, but they would also have to provide alcohol-free recreational opportunities to demonstrate that students do not have to get drunk to have fun (Wechsler 21–22).

Discussion: As I moved through the rough draft into the final paraphrase, I tried to condense and simplify the sentences in the source text while remaining comprehensive. I ended up with one paragraph instead of two, although the order of the ideas in my paraphrase still follows the order of ideas presented in the original. I'm still not sure that I like substituting "Greek" for "fraternities and sororities" in the paraphrase of the expression "crack down on them" (it may be too informal). To condense the material, I used parentheses twice to enclose material I thought was of secondary importance. Also note that I need to provide documentation only once, at the end of the paraphrased passage.

BLENDING YOUR WRITING WITH PARAPHRASED MATERIAL

Often in academic writing you will be blending your writing with material you're paraphrasing from source texts. Through documentation and attribution, you will guide your readers through the passage, clarifying which prose is yours and which is paraphrased. I have numbered the sentences in Example 7 below to make it easier to discuss the passage.

Example 7 (Using APA Documentation)

> [1]Clearly, binge drinking is a problem on many college campuses, but who is to blame? [2]Author Henry Wechsler (1998) lays part of the responsibility at the feet of fraternities and sororities. [3]According to Wechsler, although only a small number of college students actually "go Greek," fraternity and sorority members account for a disproportionate number of binge drinkers. [4]Fraternities, in particular, seem to promote binge drinking, since four out of five students living in a fraternity house report that they binge drink (p. 21). [5]If college administrators know that fraternities and sororities are a major site of binge drinking on their campuses, why don't they act to stop that behavior? [6]Wechsler believes it comes down to money. [7]They are afraid to offend alumni donors who were themselves Greeks by cracking down on fraternities and sororities (p. 21). [8]If these alumni feel that the administration is unfairly targeting Greeks, they will be less likely to donate money to the school.

Discussion: In this example, sentences 3, 4, and 7 are paraphrased from the source text and are therefore documented. Sentences 1, 2, 5, 6, and 8 are ones I wrote and therefore do not need to be documented. Note how citing the source text at the end of sentence 4 provides sufficient documentation for sentences 3 and 4.

DOCUMENTATION

Remember that any material you paraphrase from a source must be properly documented. Failing to document paraphrased material is a form of plagiarism. Although the various forms of documentation you will encounter in college are discussed in Chapter 13, remember that every discipline expects writers to document all paraphrased material properly.

Summary Chart

HOW TO PARAPHRASE MATERIAL

---

1. **Read, reread, and annotate the material.**
   - *Use a dictionary to find the meaning of any words you do not know.*
   - *Form your own opinion about the meaning of the passage.*

2. **Change words in the passage.**
   - *Substitute synonyms for key terms in the passage.*
   - *Substitute pronouns for nouns when appropriate.*
   - *Change the verbs.*

3. **Change the sentence structure in the passage.**
   - *Rearrange the order of ideas presented in the source text.*

4. **Combine sentences found in the source text.**
   - *Combine into single sentences ideas presented in two or more sentences in the source text.*

5. **Unpack sentences found in the source text.**
   - *Convey in two or more sentences ideas presented in one sentence in the source text.*

PARAPHRASE REVISION CHECKLIST

	Yes	No
1. Have you provided the full title of the source and identified its author?	_____	_____
2. Have you employed a variety of methods to paraphrase the material?	_____	_____
3. Have you checked to be sure your paraphrase accurately captures the author's ideas?	_____	_____
4. Have you remained as objective as possible in choosing language for your paraphrase?	_____	_____
5. Have you avoided offering your opinions on the topic of the reading or on the writer's style?	_____	_____
6. Have you checked your language to make sure each word you have chosen means what you think it means, has the connotation you want it to have, and fits the general tone of your paraphrase?	_____	_____
7. Have you reviewed your sentence structure for clarity and variety?	_____	_____
8. Have you provided appropriate transitions between the ideas you paraphrase?	_____	_____
9. Have you provided proper and accurate documentation?	_____	_____
10. Have you properly punctuated your documentation?	_____	_____

Chapter 4

SUMMARY

In this chapter you will learn how to

1. Differentiate among various forms of summary
2. Write effective informative and explanatory summaries
3. Write abstracts
4. Document summarized material

DEFINITION AND PURPOSE

Summarizing a reading involves two separate processes: (1) identifying the important material in the text and (2) restating the material in your own words. Because part of your job when writing a summary is deciding what to include from the reading and what to leave out, summaries are always shorter than the source text. Like paraphrases, summaries are always written in your own words (you can use quotations in a summary, but only sparingly), and they should be as objective as possible (you do not include in a summary your own opinions, beliefs, or judgments, and you try to use neutral language).

The ability to summarize readings is fundamental to academic, source-based writing. You will likely be summarizing information when you prepare a lab report, review a movie, write a research paper, or take an essay test. Instructors will often ask you to summarize articles or book chapters to be sure you can read carefully and critically, identify key ideas and important supporting evidence or arguments, and express that information clearly in your own words.

Sometimes summaries are part of a longer work. In a history research paper, for example, you may summarize the work of several different theorists while presenting an argument of your own. Other times, however, summaries will be "freestanding"—graded as independent formal essays. Your goal in writing them is to convey in your own words only the most important ideas, arguments, or findings in a reading. To write these types of assignments, you need to form a clear understanding of the source text, decide what to include in your summary and what to leave out, and choose language that clearly and objectively conveys the author's ideas.

Other times, though, you will use summaries to support a larger argument you are advancing in an essay. First, you may summarize the arguments or findings of experts who agree with the position you have assumed in your thesis; readers may accept your position if they see that other authorities support it as well. Second, you may summarize the work of experts who call into question your thesis. Doing so will help your work appear informed and balanced, again improving your credibility in the eyes of many academic readers. Be sure, however, that if you do summarize opposing views in your essay, you then somehow address them. For example, following your summary, you can critique that information—pointing out its strengths and weaknesses—and explain how the opposing ideas affect the validity of your thesis.

Whether your summary is part of a longer work or stands on its own, it must make sense to someone who has not read the source text. If, for example, you are working as a loan officer in a bank and your boss hands you a financial report to summarize, she wants to be able to understand your summary without having to read the report herself. She wants *you* to read the report carefully and distill from it the information she needs to know.

TYPES OF SUMMARIES

In college you will probably write two different types of summaries: informative and explanatory. An informative summary simply conveys the author's main ideas, data, arguments, and supporting material; an explanatory summary conveys this information as well, but also indicates the overall structure of the source text, explaining how the author develops his or her assertions. Informative summaries are shorter than explanatory summaries and are usually incorporated into longer works or take the form of an **abstract**. Explanatory summaries are longer than informative summaries, follow the organizational scheme of the source text, frequently refer to the name of the source text's author, and usually serve as independent, freestanding essays.

Below are two different summaries of the opening lines of the Gettysburg Address, one informative and one explanatory. As you read them, note the differences in content, structure, and word choice.

Example 1

Source Text

"Four score and seven years ago our fathers brought forth on this continent, a new nation, conceived in Liberty and dedicated to the proposition that all men are created equal. Now we are engaged in a great civil war, testing whether that nation, or any nation so conceived and so dedicated, can long endure. We are met on a great battlefield of that war. We have come to dedicate a portion of that field, as a final resting place for those who here gave their lives that that nation might live."

Informative Summary

> Eighty-seven years ago the United States was founded on the idea that all people are created equal. Currently a civil war is testing whether such a nation can survive. A portion of this battlefield is to be designated as a cemetery for those who fought in the war.

Explanatory Summary

> Lincoln opens the Gettysburg Address by remarking that eighty-seven years ago the United States was founded on the idea that all people are created equal. He next points out how the country is engaged in a civil war that will determine whether such a nation can survive, then acknowledges the occasion of the speech: to dedicate part of a great battlefield as a cemetery for the combatants.

Notice that the point of the informative summary is simply to capture in your own words the important ideas found in the source text. In an explanatory summary, though, you repeatedly refer to the author of the work and indicate how the piece was organized through your choice of verbs ("opens," "points out") and transition words ("next," "then").

QUALITIES OF A GOOD SUMMARY

Informative and explanatory summaries need to be comprehensive, brief, accurate, neutral, and independent.

- *Comprehensive*—it conveys all the important information in the reading.
- *Brief*—it conveys this information concisely.
- *Accurate*—it correctly conveys the author's ideas, findings, or arguments.
- *Neutral*—it avoids judgments concerning the reading's topic or style.
- *Independent*—it makes sense to someone who has not read the source text.

COMPREHENSIVE

Your summary needs to include all of the important ideas, assertions, or findings contained in the source text as well as the most significant information or arguments the author provides to support them. When you paraphrase a passage, you try to capture in your own language everything the author has written. However, when you summarize that same passage, you have to be more selective in choosing material to include. You need to identify what you believe to be the most important material in the passage and include only that in your summary. In this way your summary is comprehensive—you have not left out any important information.

Does that mean that if a number of people were summarizing the same article, all of their essays would be identical, at least in content?

No. Determining what to include in a summary requires judgment. Each individual writer must decide what is most important in the source text. Some writers will make good choices; some will make poor choices. Even those making good choices may decide to include different information. Consequently, students assigned to summarize the same reading will likely produce slightly different essays. If you carefully and critically read the source text before you begin to write your summary, and if you check your work against the source text before you turn it in to be sure you have included all of the important information, you will probably produce a comprehensive summary.

BRIEF

In writing a summary, you have to balance two concerns: you want your summary to be comprehensive, but you also want it to be brief. The point of writing a summary is to *reduce* a text to its most essential information. In a summary, brevity is usually achieved through carefully selecting your content and words. First you need to include (1) the reading's primary ideas, arguments, or findings and (2) the primary means of support the author offers for his or her contentions. Second, you must always be concerned about word count: if you can say something gracefully in four words rather than five, say it in four; if you can condense material by cutting unnecessary prepositions or adjectives, cut them. Composing a good summary requires disciplined writing.

ACCURATE

Your readers depend on you to be accurate in your summary. You have to be careful not to misrepresent—purposefully or accidentally—what the author wrote. Instead of reading the source text, your readers are depending on you to provide them with a thorough, accurate, and fair overview of the piece. Misrepresenting an author in your summary is unfair to both your reader and the original author. However, accuracy can be hard to maintain. Because in a summary you are substituting your language for the author's, even slight changes in words can drastically alter the meaning of a passage. Therefore, when you review your summary, check it against the source to be sure you have accurately represented what the author wrote. Make sure you have not misrepresented the author's ideas or findings either by omitting some important information or by using inaccurate, slanted, or vague language.

NEUTRAL

Summaries should be objective. No matter how much you would like to praise or criticize an author's argument, interpretation of data, or style of writing, such comments do not belong in a summary. In a summary you do not present your views on the topic the author is addressing, you do not comment on the quality of the author's argument or writing, and you do not voice any of your opinions at all. Instead, you try to present what the author has written accurately and objectively. When reviewing your summary, make sure you have not included your own opinions and that you have used objective language. By avoiding highly charged or judgmental terms, you can help ensure that your summary is neutral, balanced, and fair.

When there are problems with objectivity in a summary, more often than not they appear in one of three places: at the beginnings of paragraphs, in the middle of long paragraphs, and at the very end of the piece. At the beginnings of paragraphs, students sometimes react to the material contained in the previous paragraph; instead of moving on to summarize the author's next point, they respond to the previous one. In the middle of paragraphs, students sometimes begin to debate the author. They may notice that the author has presented a weak argument, for example, and feel compelled to point that out. Such criticisms are appropriate for a critique, but not for a summary. Finally, at the ends of summaries, students sometimes add the kind of concluding line commonly found in high school book reports, "Overall, I really liked this book because . . ." or "Although I found the author convincing, sometimes I had a hard time. . . ." Such statements do not belong in an objective, neutral summary.

INDEPENDENT

Your summary ought to make sense to someone who has not read the source text. Keep in mind the purpose of a summary. If, for instance, your employer asks you to summarize a report, she wants to learn from your summary the main points of the report without having to read the original text. Your summary must be able to stand on its own—read independently, it has to make sense. To achieve this goal, you need to pay special attention to word choice when drafting your summary. For example, are there any terms that, taken from the context of the source text, will need to be defined in your summary? Have you included in your summary any pronouns that refer to an antecedent in the source, not to an antecedent in your summary? Have you referred to people who were identified in the source but are not identified in your summary?

To make sure your summary is independent, let someone read it who has not read the source text before you turn it in for a grade. Ask that person to mark any words or passages he or she finds confusing.

HOW TO SUMMARIZE A TEXT

READ, REREAD, AND ANNOTATE THE SOURCE TEXT

Obviously, the first step in writing a summary is to read the material you are summarizing. As you read through it for the first time, try to get a sense of the passage's main ideas and structure—a sense of what the author covers and the order in which the ideas are presented. Next, read the material again, only more slowly this time. As you reread, carefully mark the passage, highlighting important material and taking notes in the margin that identify the main points, key supporting information, and the structure of the piece.

If you are summarizing a paragraph, locate and mark the topic sentence. If there is no topic sentence, paraphrase the main point of the paragraph in the margin. If you are summarizing an entire essay or article, locate the thesis. If the author states the thesis, underline it and make a note in the margin. If the thesis is implied rather than stated, paraphrase the main point of the piece at the end of the passage. If the source text has headings and subheadings, note how they help structure the piece.

SUMMARIZE EACH SECTION OF THE SOURCE TEXT

Identify the major sections of the piece—where the author discusses one idea or develops one argument or explores one finding. These sections may consist of a single paragraph or a group of paragraphs. In the margin of the passage or on a separate sheet of paper, briefly summarize each section of the text. Using your own words, note the primary idea, assertion, or finding being developed in each section along with the primary supporting material the author provides—the most effective example, the most telling statistic, the most important authority cited.

CHECK THE SECTION SUMMARIES AGAINST THE SOURCE TEXT

The brief summaries you produce of each section of the source text will help you incorporate the material into a longer essay you are writing, compose an abstract of the source text, or produce an explanatory summary of the reading. Now is a good time to check these brief summaries against the source text to ensure they are accurate, neutral, comprehensive, and clear.

HOW TO WRITE AN ABSTRACT

As stated earlier, the goal of an informative summary is to convey as briefly and accurately as possible the primary content of a source text or perhaps just a certain section of that text. When you incorporate summarized material into a longer essay you are writing—a report or research paper, for example—you may introduce the material by referring to the author's name and/or the title of the piece before you add it to your essay. A special form of an informative summary in academic writing is an abstract. Abstracts are usually paragraph-long informative summaries of a reading and frequently accompany scholarly texts. Most often located under the title of the text, an abstract provides a succinct overview of the reading, informing readers of the text's primary assertions, findings, or arguments. When you are engaged in a research project, abstracts can be invaluable: when you locate a source text that looks interesting, by reading the abstract alone you can decide whether to read the entire piece or move on to the next one.

After you draft your abstract, be sure to check it against the original to ensure that the abstract is comprehensive and independent—it ought to make the main points of the reading clear to someone who has not read the text. Also be sure that you are paraphrasing the source text throughout your abstract: the language you use should be yours. Sometimes you might have to quote specific terms the author has used if they are particularly important or novel.

HOW TO WRITE AN INFORMATIVE SUMMARY ESSAY

An informative summary is longer and more detailed than an abstract, covering the author's primary assertions, findings, and arguments, as well as how they are supported. Informative summaries frequently follow the source text's organization—summarizing the text's first main point first, the second main point next, and so on. This is not necessary, however, if using a different organizational strategy would make your summary stronger. In the end, your informative summary should be comprehensive, brief, accurate, neutral, and independent.

In the *opening section* of your essay, introduce the topic or context of the reading, provide the source text's full title and the full names of its authors, and state your thesis. You might also want to provide the author's credentials or the publication information of the source text (where and when it was originally published). Your thesis will be a paraphrase of the source text's thesis.

In the *body* of your informative summary, paraphrase the primary content of the source text. You may want to use the one-sentence summaries of each section you composed earlier as a guide. Just paraphrase the content of the readings—do not embellish or editorialize. Your goal is to write a thorough summary of the source text that is both clear and neutral. Do not comment on the text's content, style, or structure. Plagiarism can be a problem with summarizing a text: be sure you paraphrase the material properly. You may quote material in an informative summary, but you should use quotations sparingly.

Informative summaries do not have conclusions like other forms of source-based essays. Instead, you close your paper by summarizing the source text's last key assertion, finding, or argument. Do not editorialize at the end of your summary—do not include any judgmental statements like "Overall, the author did a good job of presenting her ideas" or "The piece was extremely interesting and easy to read." Your summary should be neutral and objective.

As always, review your rough draft against the source text as you revise to ensure that your summary is comprehensive and that you have adequately covered the source text's primary content.

HOW TO WRITE AN EXPLANATORY SUMMARY ESSAY

As with an informative summary, an explanatory summary conveys the primary content of a text. However, it describes not only what the reading says but also how it is put together through frequent references to the author's organizational strategy. When a teacher asks you to write a summary of a text, this is the type of document he or she usually has in mind: an explanatory summary of the reading that is comprehensive, brief, accurate, neutral, and independent.

In the *opening section* of your summary—usually the first paragraph or two—introduce the topic of the source text, give the title of the piece you are summarizing, mention the name and credentials of the person who wrote the piece, and include your thesis. In a summary, your thesis will likely be a paraphrase of the source text's thesis.

In the *body* of your summary, present in your own words the author's primary assertions, conclusions, or findings, as well as the supporting examples or statistics you believe your readers will need to know to understand and appreciate the author's contentions. Use as a guide the brief summaries of each section of the text you wrote earlier. An explanatory summary is different from an informative summary because in the body of your essay you will make frequent references to the author of the piece and explain how the source text is structured through your use of transitions. Assume you are working with an article by Alice Smith. Your explanatory summary will include many passages such as these: "Smith opens her essay by . . . ," "Next, Smith discusses . . . ," "Smith's third main argument is . . . ," and "Smith concludes her essay with. . . ." All of these example passages include the author's name and some listing or transition word (e.g., "first," "next," "then"). You do not have to use the author's name in every sentence, just when you are moving from your summary of one section of the source text to another section so your reader has a clear sense of the source text's structure.

Generally, summaries do not need a *conclusion*; simply end your essay with a summary of the author's last point. If you want or need a formal conclusion, make it a brief restatement of the author's thesis.

When you have finished the rough draft of your explanatory summary essay, reread the source text to ensure that you have captured all of the important content of the reading. To be sure that your summary is clear, ask someone who has not read the source text to read your summary and identify any passages he or she finds confusing. Remember: unless you are told otherwise by your teacher, assume your audience has not read the source text. Also check the tone of your summary. It ought to be objective and neutral.

DOCUMENTATION

Summarized material should be documented. Many students do not feel they need to document summarized material that is part of a larger essay because they are using their own language to convey the author's ideas. However, you still need

to give the author credit for those ideas, arguments, or findings. Documentation also tells your readers where they can locate the source text if they want
to read the whole piece themselves.

READING

After the following article, "From *Animal House* to *Big Brother:* Student Privacy and Campus Security in an Age of Accountability," by Ron Chesbrough,
you will find three summaries—an abstract, an informative summary, and
an explanatory summary. The article originally appeared in *Student Affairs
Leader*.

From *Animal House* to *Big Brother:* Student Privacy and Campus Safety in an Age of Accountability

Ron Chesbrough

Ron Chesbrough is the vice president of student affairs at Hastings College in
Nebraska. He is also a member of Student Affairs Leader's editorial board.

Two Scenarios: A student at a large university spots a gun on the desk
of a fellow student during class. Frightened, the student sends a text
message to someone outside of the classroom, who in turn contacts the
University Police Department. Members of the University Police respond
immediately, going to the classroom and removing the student and the
gun. In the process, they learn that the gun is a toy gun used in the popular
game "Assassin." They seek out the other students engaged in the game
and confiscate their toy guns. A notice is sent to the university community
describing the incident in detail and announcing the prohibition of this game
on university property.

    A student at a small private college reports to the dean of students that
she has read disturbing poems on the Facebook page of another student. The
dean reviews the postings, which contain references to being unhappy and
questioning the purpose of life. The dean calls the student in and requires
that he undergo a full psychiatric evaluation based on the poems.

Background

We have learned recently many times over, and with crushing severity, what we have long known—that college campuses are risk-inherent environments. We have also been tragically reminded of a corollary fact—that one of our greatest challenges in creating and preserving safe environments on our campuses is the ability to find and strike a proper balance between our students' rights to privacy and their rights to a safe and healthy living and learning community. This is not a new imperative for us; it is simply one that has gained importance in recent years and with recent events on our campuses.

In the wake of the tragedy of the Virginia Tech shootings of nearly a year ago and those that have followed, the intersection of student privacy rights and community safety is, now more than ever, one where the traffic light is changing erratically. With the lights blinking red, green, and yellow on all sides, institutions and professionals are left largely to their own interpretations and intuitions about when to go, stop, or proceed with caution when it comes to student privacy rights.

From emergency alert text messaging systems to patrols of Facebook and MySpace and all things in between, colleges and universities are searching for the new right relationship with students in the interest of campus safety.

Take, for example, a recent article in the *Wall Street Journal*, featured in the February 1 issue of *Student Affairs Leader*, [that] described Cornell University's new "alert team" and related university-wide training to recognize and report signs of student emotional distress and behavioral concerns ("Bucking Privacy Concerns, Cornell Acts as Watchdog," *WSJ*, December 28, 2007). These practices place Cornell "squarely in the center of a debate over the rights of American college students," according to the article. Just what is the debate, we should ask, and how have we arrived here?

FERPA in Transition

The Family Education Rights and Privacy Act (FERPA) has long governed the treatment of student privacy rights in higher education. Its protections and allowances are familiar enough by now to not bear detailed repeating here, although a refresher on the various amendments to FERPA, particularly over the past decade, is not a bad idea.

It is also useful to gain some familiarity with the shifting ground of case law in matters concerning student privacy rights and our duty to protect students from harm—whether from themselves or others.

Two recent cases worth reading again in this regard are *Shin v. Massachusetts Institute of Technology* and *Schieszler v. Ferrum College*. In both cases the courts found a special duty to care (in these cases to prevent self-harm) based on the unique relationship between students and their academic institutions.

If we set aside the legitimate and compelling question of an institution's ability to "prevent" harm to all students at all times, we can see that the real central issue here is one of discernment and disclosure.

In other words, how do we maximize our ability to detect or discern threats to safety on our campuses? And once a possible or plausible threat is discerned, to what end and to whom do we disclose this information? And finally, what are the implications of this discernment/disclosure puzzle for our relationships with students?

Disclosure

To begin, we might begin to rethink our definition of "privacy" in this scenario. We might also question the original intent of FERPA—asking who and what it was originally intended to protect, and from whom. Here it seems clear that the original and ongoing intent of FERPA is to provide reasonable protections against undue intrusions into the education records of students by those not determined under law to have legal rights to such access, and to provide students with their own due process rights to the same information pertaining to them and being held by the institution.

Where institutions keep information of a disciplinary nature, and where such records do not constitute criminal records, the same protections and rights have applied, with notable recent amendments allowing disclosure of information to certain others (e.g., parents, victims) when in relation to certain types of potentially noncriminal records (e.g., campus drug/alcohol violations, sexual violence).

Similarly, allowances exist for disclosure of certain medical or treatment records held by the college to both parents and others as directed by FERPA. Finally, the Jeanne Clery Act not only allows but also requires both annual reporting and timely warning (in cases of an ongoing threat) of criminal activity on our campuses.

Given these provisions for disclosures under FERPA and what some would argue is a gross historic misunderstanding of more general parental disclosure rights of the institution under FERPA, it is fair to say that we have often overstated protections afforded to students under this law.

It is safe to say, historically speaking, that we have often erred on the side of overprotecting these rights, especially in the grey areas of FERPA, that many would argue still exist after more than four decades and numerous amendments to the legislation. But are we moving too far, too fast into this new intersection of student privacy rights and campus safety?

Who Bears Responsibility—and to Whom

In their recent look at critical issues for student affairs professionals, Arthur Sandeen and Margaret J. Barr had this to say about the rising complexity of the question of student safety on our campuses: "Legal requirements, institutional missions, parental expectations, chronic psychological problems of students, and student behaviors require both the profession and institutions to answer this fundamental question" (Sandeen & Barr, 2006, p. xii). Their chapter entitled "Who Has the Responsibility for the Lives of Students?" is an attempt to answer this question.

I would argue, as perhaps they would, that this is not a new question, but an old one posed in a new context, with new and literal meaning imbued by recent events on our campuses nationwide. It is not the "who" in this question that has changed, but the "how."

How are we differently responsible for the lives of our students in the current era, and as importantly, how do we best fulfill that responsibility when faced with the kinds of scenarios posed at the outset? Put differently, how do we begin to rebalance the right of all students to a safe learning environment with the rights of those whom Sandeen and Barr refer to as our "disturbed" students, students whom they suggest are coming to us in increasing numbers (Sandeen & Barr, pp. 155–180)?

A Beginning Attempt

To begin, we need to revisit this concept of the disturbed student, first coined by Ursula Delworth, two decades ago in a definition that has almost eerie accuracy in today's environment of high-stakes disturbance on campus. These students, according to Delworth, can demonstrate an outward (anger and lashing out) or inward (depression and withdrawal) focus, and hold the potential to harm themselves or others (Delworth, 1989). Of particular importance, according to Delworth, is our recognition and response to those students who are both disturbed and disturbing of the campus environment.

We should refresh ourselves in the clear communication roles and responsibilities among campus administrators and health professionals established by Hollingsworth and Dunkle (2005) in our coordinated response to these students. And in this we should heed Arthur Sandeen's (1989) reminder that "an institution that decides it can not afford the resources required to address the problems of the disturbed and disturbing student may discover the costs of ignoring them are too great" (p. 61).

We should set clear behavioral expectations of our students in the classroom, in residence halls, and in the campus community at large. These are simply those norms that we insist should exist for the emotional and physical comfort of all members of the learning community, and they should be indexed to those instances where a certain behavior might reasonably be seen as imposing on or limiting the rights of other members of the community to a safe, healthy, and positive living and learning environment.

We should anticipate both the reasonable accommodations that might be made to students unable to meet certain behavioral requirements consistently or in all settings, and the absolute limits of behaviors that fall outside of the pale of the learning community. And we should clearly state what our responses would be in either case.

If we intend to not allow play guns on campus, or if concerning posts to a Facebook page are cause for college response, then students should be aware of this and the consequences of behaving in these ways. This takes hard and deliberate thought and imagination, and ought to involve a hearty dose of student and faculty input. It will lead to debate, discussion, and disagreement—but it is precisely this debate that needs to occur, in anticipation of difficult campus events rather than in response to them.

Students, and their parents, should be made to understand that college officials will exercise their full rights under FERPA to share information deemed necessary between college health officials and administrators; between administrators and parents or appropriate outside officials; and between members of the faculty, staff, and administration of the college or university as allowed by law—to ensure the safety of all members of the community to the best of their ability. And the mechanisms for said sharing should be transparent and readily understood by all members of the learning community and its constituents.

Implications

Some will point to a chilling effect of a learning environment so characterized. I would argue the opposite. What is chilling in the present environment is the relative lack of these types of safeguards in the face of clear and repeated evidence of our need for them. What is discomforting is the unease we feel at the intersection of student privacy rights and community safety—and it is discomforting not just for student affairs practitioners, but also for students, staff, faculty, and parents alike.

In this environment, it falls most logically to student affairs professionals to take the steps necessary to police this intersection and to work with others to develop the proper new traffic signals for this new environment.

It can also be said that this new posture poses new legal liability threats to institutions that may be claiming, by making such clear statements of intent, to be able to prevent bad things from happening on their campuses. Arguably, due diligence does in fact take on a new meaning in light of commitments like those described to attempt to discern and report potential threats to safety.

At the same time, we enter an environment wherein the lack of such stepped-up attempts may soon be discerned as a failure of due diligence, particularly as institutions move individually in these directions and as findings from various reports raise the question for legislators, parents, and others as to what our due diligence ought to, in fact, entail.

Still others may find such measures to have a discriminatory or dampening effect on admission for those students disclosing in that process a pre-existing diagnosis that may make them more prone to "concerning" exhibitions of behavior. All the better that college officials have more knowledge about the support needs of incoming students from the outset in order to put in place appropriate accommodations and to take the "handoff" from those who have provided supports and accommodations up to that point.

We might ask ourselves which student with special needs has the better chance of success in a college environment: the student who has disclosed what has helped him or her to succeed, or the student with special needs who is silent?

Finally, to those who herald this as a return to an even more extreme version of *in loco parentis* in our relationships with our students than we have so recently congratulated ourselves on shedding, I would say not quite, and perhaps the opposite. If we look closely at the legal doctrine of *in loco parentis,* we find that it describes a circumstance in which one assumes responsibility for a child without formally adopting the child. Applied to schools and colleges, this has typically meant that, by our actions, policies, and formal statements we agree to accept responsibility for our students "in the place of" their parents. Here I am arguing for something different.

I am arguing that we find new ways to hold our students accountable for their own actions, and that we involve parents as active partners and appropriate outside professionals whenever the need is evident. Staying with the Latin, we might call this the doctrine of *modestus pateo,* or, loosely translated, orderly openness. More simply, we might think of where we have arrived in higher education in this and many other regards as the *age of accountability*—to our students, their parents, our colleagues, and our many constituencies—in all that we do.

If campus safety at your institution is still something that the student affairs professionals are left to figure out and stew over, then it is time for change. The issues raised here about student privacy, campus safety, and our right relationship with our students in this age are not student affairs issues; they are issues of concern and importance to every member of the college community. Everyone must join the conversation. We are all standing at the same intersection, and the lights are still flashing red, green, and yellow.

References

Delworth, D., (1989). *Dealing with the Behavioral and Psychological Problems of Students.* New Directions for Student Services, no. 45. San Francisco: Jossey-Bass.

Hollingsworth, K., and Dunkle, J. "Dealing with Disturbed and Disturbing Students: Best Practices and Their Implications." Paper presented at the National Association of Student Affairs Personnel Administrators Annual Conference, Tampa, FL, 2005.

Sandeen, A., (1989). "A Chief Student Affairs Officer's Perspective on the AISP Model," in U. Oelworth (Ed.), *Dealing with the Behavioral and Psychological Problems of Students.* New Directions for Student Services, no. 45. San Francisco: Jossey-Bass.

Sandeen, A., and Barr, M. J., (2006). *Critical Issues for Student Affairs: Challenges and Opportunities.* San Francisco: Jossey-Bass.

Schieszler v. Ferrum College, 233 F.Supp.2d 796 (W.D.Va. 2002).

Shin v. MIT, 2005 Mass. Super. LEXIS 333, *32.

Wall Street Journal, "Bucking Privacy Concerns: Cornell Acts as 'Watchdog,'" 12/28/2007.

SAMPLE ABSTRACT

The author discusses a dilemma facing campus administrators: keeping students safe while protecting their privacy rights. The author argues that administrators may be reading FERPA restrictions too narrowly, failing to collect and share information that might protect students. He states that student safety is the responsibility of the entire campus community and that students' parents may play a more expanded role in forming a viable solution to the problem.

SAMPLE INFORMATIVE SUMMARY ESSAY

Ron Chesbrough's "From *Animal House* to *Big Brother*: Student Privacy and Campus Safety in an Age of Accountability" examines the tension that exists between college administrators' desire to keep students safe while at the same time protecting their privacy rights. After the fatal shootings at Virginia Tech, administrators have had to reconsider their existing policies.

Difficulties arise due to the Family Education Rights and Privacy Act (FERPA), legislation that has long served to protect student privacy. FERPA may prevent college authorities from addressing potential threats because doing so might violate a student's right to privacy. On the other hand, courts have held that colleges have a special obligation to protect the safety of students.

To address this dilemma, school administrators need to revisit the intention of FERPA, which was to ensure the privacy of student academic records and provide students due process rights. Allowances in the law enable schools to contact parents and other appropriate authorities about student health or disciplinary problems. In the past, schools have erred on the side of caution and have generally not communicated their concerns about particular students to off-campus authorities.

Particular attention needs to be paid to how schools address "disturbed" students who for medical or non-medical reasons pose a possible threat to other students. Schools must employ health care professionals who can help these students, convey to all students the school's standards of behavior, develop plans for accommodating students who need extra help coping with school, ban firearms from campus, and inform parents and students that school administrators will use all the powers FERPA provides to protect the safety of everyone on campus.

Some may find these actions too severe or opening colleges up to litigation should a tragedy occur. However, proper due diligence on the school's part is required to ensure student safety and privacy. Central to this effort is holding students accountable for their actions and enlisting the help of students and parents when formulating new school policies.

SAMPLE EXPLANATORY SUMMARY ESSAY

In "From *Animal House* to *Big Brother*: Student Privacy and Campus Safety in an Age of Accountability," author Ron Chesbrough explores how to make college campuses safer. Reacting to recent tragedies such as the killings at Virginia Tech, Chesbrough questions how best to balance the needs for student safety and student privacy, especially in light of safeguards guaranteed by the Family Education Rights and Privacy Act (FERPA). He argues that college administrators may need to operate out of a more liberal reading of FERPA regulations and enlist the aid of parents to meet the needs of students who may pose safety issues for a school.

Chesbrough opens his essay by defining a problem all college administrators face: how to ensure student safety while maintaining the privacy rights of students who may exhibit threatening or concerning behavior or actions. Central to the debate is how administrators interpret the restrictions placed on colleges through FERPA. While agreeing that FERPA has many benefits, Chesbrough notes how two recent court cases have redefined schools' responsibilities to protect students from themselves and their peers. He then poses an additional question to consider: under these new interpretations of FERPA, how do college administrators know when to release information about students who might pose a risk to the school and when to keep such information confidential?

To answer this question, Chesbrough examines the original intent of FERPA: who was it intended to protect and from what? He concludes that the act was passed primarily to protect student academic records and to ensure students due process rights concerning the release of those records. However, Chesbrough notes, FERPA allows for the release of some student medical information to parents while the Clery Act compels college administrators to act in a timely manner and with due diligence to address campus threats.

Chesbrough then offers a number of initial steps that might be taken to improve campus safety within FERPA restrictions: better define what a school means by a "disturbed" student, establish a clear communication protocol across campus to respond to any dangerous situations, share with students what constitutes acceptable and unacceptable behavior, and clarify university policy regarding firearms and Facebook postings.

Closing his essay, Chesbrough contends that taking these steps will make campuses safer while still maintaining student privacy rights. While there is a threat to privacy in identifying students who have potentially harmful mental or emotional conditions, administrators can enlist the aid of parents to help ensure that these students receive the assistance they need and that the safety of other students is protected.

Summary Chart

HOW TO SUMMARIZE TEXTS

---

1. Read, reread, and annotate the material.

Carefully read the material, paying particular attention to the content and structure of the piece.

Reread and annotate the material, being sure to note:
- *the thesis;*
- *the primary assertions, arguments, or findings; and*
- *the primary means of support for each point.*

2. Write one-sentence summaries of each section of the text.

Identify the major sections of the reading, in which the writer develops one idea before moving on to the next.

In your own words, restate the main point developed in each section of the text and primary means of support the author provides.

3. Write the first draft of your summary.

Introduce the topic of the reading.

Include, early in your essay, the author's full name and the full title of the piece.

In the body of your summary, elaborate on the one-sentence summaries, clearly explaining the important content of the reading.

4. **Check the rough draft of your summary against the source text. As you review your work, make sure your summary is:**

Brief—you have written your summary to be both clear and concise.

Comprehensive—you have included in your summary all of the author's important ideas, assertions, or findings.

Accurate—in choosing words and selecting material for your summary, you have not misrepresented the author's positions or findings.

Neutral—in choosing words and selecting material for your summary, you have attempted to be objective and fair.

Independent—your summary will make sense to someone who has not read the source text.

5. **Rewrite your summary.**

Based on your evaluation of your rough draft, make any needed changes in the content, organization, or language of your summary.

If you are writing an explanatory summary, include any transition words you need to guide your reader through your work.

SUMMARY REVISION CHECKLIST

	Yes	No
1. In the opening section of your summary have you:		
• introduced the topic of the essay?	_____	_____
• given the full title of the source text?	_____	_____
• given the full name of the author?	_____	_____
• included your thesis?	_____	_____
2. In the body of your essay do you summarize only one point at a time?	_____	_____
3. Have you accurately and fairly put into your own words all of the author's important findings, arguments, or ideas?	_____	_____
4. Have you identified the primary means of support the author provides for each finding, argument, or idea?	_____	_____
5. By cutting material or words, have you tried to make your summary as brief as possible while still being comprehensive?	_____	_____
6. To be neutral, have you avoided comments on:		
• the topic of the piece?	_____	_____
• the author's ideas?	_____	_____
• the author's style?	_____	_____
7. To help ensure that your summary will make sense to someone who has not read the original work, have you:		
• defined any unusual or technical terms?	_____	_____
• identified any people you refer to in your work?	_____	_____
• provided a sufficient context for understanding the author's assertions or findings?	_____	_____
8. Do you have adequate paragraph breaks and transitions?	_____	_____
9. Have you supplied proper documentation?	_____	_____

Chapter 5

ANALYSIS

In this chapter you will learn how to

1. Break readings down into their essential parts
2. Interpret literary and non-literary texts
3. Write effective analysis essays

DEFINITION AND PURPOSE

Analysis involves two separate but closely related skills: the ability to break down a text into its constituent parts and the ability to interpret how those parts contribute to or determine a text's meaning. While a summary conveys what a text says, an analysis examines how a text is put together. With analysis, you identify the key parts of a text in order to understand it more fully and to discover how the author employs language and/or images to achieve his or her desired goals in the piece. To reach these conclusions, you interpret the text—you determine what the text means based on your close reading of its parts. When you write an analysis of a text, however, you do not pass judgment on its quality or worth; instead, you dissect it, describe how it is put together, and explain what you think it means.

Analysis serves several purposes. First, it helps you better understand a reading. As you identify both what the text says and how it says it, you more fully comprehend the relationship between its content and construction. Second, analysis is a crucial step toward evaluating texts. Before you pass judgment on how effective a reading is, you first have to determine how its author is attempting to accomplish his or her desired goal.

Third, analysis sharpens your ability to interpret texts. When readers summarize the same text, they may have very similar responses. However, when asked to analyze and interpret that same reading, their responses are likely to vary much more widely. As they carefully examine various parts of the text and consider how these parts contribute to its meaning—in other words, when they interpret the text—their responses will reflect their unique understandings of or insights into the text.

Finally, because analysis requires strong critical reading and interpretation skills, it encourages you to focus on the *craft* of writing. When you analyze a text, you focus on its inner workings. You pay attention to the techniques of writing—*how* writers produce texts that communicate certain ideas or achieve certain goals. Studying texts this way can help make you a stronger writer. By examining how other writers craft their texts, you identify techniques you can employ when you write papers.

A wide and varied range of source-based writing assignments call on you to analyze texts. Sometimes you will write an analysis essay as a stand-alone assignment. Other times, you will analyze texts as one step in completing other assignments, such as critiques or synthesis essays. The general process for analyzing a text described here can help you work through any reading; however, certain steps will be more or less important depending on the particular assignment you are completing. Before moving on, though, read the following story.

The Story of an Hour

Kate Chopin

Knowing that Mrs. Mallard was afflicted with a heart trouble, great care was taken to break to her as gently as possible the news of her husband's death.

It was her sister Josephine who told her, in broken sentences; veiled hints that revealed in half concealing. Her husband's friend Richards was there, too, near her. It was he who had been in the newspaper office when intelligence of the railroad disaster was received, with Brently Mallard's name leading the list of "killed." He had only taken the time to assure himself of its truth by a second telegram, and had hastened to forestall any less careful, less tender friend in bearing the sad message.

She did not hear the story as many women have heard the same, with a paralyzed inability to accept its significance. She wept at once, with sudden, wild abandonment, in her sister's arms. When the storm of grief had spent itself she went away to her room alone. She would have no one follow her.

There stood, facing the open window, a comfortable, roomy armchair. Into this she sank, pressed down by a physical exhaustion that haunted her body and seemed to reach into her soul.

She could see in the open square before her house the tops of trees that were all aquiver with the new spring life. The delicious breath of rain was in the air. In the street below a peddler was crying his wares. The notes of a distant song which someone was singing reached her faintly, and countless sparrows were twittering in the eaves.

There were patches of blue sky showing here and there through the clouds that had met and piled one above the other in the west facing her window.

She sat with her head thrown back upon the cushion of the chair, quite motionless, except when a sob came up into her throat and shook her, as a child who has cried itself to sleep continues to sob in its dreams.

She was young, with a fair, calm face, whose lines bespoke repression and even a certain strength. But now there was a dull stare in her eyes, whose gaze was fixed away off yonder on one of those patches of blue sky. It was not a glance of reflection, but rather indicated a suspension of intelligent thought.

There was something coming to her and she was waiting for it, fearfully. What was it? She did not know; it was too subtle and elusive to name. But she felt it, creeping out of the sky, reaching toward her through the sounds, the scents, the color that filled the air.

Now her bosom rose and fell tumultuously. She was beginning to recognize this thing that was approaching to possess her, and she was striving to beat it back with her will—as powerless as her two white slender hands would have been. When she abandoned herself a little whispered word escaped her slightly parted lips. She said it over and over under her breath: "free, free, free!" The vacant stare and the look of terror that had followed it went from her eyes. They stayed keen and bright. Her pulses beat fast, and the coursing blood warmed and relaxed every inch of her body.

She did not stop to ask if it were or were not a monstrous joy that held her. A clear and exalted perception enabled her to dismiss the suggestion as trivial. She knew that she would weep again when she saw the kind, tender hands folded in death; the face that had never looked save with love upon her, fixed and gray and dead. But she saw beyond that bitter moment a long procession of years to come that would belong to her absolutely. And she opened and spread her arms out to them in welcome.

There would be no one to live for during those coming years; she would live for herself. There would be no powerful will bending hers in that blind persistence with which men and women believe they have a right to impose a private will upon a fellow-creature. A kind intention or a cruel intention made the act seem no less a crime as she looked upon it in that brief moment of illumination.

And yet she had loved him—sometimes. Often she had not. What did it matter! What could love, the unsolved mystery, count for in the face of this possession of self-assertion which she suddenly recognized as the strongest impulse of her being!

"Free! Body and soul free!" she kept whispering.

Josephine was kneeling before the closed door with her lips to the keyhole, imploring for admission. "Louise, open the door! I beg; open the door—you will make yourself ill. What are you doing, Louise? For heaven's sake open the door."

"Go away. I am not making myself ill." No; she was drinking in a very elixir of life through that open window.

Her fancy was running riot along those days ahead of her. Spring days, and summer days, and all sorts of days that would be her own. She breathed a quick prayer that life might be long. It was only yesterday she had thought with a shudder that life might be long.

She arose at length and opened the door to her sister's importunities. There was a feverish triumph in her eyes, and she carried herself unwittingly like a goddess of Victory. She clasped her sister's waist, and together they descended the stairs. Richards stood waiting for them at the bottom.

Someone was opening the front door with a latchkey. It was Brently Mallard who entered, a little travel-stained, composedly carrying his grip-sack and umbrella. He had been far from the scene of the accident, and did not even know there had been one. He stood amazed at Josephine's piercing cry; at Richards' quick motion to screen him from the view of his wife.

When the doctors came they said she had died of heart disease—of the joy that kills.

HOW TO ANALYZE A TEXT

READ THE SOURCE TEXT CAREFULLY

Before you begin to analyze a text, read it carefully, just as you would if you were going to summarize it. For example, if you are analyzing an argument, identify the author's thesis, primary assertions or findings, and primary means of support for those assertions or findings. If you are analyzing a piece of fiction, identify the main characters, the setting, the theme, the conflict, the imagery, and so forth. You do not want to begin to analyze and interpret a reading until you clearly understand its literal meaning and have formed an opinion concerning what the author is attempting to accomplish in the piece. Failing to do so will likely cause you to misinterpret the text.

Having carefully read "The Story of an Hour," take a few minutes to answer these questions:

1. Who are the main characters in the story?
2. What happens in the story?
3. What is the story's primary theme?
4. What images catch your attention as you read the story?
5. What changes does Louise Mallard undergo during the hour she is alone in her room?
6. What causes these changes and how do they impact her life?

IDENTIFY OR CHOOSE WHICH ANALYTICAL CRITERIA TO EMPLOY

If analysis requires you to break down a reading into its key parts, which parts do you focus on? A text can be dissected any number of ways—for example, you can analyze it in terms of its argument, its structure, its use of language, its imagery, even its punctuation. So which *criteria* do you employ when you analyze a reading—what *parts* do you focus on?

In some cases, your instructor will specify the analytical criteria you are supposed to use. For example, the instructor may ask you to analyze a reading in terms of *one or two specific aspects of the text*. The assignment might sound like this:

> *Analyze Kate Chopin's "The Story of an Hour" in terms of its references to nature.*

With this assignment, you would identify the references to nature in the story and develop an interpretation of the piece based on what you find. In other cases, the instructor may ask you to analyze a reading in terms of *a particular theory*, in which case the assignment might resemble this:

> *Analyze Kate Chopin's "The Story of an Hour" in terms of Aristotle's theory of tragedy.*

You could write this assignment in a couple of ways. You could identify where the story exemplifies Aristotle's theory and (1) explain how the theory helps you better understand Chopin's story or (2) explain how the story helps you better understand Aristotle's theory.

Other times, selecting the analytical criteria will be left up to you. Suppose you were given an assignment like this:

> *Analyze Kate Chopin's "The Story of an Hour."*

To complete this assignment, you would need to identify those aspects of the story that you believe most impact its meaning—for example, its structure, setting, or imagery. The structure, setting, or imagery would become your analytical criteria.

APPLY THE ANALYTICAL CRITERIA TO THE TEXT

When you have identified the criteria you will use to analyze a text, reread the piece several times focusing on just those parts or aspects of the reading. Carefully highlight and annotate the text, marking every instance of the criterion you encounter. Along the way, look for patterns in the criteria's use: Do they appear at regular intervals? Do they seem to be employed in particular ways, to achieve particular effects? Are they related to certain themes or arguments?

For example, suppose you are analyzing Chopin's story in terms of its references to nature. In the opening paragraphs alone, Chopin mentions how Louise Mallard, alone in her bedroom, focuses her attention on the open window. She notices the tops of trees quivering with new spring life, smells the fresh air, and hears sparrows "twittering in the eaves" (82). She drinks the "elixir of life through that open window" (83), consumed by the sounds, scents, and colors. Yet, she also feels something creeping toward her out of those blue skies, something that frightens her. Clearly, these references to nature are in the story, but what do they mean? How are they important and how might they help you understand the story more fully? Answering these questions requires interpretation.

INTERPRET THE TEXT

After you have read the text a few times focusing on your analytical criteria, determine their impact on the text. It is often useful at this point to make a list of the examples or sections you have highlighted, along with the page number of the reading on which they appear. As you examine this list, what patterns emerge? What connections can you draw between the examples you have noted and the reading's thesis, arguments, plot, or themes? Taken together, how do the criteria you have noted combine to enhance or bring meaning to the text? Develop several possible interpretations, determining which most comprehensively explains the text or most significantly adds to an understanding of the reading. Pay particular attention if your interpretation does not seem to fit or account for instances of the criteria you have noted. This may indicate that you need to revise your interpretation or decide how to explain why your interpretation does not account for them. Finally, try to articulate your interpretation in one sentence. If you are writing an analysis essay, this sentence will likely serve as your thesis statement.

If you look at all of the references to nature in Chopin's story, you may notice that Louise Mallard observes all of them through the open window. While she sits in her bedroom, the world is full of life just beyond her. Yet, she can only observe it until something from the outside world makes its way to her, a "monstrous joy" Louise begins to feel. All of the references to nature coalesce into one word for Louise: free. She begins to feel the freedom she sees in life beyond her room, understanding that with her husband's death, she can now live solely for herself. This realization fills her with terror and joy: Brently loved her and had tried to be a good husband, but she now feels liberated by his death. Chopin seems to be using nature imagery to comment on the need for freedom and self-determination even within marriage. If you reached this interpretation, you would have to test it against the story to determine its validity. Does nature imagery seem to function consistently this way in the story? Does this interpretation help you determine what the story means?

EXPLAIN AND SUPPORT YOUR INTERPRETATION

Since texts can be analyzed any number of ways, it is essential that you explain and support your particular interpretation of a reading. The support has to come from the text itself; you must be able to cite words or passages in the text that serve as the basis of your analysis and interpretation. If you cannot tie your interpretation directly to the text, your conclusions will not convince readers. As you analyzed the text, you noted patterns in the criteria that lead to your interpretation. When you explain your interpretation, you cite those same passages and explain how each can be explained by or contributes to your interpretation. Simply citing examples from the text is not enough to support your interpretation. You also need to explain how each example you cite bolsters your interpretation.

QUALITIES OF A GOOD ANALYSIS ESSAY

COMPREHENSIVE

Unless instructed otherwise, your analysis should take into account the entire source text, not just part of it. You should examine how the text works as a whole before you interpret it. Your interpretation should also explain as many instances of the criteria found in the source text as possible.

CLEAR

You should provide a clear explanation of the analytical criteria you employ. If you think your reader might be confused by your criteria, define and explain them early in your essay. Also, explain the link between examples you cite from the text and your interpretation of the reading. The connection between the two must be clear.

CONSISTENT

Whatever criteria you employ to analyze a text should be applied consistently to the reading. That is, you should not change criteria as you analyze a text or change your definition of the criteria to assist your interpretation. If you analyze a text using multiple criteria, consistently apply each one separately—don't confuse or conflate the two in your analysis.

TIED TO THE SOURCE TEXT

Your analysis should be tied to the reading. Examples you cite in your analysis should come directly from the source text and your interpretation of a reading should focus on that text.

INFORMATIVE

Your analysis should pass the "So what?" test. The criteria you use to analyze a text and the interpretation of the reading you offer should be consequential, not trivial. Both should add to your reader's understanding of and/or appreciation for the text.

HOW TO WRITE AN ANALYSIS ESSAY

If you are assigned to write an analysis essay, these instructions may serve as a helpful guide. However, because analysis assignments vary so widely across disciplines, talk with your instructor to clarify any questions you have or to get more specific instructions.

OPENING SECTION

In the opening section of your essay (typically one or two paragraphs) introduce the topic of the reading you are analyzing. To capture reader interest, you might bring up questions concerning the meaning of the text (which you will address in your analysis), provide some relevant information about the text's author or publication history, or employ a quotation from the text that can focus your essay. Provide your reader the full title of the piece you are analyzing and the author's full name. Finally, include your thesis statement.

You may use either an open or closed thesis statement. In an open thesis statement, you state your interpretation of the piece. In a closed thesis statement, you also include the analytical criteria you employed to reach that interpretation.

Open thesis:

> In "The Story of an Hour," Kate Chopin indicts marriage as an enslaving institution that stultifies the desire to be free.

Closed thesis:

> A close examination of nature imagery in "The Story of an Hour" demonstrates Kate Chopin's view of marriage as an enslaving institution that stultifies the desire to be free.

BODY

In the body of your essay, you will explain and support your interpretation through specific references to and explanations of the source text. If you are employing only one analytical criterion, you may organize the body of your essay this way, explaining how a series of passages from the text support your interpretation:

First example of criterion to be examined:

- Introduce first example.
- Illustrate example with passage(s) drawn from the text.
- Explain how example contributes to the meaning of the text.

Second example of criterion to be examined:

- Introduce second example.
- Illustrate example with passage(s) drawn from the text.
- Explain how example contributes to the meaning of the text.

Last example of criterion to be examined:

- Introduce last example.
- Illustrate example with passage(s) drawn from the text.
- Explain how example contributes to the meaning of the text.

If you are employing multiple analytical criteria, then you examine them one at a time, explaining how each one supports your interpretation, with evidence drawn from the source text. Your essay might be organized like this:

First criterion:

- Introduce first criterion and state how it contributes to the meaning of the text.
- Illustrate with examples of the criterion drawn from the text.
- Explain how each example contributes to the meaning of the text.

Second criterion:

- Introduce second criterion and state how it contributes to the meaning of the text.
- Illustrate with examples of the criterion drawn from the text.
- Explain how each example contributes to the meaning of the text.

Last criterion:

- Introduce last criterion and state how it contributes to the meaning of the text.
- Illustrate with examples of the criterion drawn from the text.
- Explain how each example contributes to the meaning of the text.

Regardless of which approach you take—employing a single analytical criterion or several—your goal is the same: support your interpretation of the text by citing and explaining specific passages from the source text.

CONCLUDING SECTION

In the concluding section, bring your essay to a satisfying close by reminding readers of your thesis, reiterating the importance or significance of your interpretation, explaining how your interpretation helps readers better understand the text or answer a key critical question, or showing how your interpretation differs from other readings of the text.

REVISING YOUR ESSAY

As you revise your analysis essay, check for accuracy, development, clarity, and balance.

ACCURACY

Be sure you have not misrepresented the source text either in the examples you use or the explanations you offer. Base your analysis and interpretation on a clear, accurate understanding of the source text.

DEVELOPMENT

Any interpretation of the source text you provide needs to be fully developed. You may want someone else to read your rough draft and ask that person to tell you where any assertion or explanation needs further support or explanation. Be sure you have enough examples from the source text to convince your reader that your interpretation is well grounded.

CLARITY

Pay close attention to word choice and sentence structure. Do any terms or references need to be explained? Does the meaning of any sentence get lost due to poor syntax? Are the connections between the various sections of your essays clear—for example, does the discussion in one of your body paragraphs flow logically from the discussion in the previous paragraph?

BALANCE

Have you purposely or inadvertently ignored instances when your interpretation of the text does not explain one or more instances of the criteria you used to analyze the reading? If so, consider how you can change your interpretation to account for the outlying examples or explain in your essay why those examples do not damage the credibility of your interpretation.

DOCUMENTATION

Summarized, paraphrased, or quoted material needs to be properly documented.

SAMPLE ANALYSIS ESSAY

Nature, Freedom, and Will in "The Story of an Hour"

> When she abandoned herself a little whispered word escaped her slightly parted lips. She said it over and over under her breath: "free, free, free!" (Chopin 83)

Kate Chopin's "The Story of an Hour" is built around a series of ironies. In the opening of the story, Louise Mallard learns that her husband, Brently, has been killed in a train accident. However, this was a false report; Brently Mallard is very much alive. During the brief hour that Louise thinks her husband is dead, she comes to realize a "monstrous joy" (83) at the thought of being free from Brently, even though he "had never looked save with love upon her" (83). Ironically, Louise is filled with excitement at the thought of being free from what appears to be a happy marriage. Yet, was the marriage that happy? Could it ever have been a source of joy in Louise's life? Through her repeated use of nature imagery, Chopin makes clear that the desire for individual liberty and self-determination are more important for human happiness than is socially sanctioned marriage, more important even than love.

"The Story of an Hour" has a surprise ending. When Louise finds out that Brently is alive after all, she collapses. Her doctors say she "died of heart disease—of the joy that kills" (84). In other words, Louise's heart was too weak to withstand the surge of joy sweeping through her when she sees Brently. A closer look at the story, however, reveals the irony of the doctors' diagnosis. They were half right—heart disease killed Louise. However, her death was due to the happiness and joy suddenly denied her, not suddenly returned to her, a point Chopin makes clear through her use of nature imagery.

After Louise learns of Brently's death, she retires to her bedroom, locks the door, and sinks into an armchair near an open window. Exhausted, she sees outside the window a city square and trees "all aquiver with the new spring life" (82). Rain has freshened the air, a distant song reaches her ears, and "countless sparrows were twittering in the eaves" (82). In short, at a time when death has entered her life, she is confronted by images of life and renewal. Beyond that open window the world is full of joyous life—it's spring, the birds are twittering, people are singing.

The scene captivates Louise and freezes her in the chair. She ceases "intelligent thought" (83) and opens her heart to her emotions. As soon as she does, however, a fearful, terrible thought occurs to her. The life she had been living with Brently was not joyous or life affirming. The lines in Louise's face "bespoke repression" (83), but she fights against the epiphany building within her, "creeping out of the sky, reaching toward her through the sounds, the scents, the color that filled the air" (83). Her heart beats more rapidly and "the coursing blood warmed and relaxed every inch of her body" when she names this feeling: "free, free, free!" (83).

With Brently dead, Louise is now free of her marriage—years of freedom lay ahead of her and "she opened and spread her arms out to them in welcome" (83). Interestingly, though, Brently had not been a cruel or demanding husband. He had loved her and treated her kindly. Louise realizes that she too loved him, "sometimes" (83). Yet, love and marriage are incompatible with the freedom she now experiences. By its very nature, marriage makes both husband and wife feel the right to "impose a private will upon a fellow-creature" (83). And love? Love counts for nothing in light of "the possession of self-assertion which [Louise] suddenly recognized as the strongest impulse of her being!" (83). Instead of wallowing in grief over her husband's death, Louise is "drinking in a very elixir of life through that open window" (83).

Thus, when Louise opens the door and walks to the stairs with her sister, she is filled with joyous notions of individual freedom promised by nature. Those visions of a bright future are snatched away when Brently enters the house and the sorrow breaks her heart. "The joy that kills" Louise is the joy denied her, an insight into her character that becomes clear after a careful analysis of nature imagery in the story.

Summary Chart

HOW TO ANALYZE TEXTS

---

1. Read the source text carefully.

Read the material as if you were going to summarize it, identifying exactly what it is saying and how it is organized.

If you are analyzing a piece of fiction, pay special attention to
- *the main characters*
- *the structure*
- *the themes*
- *the setting*
- *the images*

If you are analyzing a piece of non-fiction, pay special attention to the thesis statement
- *the primary assertions, conclusions, or findings*
- *the primary means of support provided for claims*
- *the structure of the piece*

---

2. Identify or choose which analytical criteria to employ.

Note which criteria, if any, are identified in the assignment.

If you are to choose your own criteria, identify which elements of the text most impact its meaning and employ one or more of them in your essay.

---

3. Apply the analytical criteria to the text.

Carefully reread the text with the analytical criteria in mind.

Mark every instance of the criteria in the text you find.

Note in the margins of the text any patterns you begin to see in the criteria.

Be imaginative: identify elements of the text that might be related to your criteria even if you are not entirely sure they are.

---

4. Interpret the text.

When read together, what meaning emerges from the criteria you have noted?

What relationships do you find among the criteria you noted and the text's thesis or goal?

Capture your interpretation in one sentence.

5. Explain and support your interpretation.

Explain how each example of the criteria you used to analyze the text supports the claim you make in your interpretation.

Explain the relationship between each example you use to other examples.

Explain the relationship between each example you use to the overall meaning of the text.

Summary Chart

HOW TO WRITE AN ANALYSIS ESSAY

1. Opening Section

Introduce the topic of the reading you are analyzing.

Provide the author's full name and the full title of the reading.

Capture reader interest.

Provide your thesis statement.

2. Body Section

Develop your essay in line with your thesis statement. Do not stray from your thesis. If you do stray, decide whether to cut that part of your essay or to revise your thesis statement to accommodate it.

Organize your essay around the criteria you employed.

Provide specific examples from the text to illustrate each criterion you employ.

Fully explain the link between each of the examples you draw from the text and your interpretation of that text. Do not expect your reader to understand the link—explain it for them.

3. Conclusion

Bring your essay to a satisfying close. Perhaps repeat the strategy you used to open your essay: if you opened with a quote from the source text, close with one; if you opened with a rhetorical question, answer that question.

Remind readers of your thesis.

Be sure you have answered the "so what?" question: how does your interpretation help readers better understand the text or address key questions about it?

ANALYSIS ESSAY REVISION CHECKLIST

	Yes	No
1. Have you included the title of the reading and author's name in your introduction?	_____	_____
2. Does your thesis clearly indicate your interpretation of the text?	_____	_____
3. If you are using a closed thesis, do you list the analytical criteria you employ in the same order as you address them in the body of your essay?	_____	_____
4. Is each statement of your interpretation clearly worded in the body of your essay?	_____	_____
5. Do you support each of your interpretive claims with specific examples from the reading?	_____	_____
6. Do you fully explain the link between each example you cite and your interpretation of the reading?	_____	_____
7. Have you employed your criteria consistently in your essay?	_____	_____
8. Have you comprehensively analyzed all of the text unless assigned to do otherwise?	_____	_____
9. Have you defined any terms or references that might confuse your readers?	_____	_____
10. Have you included clear transitions between the major sections of your essay?	_____	_____
11. Have you checked the accuracy of all quoted and paraphrased material against the original passages in the source text?	_____	_____
12. Have you checked to be sure you have documented your essay correctly?	_____	_____
13. Have you proofread your essay?	_____	_____
14. Does your essay accurately communicate your interpretation of the text?	_____	_____

Chapter 6

RESPONSE ESSAYS

In this chapter you will learn how to

1. Differentiate response from summary and analysis

2. Identify and articulate your responses to a text

3. Write effective response essays

DEFINITION AND PURPOSE

Response essays ask you to examine, explain, and often defend your personal reaction to a reading. In this type of essay you explore why you liked the reading, agreed with the author, found the piece informative or confusing—whatever your response might be. There are not necessarily any "right" or "wrong" reactions to material; instead, response essays are usually evaluated on the basis of how well you demonstrate an understanding of the reading and how clearly you explain your reactions.

Sometimes teachers grade response essays the same way they grade any other assignment. Other times they assign ungraded response essays—usually as a way to help students develop material for graded essays. Still other teachers combine response essays with other types of papers; for example, they might ask students to summarize and then respond to a reading, or to respond to a reading and then critique it. Sometimes teachers will specify which aspects of the text they would like you respond to in your essay (for example, the author's thesis or use of figurative language); other times they will leave the choice of content up to you. In short, the response essay is a very flexible assignment employed widely by teachers in college. Writing this type of paper helps you understand your personal reaction to what you read: what you think about the topic, how you judge the author's ideas, and how the words on the page affect you as a reader.

Effective response essays demonstrate a strong connection between the source text and your reaction. Your responses are triggered by what you read, by certain words on the page. It is important to keep that connection strongly in mind as you compose your response essay. First, you need to put into words your responses to the source text. Second, you need to identify which words on the page triggered those responses. Third, you need to determine—and then explain for your reader—why and how those words triggered those responses.

In writing this type of essay, you cannot simply state your response and move on: "I liked this. I didn't like that." "This interested me; that puzzled me." Instead, you must develop and explain your response: what, *exactly*, is your response; what part of the text triggered it; what, *exactly*, is the relationship between the words on the page and your reactions to them? Although the idea of "developing" your response may seem odd, remember that you are writing for a reader, not just for yourself. You want your reader to be able to understand and appreciate both your response and what led you to have it. Clearly, writing a response essay is more difficult than it might first appear.

QUALITIES OF A GOOD RESPONSE ESSAY

Part of what makes a good response essay difficult to write is that it must be honest, informed, clear, and well supported.

- *Honest*—it reflects your true responses.
- *Informed*—it reflects an accurate and thorough understanding of the source text.
- *Clear*—it makes sense to your readers.
- *Well supported*—it demonstrates a close link between your responses and the source text itself.

HONEST

A response essay should focus on your sincere, thoughtful reactions to what you read. You want to identify your responses to the material and explore their relationship to the text itself: What gives rise to your reactions? How do they affect your reading of the author's work? These essays are highly subjective—you focus on *your* reactions to the text. Consequently, you should not pretend your responses are other than what they truly are. If you found a work boring, for example, do not claim that you found it intriguing simply because you think that is the way you are *supposed* to respond.

INFORMED

Can your responses, then, ever be "wrong"? In one sense, they cannot—your responses are your responses. That does not mean, however, that all responses to a reading are equally informed. For example, if your response is based on a misunderstanding of the source text—if you criticize an author for saying something she never said—then your response is misguided. Responses can also be naïve, shortsighted, or biased. These responses are not, in a sense, "wrong," but neither are they very insightful. Informed response essays are based on a clear understanding of the source text: the more you know about a topic, author, or reading, the more likely your response will be informed.

Take, for example, an experience I had a few years ago. I asked a group of students to respond to a satirical political essay before we discussed the piece in class. The students who recognized the satire produced fine response essays. However, the students who did not understand that the author was being satirical terribly misread the piece and produced misguided essays. Their responses were honest—the responses accurately reflected their reading of the text—but they were not informed.

CLEAR

When your readers finish your response essay, they should understand (1) how you reacted to the reading and (2) how your reactions are tied to the source text. Problems with clarity often arise from weak content, weak organization, or poor word choice.

Problems with clarity involving **content** occur when the person writing the response essay fails to state clearly the nature of his or her response, fails to identify which aspect of the source text gave rise to that response, or fails to explain the relationship between his or her response and those aspects of the text. Unless all three are clearly stated and explored, readers can be left confused about the nature of your response to the reading.

Other problems with clarity involve **organization**. Be sure that your essay has a fully developed opening and closing section and a clearly stated thesis. A good response essay also explores only one reaction at a time and provides clear transitions between the various sections of the paper. Problems with clarity can occur when you shift too quickly from discussing one response to discussing another—without a good transition, the change of focus might not be clear to your reader.

Finally, problems with clarity often involve the **language** used in response essays. Too often students use vague language to explore their reactions—words that mean something to them but nothing to their readers. Though response essays are highly subjective, when you turn them in for a grade, they must be addressed to a more public audience. Good response essays can be difficult to write for just this reason: you have to find language that clearly and efficiently communicates to others your subjective responses to a reading.

WELL SUPPORTED

In good response essays, students support and explain their reactions to the text with specific, elaborated examples. For example, if a student claims that she was offended by an author's illogical assertions, she should quote some of those passages and explain why she finds them illogical. If another student reads the same work and finds the same passages convincing because they match his experiences, he should also quote some examples and explain why he finds them convincing. In either case, the student supports her or his responses by citing from the source text examples that gave rise to them and then clearly explaining the relationship between those examples and their responses.

WRITING THE RESPONSE ESSAY

CAREFULLY READ THE MATERIAL

The problem with many response essays is that the students have not *fully* understood the source text before they begin to write. Some students respond to only part of the reading, without indicating they understand how the material fits into the author's overall thesis. As a result, their responses often seem limited or even biased; their work tends to ignore important issues raised in the source text. Other students simply misread the source text—basing their response on something the author neither wrote nor intended.

Therefore, when you are assigned to respond to a reading, read it several times and briefly summarize it before you write your essay (see Chapter 4 for advice on writing summaries). Summarizing the piece first can help ensure that your response will be based on a full and accurate understanding of the text's content, structure, tone, and thesis.

Explore Your Responses to the Reading as You Annotate the Text

To develop material for your response essay, as you read and annotate the text, note your responses briefly in the margin of the piece. Sometimes just jotting down a key word or two will do; other times you may need to write out a question you have. Even punctuation marks, such as exclamation points or question marks, can help you keep track of your reactions. When you are finished, expand on these notes at the end of the reading or on a separate sheet of paper. Your goal is to capture in a few sentences your overall response to what you have just read. These notes will form the basis of your response essay. In deciding what to mark and what kinds of comments to write as you read the source text, try answering the following questions.

How Do You React Emotionally to What the Author Has Written?

Your subjective, emotional reaction to a reading is a good place to start generating material for a response essay. Does the text make you angry? Excited? Bored? To explore these reactions, ask yourself several questions:

1. What, exactly, has the author written that makes you feel this way?
2. At what point in your reading did you have these reactions?
3. Which words on the page or ideas caused this response?
4. In short, what has the author done to make you respond this way? Examine the choices the writer made concerning content, organization, and style. What aspects of the text contribute to your response?

As you try to capture your responses in writing, carefully examine your reactions and, when possible, tie them to specific words, passages, or graphics in the text.

How Do the Ideas Offered in the Reading Compare with Your Experience or Your Sense of Reality?

We have all had the experience of hearing or reading something that has a ring of truth or falsehood. Something in a reading makes sense to us because it squares with our experience; it sits right with what we have come to understand about the world. As you reread and annotate a reading, note which of the author's ideas you tend to agree with or question based on how they match your own experience.

There is a real danger, though, in judging what others say by the standards of our experience alone. All of us bring to a reading important but limited experiences. When an author's statements do not match our sense of reality, we should not act defensively and immediately dismiss her ideas. Likewise, simply because we tend to agree with an author does not mean we ought to accept her ideas uncritically. Writing a response essay will give you the chance to question what you believe in light of what the author writes and to understand how your experiences influence the way you react to new ideas.

How Do the Ideas Offered in the Source Match What Others Have Had to Say on the Topic?

When you read a source, you bring with you not only what you think and feel based on your own experience, but also what you know, what you have already learned from your reading and education. There is no reason to ignore this knowledge when you write your response essay. In fact, whether the source text confirms or contradicts what you already know about the topic may be one of the reasons for your reaction to the piece. Be sure to note any reactions you have based on the match between the author's ideas and those proposed by other authors you have read.

COMPOSE YOUR ROUGH DRAFT

When you write your response essay, you will need to introduce the source text, provide your reader with a brief summary of its content, and then develop and clarify your reactions.

Introduce Your Topic, Source Text, and Thesis

When composing the opening of your response essay, you have four goals: introduce the topic of your essay, introduce your source text, state your thesis, and capture reader interest. After you introduce the source text's topic, provide its title and its author's full name. Your thesis for this type of essay will be a statement of your overall response to the reading and, if you like, an indication of how you will develop or explore that response in the body of your paper.

If you employ an "open" thesis statement for your essay, you will indicate your overall response to the piece:

- I found parts of the essay confusing.
- Reading this essay proved to be an emotional challenge.

If you employ a "closed" thesis statement for your essay, you will indicate your overall response to the source text and also indicate how you will develop that response in the body of your paper:

- I found parts of the essay confusing, especially its structure and many of its allusions.
- Because members of my family have been touched by the issues the author discusses, reading this essay proved to be an emotional challenge.

Either type of thesis can work equally well.

Finally, to capture reader interest you may want to use one of the following strategies:

- Open your essay with a provocative or interesting question raised by the reading or your response to it.
- Open your essay with an interesting quotation from the reading.
- Open your essay with a personal anecdote or hypothetical story related to the topic of the reading.
- Open your essay with a reference to a current controversy or public issue related to the topic of the reading.

Summarize the Source Text

After introducing the source and stating your thesis, give a brief summary of the reading. Generally, this summary will be only a paragraph or two long, highlighting the reading's most important findings, conclusions, or arguments. In the summary, anticipate what you will address in the body of your response. For example, if you know you will be questioning the validity of some of the author's claims, summarize his claims in this part of your essay. When they come up again in the body of your response, your reader will remember them and will be able to follow your assertions more easily.

State and Explain Your Responses Clearly and Concisely

In the body of your essay, you explore your responses, clearly and thoroughly, one at a time. This process might sound simple, but clearly and thoroughly stating and explaining your response to a reading can be difficult primarily because it is *your* response. The language you use when describing your reaction may make perfect sense to you but might well be unclear to your reader. For instance, if you were reading someone else's response essay and the writer complained that the source text made her feel "wheezy," would you really know what the person meant? Perhaps her explanation would make it clear, but the language she uses to characterize her response may hinder her readers' ability to understand her reaction. Therefore, a first step in clarifying your response for a reader is to choose language that others can understand. Likewise, explain the terms you use. For example, if you contend that a source is "confusing," explain whether you had difficulty understanding the writer's language, findings, structure, or some other aspect of the text.

Next, be sure to provide specific examples from the source text to help your reader understand each response. When you have a particular response to a reading, something on the page triggered it. In your essay, identify those "triggering" passages before you explain the dynamics of your response. For example, if you contend that a source text is confusing, identify and perhaps quote a passage that you cannot understand, then explain what it is about the writing you find difficult to follow (the logic of the passage? the wording? the structure?).

WRITE YOUR CONCLUSION

With a response essay, your conclusion should restate your overall response to the source text, echoing your thesis. To give a sense of closure to your essay, you should also try to mirror the strategy you employed to capture reader interest in the opening of your essay. For example, if you opened your essay with a question, return to that question in your conclusion and provide an answer. If you opened with an anecdote or story, refer back to it in your conclusion, perhaps indicating how that anecdote or story turned out. If you opened with a quotation from the source text, consider closing with a quotation as well.

REVISE YOUR ROUGH DRAFT

As you revise the rough draft of your response, pay particular attention to your assertions, organization, language, and support.

Review Your Assertions

When you review the assertions you make in your response essay, your primary concern is accuracy:

- Have you truly captured your reactions to the reading?
- Have you openly, honestly, and thoroughly explored your response to the material?
- Does your essay offer an accurate representation of your reaction?
- When other people read your essay, will they be able to understand and appreciate your reaction?

To check your assertions, first reread the source text and see whether you still feel the same way about it. Even a short time away from a reading may enable you to reconsider your reactions—maybe your views have changed. If they have changed, revise your essay. Also, in reviewing the source text, be sure you reread the annotations you originally made. Have you addressed the concerns, questions, and reactions you noted as you earlier annotated the piece?

Review Your Support and Explanations

As you revise your response, examine the way you illustrate and explain each of your responses. Remember that your responses should be tied to specific aspects of the source text, such as words, images, and graphics. When you compose your response, you need to explain for your reader the link between the source text and your reaction. In the body of your essay, you should state a response, point out what aspect of the reading led to that reaction (perhaps quoting the passage), and then explain clearly and thoroughly how that material led you to that response. As you revise your draft, make sure you accomplish all three goals in each section of your essay.

Review Your Organization

Next, when you review the organization of your rough draft, check to be sure you have fully developed opening and closing sections and have a clearly stated thesis. In the body of your essay, be sure that you are developing only one response at a time. Often when you write your rough draft, examining one reaction will lead you to a new response, one you have not previously considered. That is one of the real powers of writing: it not only helps you capture ideas in words but often will help you generate new ideas as well. When this happens, some writers will follow that new idea even if it does not belong in that part of the essay, knowing that in the next draft they can place it elsewhere. Other writers prefer to write a note to themselves to explore that new idea later, not wanting to lose track of the idea they are currently exploring. When you review your rough draft, check to see that you are developing only one response at a time in your essay.

Finally, be sure you indicate to your reader—through paragraph breaks and transition words—when you shift focus from one response to the next. Adding these signals to your paper makes it easier for your reader to follow your line of thought. Since you are writing about *your* responses, you know when you have changed focus; your readers, though, may have a harder time recognizing the structure of your essay. Adding appropriate paragraph breaks and transitions can help.

Review Your Language

As indicated earlier, word choice—finding and choosing appropriate terms to express your reactions—can be truly problematic when you are writing response essays. First, your initial reactions to what you read may be so emotional or so abstract that you cannot put them into words. You may struggle to find appropriate language. Second, your first efforts at finding words may result in highly "private" writing; since they arise from your own knowledge and experience, the terms you use may make sense only to you. In this case, you need to find terms that can communicate your responses to others. Before you turn in the final draft of your response essay, be sure to have someone else read your work, someone you trust to give you an honest appraisal of your language. Ask that person to indicate any part of the response he or she does not understand because of the words you are using.

SAMPLE RESPONSE ESSAY

This sample essay is responding to the article "From *Animal House* to *Big Brother*: Student Privacy and Campus Safety in an Age of Accountability" by Ron Chesbrough, found in Chapter 4 of this text. If you are unfamiliar with the article, read it before you read the following response essay.

A RESPONSE TO "*FROM ANIMAL HOUSE TO BIG BROTHER*: STUDENT PRIVACY AND CAMPUS SAFETY IN AN AGE OF ACCOUNTABILITY"

As Ron Chesbrough notes in his essay "From *Animal House* to *Big Brother*: Student Privacy and Campus Safety in an Age of Accountability," violent episodes, like the shootings at Virginia Tech a few years ago, have raised serious concerns about campus safety. Though my roommates and I have discussed this issue a few times and we had a floor meeting to talk about emergency evacuation plans at the beginning of the term, Chesbrough's essay offers a perspective on the problem I hadn't considered: what policies can the administration at a school adopt to keep students safe? As a first-year college student, I found Chesbrough's essay informative but not very helpful. In the end, he fails to offer very satisfying answers to the problems he raises.

Campus safety happens to be an issue I deeply care about. When the shootings took place at Virginia Tech, my sister was attending Radford College, which is not far from Blacksburg. When I saw the news coverage on television, I started texting my sister immediately to be sure she was safe. She told me the students at her school were also keeping up with the story and were a little nervous, but that I shouldn't worry because nothing like that had ever happened at her school. I felt better, but when I thought about it, what happened at Virginia Tech could happen at any college in the country.

In his article, Chesbrough explores why the violence erupted at Tech and offers a few explanations I had not considered. For example, I had not realized the kinds of restrictions administrators face due to FERPA (the Family Education Rights and Privacy Act). From orientation, I knew that my school could not release my grades to anyone without my permission, even to my parents. I was surprised to learn that FERPA regulations might have kept the administrators at Virginia Tech from acting to prevent the attack. According to news reports, the shooter, Seung-Hui Cho, had a history of mental illness and had received treatment while a high school student. Virginia Tech officials were not informed of Cho's past problems, and when they started to emerge on campus, FERPA regulations kept administrators from telling his teachers or others because Cho did not authorize the release of that information.

This whole scenario is just frustrating, especially for college students like me who could be facing similar dangers and not know it. Respecting a student's privacy is important, but should privacy concerns override safety concerns? I think they should not, but Chesbrough explains why Tech officials did not act. "Due diligence" requirements would seem to mandate that school officials step in to restrain students whose behavior is dangerous. Not acting could open them to lawsuits should something terrible happen. However, if the officials act and nothing happens, they can be sued for violating the student's privacy. I agree with Chesbrough that parents should inform the administration of any pre-existing emotional problems a student has when he or she enters school. Instead of using this information to keep these students from enrolling at the school, administrators can use it to provide the students the help and support they need.

Chesbrough's ideas all seem reasonable, but I do not think they offer a satisfying response to the problem. When balancing the privacy needs of potentially dangerous students against the safety of the entire student body, schools should take greater action to protect the campus. Simply knowing up front which entering students have emotional and psychological problems does not guarantee that the students will seek appropriate treatment on campus. Instead, schools should consider provisional admission for these students— they can stay enrolled on campus as long as they verify that they are getting appropriate treatment. The treatment can remain private, but the administration has to make sure it is taking place. The campus health center could be charged with monitoring the students' treatment, ensuring that they are taking the medicines or receiving the counseling they need. If these students do not keep up with the treatments prescribed by their physician or therapist, they are expelled from school. This solution is not perfect because treatments are not perfect, but it would help ensure that troubled students are receiving help while maintaining their privacy.

Most of the time I do not worry about campus safety. If students take the right precautions on our campus (like never going out alone at night, staying with groups of people, locking doors and windows at night), they can avoid problems. After reading this article though, I am more concerned. How many students on campus have severe emotional or psychological problems? How many of them are getting help so that our school does not become another Virginia Tech?

Summary Chart

HOW TO WRITE A RESPONSE ESSAY

1. **Carefully read the material.**

   Your goal is to form a clear understanding of what the writer has to say.

   Identify and be able to paraphrase the writer's thesis and main assertions or findings.

2. **Reread and annotate the text.**

   As you reread the material, begin to examine your responses by asking yourself the following questions:
   - *How do I react emotionally to what the author has written?*
   - *How do the ideas offered in the source text match my experience and my sense of reality?*
   - *How do the ideas offered in the text match what others have had to say about the topic?*

   Note in the margin your responses to these questions using some combination of the following:
   - *key words*
   - *questions*
   - *statements*
   - *punctuation marks*

   When you are finished, write out in a few sentences your response to the material.

3. **Compose your rough draft.**

   Introduce the topic, your source text, and the full name of the author or authors.

   Summarize the source text.

   State and explain your responses clearly and concisely one at a time.
   - *State your response. (For example, the material made you angry.)*
   - *Explain the terms you are using. (What do you mean by "angry"?)*
   - *Tie that response to some aspect of the source text.*

     What material in the reading made you feel that way?
   - *Explain how that material gave rise to that response.*

     Why or how did that material make you feel angry?
   - *Write your conclusion.*

     What was your overall response to the material?

SUMMARY CHART: HOW TO WRITE A RESPONSE ESSAY *(CONTINUED)*

---

4. Revise your rough draft.

Review your assertions about your reactions.
- *Are they honest?*
- *Are they informed?*
- *Are they clear?*
- *Are they well supported?*

Review your organization.
- *Are your opening and closing sections constructed well?*
- *Are you addressing one response at a time?*
- *Are there clear transitions between the responses you explore?*
- *Are your responses tied to some guiding thesis?*

Review your language.
- *Are you using terms your readers are likely to understand?*
- *Are you invoking a consistent tone, not becoming too informal, too angry, or too satiric when that does not match the tone of your response as a whole?*

Review your support.
- *Have you tied each response to some aspect of the text?*
- *Have you added enough textual references to make clear the connections between the reading and your response?*
- *Have you attempted to explain those connections?*

RESPONSE ESSAY REVISION CHECKLIST

	Yes	No
1. In the introductory section of your essay, have you:		
• introduced the topic of the reading?	_____	_____
• included the full and exact title of the reading?	_____	_____
• included the full name of the author?	_____	_____
2. Have you included a thesis statement that captures your overall response to the reading, a response you develop in the body of your essay?	_____	_____
3. Have you considered the accuracy and honesty of the responses you include in your essay?	_____	_____
4. Have you clearly stated each of these responses?	_____	_____
5. Have you explained the terms you used to characterize each of your responses?	_____	_____
6. Have you tied each of your responses to some aspect of the source that gave rise to it?	_____	_____
7. Have you explained how the material in the source text gave rise to your response?	_____	_____
8. Have you developed only one response at a time in each section of your essay?	_____	_____
9. Have you used language that helps your reader understand when you are moving from your discussion of one response to the next?	_____	_____
10. Have you explained the connection between each response you explore and your overall thesis?	_____	_____
11. Have you reviewed the language you use to make sure your word choice is clear and accurate?	_____	_____

Chapter 7

··

CRITIQUE

In this chapter you will learn how to

1. Identify appropriate evaluative criteria and standards

2. Apply those criteria and standards to evaluate a reading

3. Write an effective critique essay

DEFINITION AND PURPOSE

While response essays focus on your personal reactions to a reading, critiques offer a more formal evaluation. Instead of responding to a reading in light of your experience and feelings, in a critique you evaluate a source text's quality or worth according to a set of established criteria. Based on your evaluation, you then assert some judgment concerning the text—whether the reading was effective, ineffective, valuable, or trivial. Critiques, then, are usually argumentative. Your goal is to convince your readers to accept your judgments concerning the quality of the reading.

These judgments will be based on certain criteria and standards. **Criteria** are certain aspects of a reading that serve as the basis of your assessment—for example, the text's style or use of evidence. **Standards** serve as the basis for evaluating a criterion—what makes a certain "style" good or bad, acceptable or unacceptable? What counts as "valid" evidence in a reading? When you critique a reading, you will employ either **general** academic criteria and standards (those used to evaluate source material in many fields) or **discipline-specific** criteria and standards (those used by scholars in a particular field of study and generally not applicable to material studied in other disciplines).

In college composition courses you may learn how to critique a source text using general evaluative criteria—for example, how to assess the quality of a reading based on its structure, style, or evidence. These criteria can help you evaluate source material in a variety of classes. In your other college courses you may learn discipline-specific evaluative criteria typically used to assess source material in that field of study. For example, in an English literature course you may learn the criteria used by scholars to critique a poem or a play; in an accounting class, you may learn to employ the criteria and standards experts in that discipline use to critique a financial report or prospectus.

Students often find the idea of writing a critique intimidating: they are not sure what the assignment is asking them to do, how to generate material for their paper, what to include in their essay, how to support their assertions, or what tone to assume. However, you are probably more familiar with this type of writing than you realize since you are often exposed to one special form of critique: the movie review. If you ever listened to movie critics argue over a film, you are familiar with the basic structure of a critique. If you ever discussed the strengths and weaknesses of a movie and tried to get a friend to go see it (or to avoid it), then you have already engaged in critique. Examining how a film critic writes a review of a movie can help you understand how to write a critique of a reading.

THE FILM REVIEW AS CRITIQUE

First, consider the nature of a movie critic's job: he watches a film, analyzes and evaluates what he sees, forms some judgment based on that analysis and evaluation, then writes his review, trying to clarify and defend his judgments with specific references to the film and clear explanations of his assertions. In writing his review, the critic does not address every aspect of the film; he addresses only those aspects of the movie that best support his judgment of it. If, for instance, he thought a film was wonderful, he would address in his review only the aspects of the film that, in his opinion, made it exceptional—for example, the direction, the photography, and the acting. If he thought the film was uneven—some parts good, other parts weak—he would offer in his review examples of what made the film effective (maybe the plot or the lighting) and examples of what made it ineffective (maybe the musical score and the special effects).

Think about the way you discuss a film with someone. Maybe the conversation runs something like this:

"So, did you like the movie?"

"Yeah, pretty much. I wasn't too sure about some of the dialogue—sounded pretty lame sometimes—but the special effects were good and the acting was ok."

"The acting was just 'ok'? What didn't you like? I thought the acting was great."

"Well, there was that scene early in the film, right before he shot the guy; I just didn't buy it when he . . ."

In this conversation, one friend asserts a position about the film, is challenged, then begins to defend or explain her view. To convince her friend to accept her judgment, she will likely discuss specific aspects of the film she believes best illustrate her views.

Most of us are accustomed to talking about movies, television shows, or music this way—we form and defend judgments about what we see, hear, and read all the time. However, we are usually more comfortable evaluating movies than we are critiquing arguments, book chapters, or lab reports. First, when it comes to movies, we are probably familiar with many of the source texts—we have seen lots of films—and most of us feel we can knowledgeably discuss what we have seen. We can generate, fairly easily, lots of examples from a movie to support our views. Second, we know *how* to talk about films: we know how to identify and discuss particular aspects of a movie—certain criteria—that influence our judgment. We know that when we analyze a movie we can address the dialogue, the acting, the special effects, and so forth. Finally, we know the standards usually applied to evaluate various aspects of a film; we know what passes for good dialogue, good acting, good special effects, and so on. In short, when we discuss a movie, we know how to *analyze* it (what parts to focus on for review), *evaluate* it (what kinds of questions to ask of each part when assessing its quality), and *defend* our assertions (how to examine specific scenes from the film that support our judgments).

These are the same basic skills you employ to critique readings in college. To critique readings, you need to engage in:

- *Analysis*—break readings down into their essential parts.
- *Evaluation*—assess the quality of those various parts.
- *Explanation*—link your judgments to specific aspects of the readings and make those connections clear and convincing to your reader.

Even though you have probably engaged in this process quite often when discussing movies or television shows, you may have a hard time using these skills to critique readings. First, you are probably less familiar with how critiques look and sound than you are with how movie reviews look and sound. When you are assigned to write a critique, no model may come to mind. Second, the readings you are asked to critique in college can be hard to understand. You cannot critique a reading until you are certain you know what it has to say. Finally, you are probably less familiar with the criteria and standards used in college to analyze and critique readings than you are with the criteria and standards used to review films. When you are asked to critique a philosophical essay on the nature of knowledge, do you know how to break that reading down into its key parts and what kinds of questions to ask of each part to determine its quality? When asked to critique a chapter of your history book, do you know what to look for, what questions to ask? Learning how to critique readings such as these is a central goal of your college education, a skill you will obtain through practice in many different disciplines.

Examining how a movie critic organizes a review can also help you understand how to structure a critique. For example, a critic typically opens her review with a "thesis" that captures her overall assessment of the film. This thesis may take the form of a statement early in the review, a graphic placed beside the review—for example, five stars or two stars—or frequently a comment at the end of the review. Sometimes the critic will love the film; she will give it five stars and a rave review. Sometimes she will hate the movie; she will give it one star and a terrible review. Still other times she will have a split decision; she will give it two and a half stars and in her review acknowledge the strengths and weaknesses of the movie. Next, the critic will typically offer a brief summary of the film so her readers can follow what she has to say in the review. Then, in the body of the review, she will address only the aspects of the film that best illustrate or defend her thesis: she will introduce a particular element of the film (for example, the special effects), comment on its quality (claim they were especially effective), describe a specific example or two from the film (perhaps the climactic battle scene), and explain how that specific example illustrates or supports her judgment (what made the special effects in that battle scene especially good).

Writing a critique involves much the same process. After reading the text, you'll form a judgment of its quality or worth based on some set of criteria and standards. This judgment will form the thesis of your critique, which you will explain or defend in the body of your essay, with specific references to the reading. As you draft your thesis, keep in mind the range of judgments open to the film critic. To critique a reading does not necessarily mean only to criticize it. If you honestly think a reading is weak, based on your evaluation of its various parts, then say so in your thesis. If, however, you think the writing is quite strong, say that. If your judgments fall somewhere in the middle—some parts are strong while others are weak—reflect *that* in your thesis. Your thesis should reflect your carefully considered opinion of the reading's overall quality or worth, whatever that judgment may be.

Next, you will offer a brief summary of the text so your reader can follow what you later have to say about the piece. In the body of your critique, you will choose for examination only the parts of the reading that best illustrate or defend your thesis: you will introduce a particular aspect of the reading (for example, its use of statistical evidence), describe a specific example or two from the reading (perhaps the way statistics are used to support the author's second argument), and explain how that specific example illustrates or supports your judgment (what makes the statistical evidence especially compelling in this section of the text).

Your goal, then, in writing a critique mirrors in many ways the goal you would have in writing a movie review. Your task is to analyze and evaluate a reading according to a set of established criteria and standards, pass judgment on the reading's quality or worth, then assert, explain, and defend that judgment with specific references to the reading.

WRITING A CRITIQUE

Writing a critique typically involves five steps:

1. Read and annotate the text.
2. Analyze and evaluate the piece: break it down into its primary parts and judge the quality of each part.

3. Write your thesis and decide which aspects of the reading you will focus on in your essay.
4. Compose your rough draft.
5. Rewrite your critique.

This is only a general guide. Throughout college you will learn much more specific, specialized ways to critique readings.

STEP 1—CAREFULLY READ AND ANNOTATE THE SOURCE TEXT

Before you start to write a critique, you first need to develop a clear understanding of the reading you are about to analyze and evaluate. The material you read in college is often challenging; you have to work hard to understand exactly what the author is asserting. However, this work is unavoidable; it makes little sense to evaluate a piece of writing when you are not completely sure what point the author is attempting to make. As you annotate a reading for a critique, keep in mind the following suggestions.

Note the Author's Thesis, Primary Assertions, and Primary Means of Support

Be sure that you mark the author's thesis, highlight and summarize each major point the author makes, and highlight and summarize how the author supports each idea, argument, or finding. Are the thesis and primary assertions clearly stated? Does the thesis direct the development of the paper? Are the assertions supported?

Note the Author's Use of Graphics, Headings, and Subheadings

What graphics does the author provide? What is their function? How do the headings and subheadings organize the piece? Are the headings and graphics effective? How so?

Note the Author's Diction and Word Choice

Consider the kind of language the writer is employing. Is it formal or informal? Is it overly technical? Is it appropriate? Do you notice any shifts in diction? Are some sections of the text more complicated or jargon laden than others? Note any strengths or weaknesses you see in the author's language.

Note the Author's Tone

What seems to be the author's attitude toward the topic? Is he being serious, comical, or satiric? Does the tone seem appropriate, given the writer's topic and thesis? Are there any places in the text where the tone shifts? Is the shift effective?

Note the Author's Audience

When you finish the piece, determine what the writer seemed to assume about his readers. For example, is the writer addressing someone who knows something about the topic or someone likely reading about it for the first time? Is the author assuming readers agree or disagree with the position being forwarded in the piece? Judging from the content, organization, diction, and tone of the piece, which type of reader would tend to accept the author's position and which would tend to reject it?

Note the Author's Purpose

Decide, in your own mind, the primary aim of the piece. Is the author attempting to entertain, inform, or persuade readers? Where in the text has the author attempted to achieve this aim? How successful are those attempts? Note at the beginning or end of the reading your comments concerning the author's purpose.

Summarize the Piece

After you have read and studied the text, write a brief summary of the piece, either at the end of the reading or on a separate sheet of paper (see Chapter 4 for tips on summarizing a reading).

When you have finished reading, rereading, and annotating the source text, you should have a clear understanding of its content, organization, purpose, and audience. Try to clear up any questions you have about the reading before you attempt to critique it. You want your critique to be based on a thorough and clear understanding of the source text.

STEP 2—ANALYZE AND EVALUATE THE READING

Think back to the process of putting together a movie review. When a movie critic watches a film, she forms a judgment of its quality based on certain things she sees or hears. As she watches the movie, she will examine and judge certain aspects of the film, including its

acting	scenery	lighting
direction	costuming	plot
special effects	dialogue	action
theme	pacing	makeup
cinematography	stunts	music

Her evaluation of these various elements of the film, either positive or negative, will form her overall judgment of the movie—her thesis.

What, then, should you look for when analyzing a reading? What parts of a text should you be isolating for evaluation as you read and reread the piece? In part, the answer depends on the course you are taking: each discipline has generally agreed-on ways of analyzing a reading. As you take courses in anthropology or physical education, you will learn how experts in those fields analyze readings. However, analyzing certain general aspects of a reading can help you better understand material in a wide variety of classes. Regardless of the course you are taking, you might start to analyze a reading by identifying its

- thesis and primary assertions or findings,
- evidence and reasoning,
- organization, and
- style.

After you have analyzed a reading, isolating for consideration its essential elements, your next task in writing a critique is to evaluate the quality of each element. Here, writing a critique differs from writing a response essay. In a response essay, your goal is to articulate your personal, subjective reaction to what you have read. In a critique, though, you are expected to evaluate the reading according to an established set of standards. Think about the movie critic's job again. Most reviewers employ similar criteria and standards when evaluating a film. If a reviewer decides to critique the musical score of a film, she knows the types of evaluative questions one usually asks about this aspect of a movie: How did the music contribute to the overall mood of the film? Was it too intrusive? Did it add humor or depth to the scenes? Did it heighten drama? Was it noteworthy because of the performers who recorded it? Her answers to these questions will lead to her final assessment of this particular aspect of the film. (Of course, another reviewer employing the same criteria and applying the same standards could come to a different judgment concerning the quality of the music in the film; for example, one reviewer might think it heightened the drama in a particular scene while another might think that it did not.)

In college, you will quickly discover that the criteria and standards used to evaluate readings vary from discipline to discipline. Teachers often employ evaluative criteria unique to their field of study, especially in upper-level courses in which the professor is preparing students to enter a profession. In lower-level courses designed to introduce you to a field of study, you may encounter a different sort of problem. Teachers in different fields may be asking you to employ the same or similar criteria, but their standards are very different. Suppose, for example, you are asked to evaluate the style of a particular reading in both an education and an English course. Your job is the same—determine, stylistically, whether this is a well-written essay. Your answer might be different in each class. According to the stylistic standards advocated by the school of education, you might have before you a well-written essay. According to the standards advocated by the English department, however, the same piece of writing might not fare so well. As always, work closely with your teacher when evaluating a reading to be sure you are applying an appropriate set of criteria and standards.

Following is a series of questions you can ask to begin your analysis and evaluation of a reading's thesis, assertions, evidence, reasoning, organization, and style. The questions are meant to serve only as general guidelines. Your teacher may have much more specific questions he would like you to ask of a reading or evaluative criteria he would like you to employ. Together, analysis and evaluation enable you to critique a reading. After breaking a reading into its essential parts and judging their effectiveness, you will form the thesis of your critique—a judgment of the reading's quality or worth—which you will develop and defend in your essay.

Analyzing and Evaluating a Reading's Thesis and Primary Assertions or Findings

Sometimes identifying an author's thesis can be relatively easy—you can point to a specific sentence or two in the text. Other times, though, an author will not state his thesis. Instead, the thesis is implied: some controlling idea is directing the development of the piece even though the author never puts it into words. If this is the case, you will need to identify and paraphrase this controlling idea yourself and evaluate it as if it were the thesis.

Many times, identifying the author's primary assertions or findings can be easy, too. For example, if the author has made effective use of paragraph breaks, topic sentences, headings, or graphics, you can usually locate his primary assertions fairly easily. However, do not rely on these means alone to identify the author's main ideas. Not every source text is well written. Often, important assertions get buried in an article; key findings may be glossed over. As you analyze a reading, make up your mind about its primary assertions or findings independently of what the author may indicate. Also, be sure to distinguish between primary assertions and their evidence or support. Often a student will identify as a primary argument of a reading some statistic or quotation that the author is using only as a piece of evidence, something to support the actual assertion he is trying to make. In short, to analyze a reading's thesis and primary assertions, consider the following questions:

- What is the author's thesis? Is it stated or unstated? If stated, highlight it; if unstated, paraphrase it.
- What are the primary assertions in the reading? Highlight each one and paraphrase it in the margin of the text.
- What is the primary means of support offered to illustrate or defend each assertion? Again, highlight this material.

In determining the quality of a reading's thesis and primary assertions or findings, you can begin by questioning their clarity, effectiveness, and organization. The thesis, whether stated or implied, should direct the development of the piece. Each major finding or assertion should be clearly stated and linked to that thesis through the effective use of transitions, repetition of key terms, or headings. To evaluate an author's thesis and findings, you might begin by asking the following questions. If your answers are positive, you can likely claim that the author has effectively presented and developed his thesis; if your answers are negative, be sure to articulate exactly where the problems exist.

- Is the thesis clearly stated? Does it control the organization of the piece? Is it consistently held or does the author shift positions in the essay?
- If the thesis is implied rather than stated, does it still serve to direct the organization of the piece? Are you able to paraphrase a comprehensive thesis on your own, or does the material included in the piece preclude that?
- Are the author's assertions or findings clearly stated?
- Are the author's assertions or findings somehow tied to the thesis?

Analyzing and Evaluating a Reading's Evidence and Reasoning

Here you identify two separate, but related, aspects of a reading: (1) the evidence an author provides to support or illustrate her assertions and (2) the author's reasoning process or line of argument.

First, try to identify the types of **evidence** the author uses to support her thesis. (At this point do not try to evaluate the effectiveness of the evidence—that comes later.) The types of evidence used to support a thesis vary greatly in academic writing, so again be cautious when using these guidelines to analyze the readings in any particular course. However, to begin your analysis of the evidence an author employs, you might try asking yourself this series of questions:

- In supporting her assertions or findings, what kinds of evidence has the author employed? Has the author used any of these forms of evidence:

statistics	empirical data	precedent
expert testimony	emotional appeals	case histories
personal experience	historical analysis	analogies

- Where in the article is each type of evidence employed?
- Is there a pattern? Are certain types of evidence used to support certain types of claims?
- Where has the author combined forms of evidence as a means of support?

Analyzing an author's **reasoning process** is more difficult because it is more abstract. First, you identify how the author uses evidence to support her thesis and how she develops and explains her ideas, her line of reasoning. Second, you examine the assumptions an author makes concerning her topic and readers. As she wrote the piece, which aspects of the text did she decide needed more development than others? Which terms needed clarification? Which argument or explanation needed the most support? In analyzing the author's reasoning process, these are the kinds of questions you might ask:

- In what order are the ideas, arguments, or findings presented?
- What are the logical connections between the major assertions being made in the piece? How does one idea lead to the next?

- What passages in the text explain these connections?
- What assumptions about the topic or the reader is the author making?
- Where in the text are these assumptions articulated, explained, or defended?

Standards used to assess the quality of an author's evidence and reasoning will vary greatly across the disciplines. For example, you might want to determine whether an author offers "adequate" support for his or her thesis. However, what passes for adequate support of a claim will be quite different in an English class from what it will be in a physics course or a statistics course: these fields of study each look at "evidence" and the notion of "adequacy" very differently. In other words, a good general strategy to employ when critiquing a reading is to determine the adequacy of its evidence; however, how that strategy is implemented and what conclusions you reach employing it can vary depending on the course you are taking. Part of learning any subject matter is coming to understand how scholars in that field evaluate evidence; therefore, answer the following questions thoughtfully:

- Does the author support her contentions or findings?
- Is this support adequate? Does the author offer enough evidence to support her contentions?
- Is the evidence authoritative? Does it come from legitimate sources? Is it current?
- Does the author explain *how* the evidence supports or illustrates her assertions?
- Has the author ignored evidence, alternative hypotheses, or alternative explanations for the evidence she offers?
- In developing her position, are there any problems with unstated assumptions? Does the author assume something to be the case that she needs to clarify or defend?
- Are there problems with logical fallacies such as hasty generalizations, false dilemmas, or appeals to false authorities?
- Has the author addressed the ethical implications of her position?
- Is the author's reasoning a notable strength in the piece? Is it clear and convincing?

Your answers to these questions will help you determine whether there are serious problems with the evidence and reasoning employed in the reading.

Analyzing and Evaluating a Reading's Organization

At this point you want to identify how the author orders the material contained in the reading. As the author develops a set of findings or ideas, lays out his reasoning for the reader, and offers examples and explanations, what comes first? Second? Third? How has the author attempted to mold these parts into a coherent whole? When analyzing the organization of a reading, you might begin by considering the following questions:

- In what order are the ideas or findings presented?
- How has the author indicated that he is moving from a discussion of one point to the discussion of another point?
- What is the relationship between the thesis of the piece (stated or unstated) and the order in which the assertions or findings are presented?
- How has the author tried to help the reader understand the organization of the reading? Identify where in the text the author has used any of the following to help guide his readers through the text:

headings and subheadings	repetition of key terms
transition words or phrases	repetition of names or titles
transition paragraphs	repetition of language from the thesis

If any aspect of a reading's organization makes it difficult for you to understand the author's message, you may want to examine it in your critique. Clearly explain the nature of the problem and how it damages the reading's effectiveness. Likewise, if the organization is especially strong—if it significantly enhances the reading's clarity or effectiveness—you can point that out in your critique and explain how it helps the text. Here are some questions to consider when evaluating the source text's organization:

- Is there a clear connection between the major assertions of the essay? Does there seem to be some reason why one idea precedes or follows another?
- Are all the assertions clearly related to the overall thesis of the piece?
- Has the author provided headings or subheadings to help readers follow his line of thought? How effective are they?
- Has the author provided adequate transitions to help readers move through the writing and see the logical connection between the assertions he is making? How effective are they?

Analyzing and Evaluating a Reading's Style

Stylistic analysis is a complicated process—an academic specialty in and of itself within the field of English studies. In most of your college courses, though, when analyzing style you will likely focus on issues of clarity and convention. First, when you critique a reading, you might comment on its clarity. You will want to identify which aspects of the writer's word choice and sentence structure help you understand what she has to say or which serve to complicate your reading of the text. Other times, you may ask a different set of questions concerning style, especially in upper-division courses. Your assignment will be to assess how well an author adheres to the stylistic conventions of a discipline. For example, you might explore whether the author's language, tone, and syntax are appropriate for a particular type of writing or field of study. To begin your analysis of style, here are some questions you might ask about a reading:

- What level of diction is the writer employing (how formal is the prose)?

  formal   conversational
  informal   a mixture

  Identify which words or passages lead you to this conclusion.
- What is the tone of the piece (what is the author's apparent attitude toward the topic)?

  serious   satiric   involved
  humorous   angry   detached

  Identify which words or passages lead you to this conclusion.
- What kind of language is used in the piece? Identify any passages using specialized language, emotional language, or jargon.
- What types of sentences are used in the reading?

  simple, compound, complex, complex-compound
  long or short
  active or passive
  a mixture of types

When critiquing a reading's style, you evaluate elements of the author's prose such as diction, tone, word choice, and syntax. Again, stylistic standards vary greatly across the disciplines. Although teachers in various disciplines may use similar terms when describing "good" style in writing—that it should be clear and concise, for example—how they define their criteria is likely to vary. Clear and concise writing in a chemistry lab report may have little in common, stylistically, with clear and concise writing in a philosophy research report. Below are some questions that might help you begin to evaluate certain aspects of an author's style. Remember, though, that your answers may well depend on the stylistic standards accepted by a particular discipline:

- How would you characterize the diction of the piece: formal, informal, or somewhere in the middle? Is it consistently maintained? Is it appropriate? Does it contribute to the effectiveness of the piece?
- How would you characterize the tone of the piece? Is it inviting, satiric, or humorous? Is it appropriate, given the topic and intent of the piece? Does the tone enhance or damage the effect of the writing?
- Is the author's word choice clear and effective? Or does the writer rely too heavily on jargon, abstractions, or highly technical terms?
- Is the author's word choice needlessly inflammatory or emotional? Or do the words convey appropriate connotations?

- Are the sentences clearly written? Are any of the sentences so poorly structured that the source is difficult to read and understand?
- Are the sentence types varied? Is the syntax appropriate given the audience and intent of the piece?

STEP 3—WRITE YOUR THESIS AND DECIDE WHICH ASPECTS OF THE READING WILL BE THE FOCUS OF YOUR ESSAY

At this point you need to develop your thesis and decide which aspects of the reading you will use to develop your critique. To formulate your thesis, you need to decide which elements of the source text best illustrate or defend your judgment. You want your reader to understand and accept your thesis, but this acceptance can come about only if you clearly explain each claim you make about the reading and offer convincing examples from the text to illustrate and defend your contentions.

In your critique, you do not need to address every aspect of the source text. Remember how the movie critic supports her assertions about a film. No review addresses every aspect of a movie. Instead, the critic chooses to discuss in her review only those elements of the movie she thinks most clearly and effectively illustrate her judgment. Maybe she will address only the acting and direction, perhaps only the dialogue, plot, and special effects. Perhaps she will choose to mention, only briefly, the costuming and musical score, then concentrate more attention on the film's cinematography.

Follow the same line of thinking when you decide which aspects of the reading to address in your critique. To illustrate and defend your thesis, you may choose to look only at the logic of the piece and its structure. However, you may choose to ignore both of these and concentrate, instead, on the writer's style. Maybe you will decide to look briefly at the evidence the author offers, and then concentrate most of your attention on the organization of the piece. Your decisions should be based on two fairly simple questions: (1) Which aspects of the reading most influenced your judgment of its quality and worth? (2) Which aspects will best illustrate and support your thesis? Choose only those aspects of the reading for examination in your critique.

Your thesis in a critique is a brief statement of what you believe to be the overall value or worth of the source text based on your analysis and evaluation of its parts. In stating your thesis, you have several options. You can say only positive things about the reading, only negative things, or some mixture of the two. Your main concern at this point is that your thesis honestly and accurately reflects your judgment.

Also, your thesis statement can be either open or closed. In an open thesis statement, you offer your overall judgment of the piece and nothing else. In a closed thesis statement, you offer your judgment and indicate which aspects of the reading you will examine when developing your essay. Following are some sample open and closed thesis statements for a critique—positive, negative, and mixed.

Positive Thesis Statement

Open

Jones presents a clear, convincing argument in favor of increased funding for the school district.

Closed

Through his use of precise examples and his accessible style, Jones presents a clear and convincing argument in favor of increased funding for the school district.

Negative Thesis Statement

Open

Jones's argument in favor of increased funding is not convincing.

Closed

Due to numerous lapses in reasoning and problems with the organization, Jones's argument in favor of increased funding is not convincing.

Mixed Thesis Statement

Open

Although uneven in its presentation, Jones's argument in favor of increased funding for the school district is, ultimately, convincing.

Closed

Even though there are some problems with the organization Jones employs in his report, his use of expert testimony makes his argument for increased funding for the schools convincing.

STEP 4—WRITE YOUR ROUGH DRAFT

Although there are many ways to structure a critique, the suggestions that follow can serve as a general guide.

Introductory Section

- Introduce the topic of the reading.
- Give the title of the piece and the name of its author.
- Give your thesis.
- Summarize the source text.

In the opening section of your critique, you should introduce the topic of the reading and give your reader its exact title and the full name of its author. You will also include here your thesis and a brief summary of the reading (one or two paragraphs long). The exact order you choose to follow when covering this material is up to you. Some writers like to begin with the summary of the source text before giving the thesis; some prefer to give the thesis first. Overall, though, your introductory section should only be two or three paragraphs long.

Body

- Examine one element of the reading at a time.
- Cite specific examples of this element from the reading.
- Explain your evaluation of each example you offer.

State the Criteria and Your Judgments

In the body of your critique, you will explain and defend the judgment you made in your thesis, focusing on one aspect of the reading at a time. Topic sentences in a critique usually indicate the element of the reading you will be examining in that part of the essay and whether you found it to be a strength or liability—for example, "One of the real strengths of the essay is the author's use of emotional language."

Offer Examples

Whatever aspect of the reading you are examining—logic, word choice, structure—give your readers specific examples from the source text to clarify your terms and demonstrate that your judgment is sound. For example, the student who hopes to prove that the author's use of emotional language is one of the reading's strengths will need to quote several examples of language from the text he believes are emotional. Offering only one example might not be convincing; readers might question whether the student isolated the single occurrence of that element in the text for praise or criticism.

Explain Your Judgments

After you have specified the aspect of the reading you are examining in that part of your critique and have offered your readers examples from the text, you need to explain and defend your judgment. After the student mentioned above cites a few specific examples of the author's emotional language, he will need to explain clearly and convincingly *how* that language strengthens the author's writing. Simply saying it does is not good enough. The student will have to explain how this type of language helps make the author's article clearer or more convincing.

In this section of the critique you will likely develop and explain your unique perspective on the reading. Suppose you and your friend are critiquing the same reading. You could both agree that it is effective and could even choose to focus on the same elements of the reading to defend and illustrate this judgment; for example, you could both choose to focus on the author's use of evidence. The two of you will probably differ, though, in your explanation of how and why the author's use of evidence is strong. You will offer your individual assessments of how the writer effectively employed evidence to support his thesis.

Conclusion

- Wrap up the paper.
- Reassert the thesis.

In your concluding section, try to give your reader a sense of closure. Consider mirroring in your conclusion the strategy you used to open your critique. For example, if you opened your essay with a question, consider closing it by answering that question; if you began with a quotation, end with a quotation; if you opened with a story, finish the story. You might also consider restating your thesis—your overall assessment of the piece—to remind your readers of the judgments you developed in the body of your essay.

STEP 5—REWRITE YOUR CRITIQUE

In rewriting your critique, check to make sure your work is accurate, thorough, organized, and clear.

- *Accurate*—it reflects your true assessment of the source text.
- *Thorough*—you completely explain your assertions.
- *Organized*—readers can easily follow the development of your critique.
- *Clear*—you have explained all the terms you need to explain and supported any assumptions that might reasonably be questioned.

Check for Accuracy

When reviewing your work, first check for accuracy. You want to be sure that your essay reflects your honest assessment of the source text. Starting with your thesis, look through your essay to make sure the assertions you make, the supporting material you employ, and the explanations you offer accurately reflect your point of view.

Check the Development of Your Assertions

Next, make sure you have been thorough in developing your critique. Check to be sure you have offered examples from the source text to support and illustrate your claims and that you have explained your reasoning clearly and completely. Add material—quotations, examples, and explanations—where you think it is needed.

Check the Organization

As you review the organization of your critique, make sure your thesis guides the development of your essay. Are you examining only one aspect of the reading at a time? If not, move material around to improve the organization in your essay. Have you provided adequate transitions to help your reader move through the piece? Do you repeat key terms or provide transition words that remind your reader of your thesis or signal the relationship between the various assertions you make?

Check for Clarity

Check your critique for clarity. Have you used any terms that need to be defined? Have you made any assertions that readers would find unclear? Have you made any assumptions that need to be explained or defended? When necessary, change the content, word choice, or sentence structure of your essay to make your ideas more accessible to your readers.

READINGS

The essay "The Doctrine of Academic Freedom" by Sandra Y. L. Korn was published in *The Harvard Crimson*. Michael LaBrossiere critiques Korn's argument in "Academic Freedom vs. Academic Justice" which appeared on *The Philosopher's Blog*. Following both readings is a sample critique essay that also examines Korn's argument.

The Doctrine of Academic Freedom

Sandra Y. L. Korn

Sandra Y. L. Korn *is an editorial writer for* The Harvard Crimson.

In July 1971, Harvard psychology professor Richard J. Herrnstein penned an article for *Atlantic Monthly* titled "I.Q." in which he endorsed the theories of UC Berkeley psychologist Arthur Jensen, who had claimed that intelligence is almost entirely hereditary and varies by race. Herrnstein further argued that because intelligence was hereditary, social programs intended to establish a more egalitarian society were futile—he wrote that "social standing [is] based to some extent on inherited differences among people."

When he returned to campus for fall semester 1971, Herrnstein was met by angry student activists. Harvard-Radcliffe Students for a Democratic

Society protested his introductory psychology class with a bullhorn and leaflets. They tied up Herrnstein's lectures with pointed questions about scientific racism. SDS even called for Harvard to fire Herrnstein, along with another of his colleagues, sociologist Christopher Jencks.

Herrnstein told *The Crimson*, "The attacks on me have not bothered me personally. . . . What bothers me is this: Something has happened at Harvard this year that makes it hazardous for a professor to teach certain kinds of views." This, Herrnstein seems not to have understood, was precisely the goal of the SDS activists—they wanted to make the "certain kinds of views" they deemed racist and classist unwelcome on Harvard's campus.

Harvard's deans were also unhappy. They expressed concerns about student activists' "interference with the academic freedom and right to speak of a member of the Harvard faculty." Did SDS activists at Harvard infringe on Herrnstein's academic freedom? The answer might be that yes, they did—but that's not the most important question to ask. Student and faculty obsession with the doctrine of "academic freedom" often seems to bump against something I think much more important: academic justice.

In its oft-cited Statement of Principles on Academic Freedom and Tenure, the American Association of University Professors declares that "Teachers are entitled to full freedom in research and in the publication of the results." In principle, this policy seems sound: It would not do for academics to have their research restricted by the political whims of the moment.

Yet the liberal obsession with "academic freedom" seems a bit misplaced to me. After all, no one ever has "full freedom" in research and publication. Which research proposals receive funding and what papers are accepted for publication are always contingent on political priorities. The words used to articulate a research question can have implications for its outcome. No academic question is ever "free" from political realities. If our university community opposes racism, sexism, and heterosexism, why should we put up with research that counters our goals simply in the name of "academic freedom"?

Instead, I would like to propose a more rigorous standard: one of "academic justice." When an academic community observes research promoting or justifying oppression, it should ensure that this research does not continue.

The power to enforce academic justice comes from students, faculty, and workers organizing together to make our universities look as we want them to do. Two years ago, when former summer school instructor Subramanian Swamy published hateful commentary about Muslims in India, the Harvard community organized to ensure that he would not return to teach on campus. I consider that sort of organizing both appropriate and commendable. Perhaps it should even be applied more broadly. Does Government Professor Harvey Mansfield have the legal right to publish a book in which he claims that "to resist rape a woman needs . . . a certain ladylike modesty?" Probably. Do I think he should do that? No, and I would happily organize with other feminists on campus to stop him from publishing further sexist commentary under the authority of a Harvard faculty position.

"Academic freedom" might permit such an offensive view of rape to be published; academic justice would not.

Over winter break, Harvard published a statement responding to the American Studies Association's resolution to boycott Israeli academic institutions until Israel ends its occupation of Palestine. Much of the conversation around this academic boycott has focused on academic freedom. Opponents of the boycott claim that it restricts the freedom of Israeli academics or interrupts the "free flow of ideas." Proponents of the boycott often argue that the boycott is intended to, in the end, increase, not restrict, academic freedom—the ASA points out that "there is no effective or substantive academic freedom for Palestinian students and scholars under conditions of Israeli occupation."

In this case, discourse about "academic freedom" obscures what should fundamentally be a political argument. Those defending the academic boycott should use a more rigorous standard. The ASA, like three other academic associations, decided to boycott out of a sense of social justice, responding to a call by Palestinian civil society organizations for boycotts, divestment, and sanctions until Israel ends its occupation of Palestine. People on the right opposed to boycotts can play the "freedom" game, calling for economic freedom to buy any product or academic freedom to associate with any institution. Only those who care about justice can take the moral upper hand.

It is tempting to decry frustrating restrictions on academic research as violations of academic freedom. Yet I would encourage student and worker organizers to instead use a framework of justice. After all, if we give up our obsessive reliance on the doctrine of academic freedom, we can consider more thoughtfully what is just.

Academic Freedom vs. Academic Justice

Michael LaBossiere

Michael LaBossiere *is a philosophy professor at Florida A&M University.*

Sandra Y. L. Korn has proposed dispensing with academic freedom in favor of academic justice. Korn begins by presenting the example of Harvard psychology Professor Richard Herrnstein's 1971 article for *Atlantic Monthly*.

In this article, Herrnstein endorsed the view that intelligence is primarily hereditary and linked to race. Herrnstein was attacked for this view, but defended himself and was defended by others via appeals to academic freedom. Korn seems to agree with Herrnstein that the attacks against him infringed on academic freedom. However, Korn proposes that academic justice is more important than academic freedom.

Korn makes use of the American Association of University Professors view of academic freedom: "Teachers are entitled to full freedom in research and in the publication of the results." However, Korn regards the "liberal obsession" with this freedom as misplaced.

Korn's first argument seems to be as follows. Korn notes that there is not "full freedom" in research and publication. As Korn correctly notes, which proposals get funded and which papers get published is largely a matter of academic politics. Korn then notes that no academic question is free from the realities of politics. From this, Korn draws a conditional conclusion: "If our university community opposes racism, sexism, and heterosexism, why should we put up with research that counters our goals simply in the name of 'academic freedom'?"

It might be suspected that there is a false dilemma lurking here: either there is full academic freedom or restricting it on political values is acceptable. There is not full academic freedom. Therefore restricting it on political values is acceptable. The reason why this would be a false dilemma is that there is a considerable range of options between full academic freedom (which seems to be complete freedom) and such restrictions. As such, one could accept the obvious truth that there is not full (complete) freedom while also legitimately rejecting that academic freedom should be restricted on the proposed grounds.

To use the obvious analogy to general freedom of expression, the fact that people do not possess full freedom of expression (after all, there are limits on expression) does not entail that politically based restrictions should thus be accepted. After all, there are many alternatives between full freedom and the specific restrictions being proposed.

To be fair to Korn, no such false dilemma might exist. Instead, Korn might be reasoning that because the reality is such that political values restrict academic expression it follows that adding additional restrictions is not problematic. To re-use the analogy to general free expression, the reasoning would [be] that since there are already limits on free expression, more restrictions are acceptable. This could be seen as a common practice fallacy, but perhaps it could be justified by showing that the additional restrictions are warranted. Sorting this out requires considering what Korn is proposing.

In place of the academic freedom standard, Korn proposes "a more rigorous standard: one of 'academic justice.' When an academic community observes research promoting or justifying oppression, it should ensure that this research does not continue."

While Korn claims that this is a more rigorous standard, it merely seems to be more restrictive. There is also the rather obvious problem of presenting an account of what it is for research to promote or justify oppression in a way that is rigorous and, more importantly, accurate. After all, "oppression" gets thrown around with some abandon in academic contexts and can be a rather vague notion. In order to decide what is allowed and what is not, Korn proposes that students, faculty and workers should organize in order to "to make our universities look as we want them to do." While that sounds somewhat democratic, there is still the rather important concern about what standards will be used.

While there are paradigm cases (like the institutionalized racism of pre-civil rights America), people do use the term "oppression" to refer to what merely offends them. In fact, Korn makes reference to the offensiveness of a person's comment as grounds for removing a professor from a faculty position.

The obvious danger is that the vagueness of this principle could be used to suppress and oppress research that vocal or influential people find offensive. There is also the obvious concern that such a principle would yield a political hammer with which to beat down those who present dissenting or unpopular views. For example, suppose a researcher finds legitimate evidence that sexual orientation is strongly influenced by choice and is accused of engaging research that promotes oppression because her research runs counter to an accepted view among certain people. As another example, imagine a faculty member who holds conservative views that some might find offensive, such as the view that people should work for their government support. This person could be seen as promoting oppression of the poor and thus be justly restricted by this principle.

Interestingly, Korn does present an example of a case in which a Harvard faculty member was asked not to return on the basis of objections against remarks that had been made. This would seem to indicate that Korn's proposal might not be needed. After all, if academic freedom does not provide protection against being removed or restricted on these grounds, then there would seem to be little or no need to put in place a new principle. To use an analogy, if people can already be silenced for offensive speech, there is no need to restrict freedom of speech with a new principle—it is already restricted. At least at Harvard.

In closing, I am certainly in favor of justice and even more in favor of what is morally good. As such, I do endorse holding people morally accountable for their actions and statements. However, I do oppose restrictions on academic freedom for the same reason I oppose restrictions on the general freedom of expression (which I have written about elsewhere). In the case of academic freedom, what should matter is whether the research is properly conducted and whether or not the claims are well-supported. To explicitly adopt a principle for deciding what is allowed and what is not based on ideological views would, as history shows, have a chilling effect on research and academics. While the academic system is far from perfect, flawed research and false claims do get sorted out—at least fairly often. Adding in a political test would not seem to help with reaching the goal of truth.

As far as when academic freedom should be restricted, I also go with my general view of freedom of expression: when an action creates enough actual harm to warrant limiting the freedom. So, merely offending people is not enough to warrant restrictions—even if people are very offended. Actually threatening people or engaging in falsification of research results would be rather different matters and obviously not protected by academic freedom.

As such, I am opposed to Korn's modest proposal to impose more political restrictions on academic freedom. As Korn notes, there are already many restrictions in place—and there seem to be no compelling reasons to add more.

SAMPLE CRITIQUE

AN UNCONVINCING ARGUMENT CONCERNING ACADEMIC FREEDOM

Academic freedom is a cornerstone of American higher education. Under the protection of academic freedom, faculty are free to conduct their research and publish their results without fear of retaliation from the college or university even if the topics they investigate are controversial. In a recent article published in *The Harvard Crimson*, student and editorial writer Sandra Korn argues that academic freedom should be abolished in favor of "academic justice." Under a policy of academic justice, colleges and universities could fire or otherwise punish faculty who conduct research concerning topics the institution, its students, or its other faculty deem inappropriate, immoral, or counter to the stated school's stated goals. Korn's argument, though interesting and provocative, is unconvincing due to numerous flaws in her reasoning.

One of the ways Korn supports her argument is by citing precedent. In 2012, Subramanian Swamy, an economics professor who taught summer courses at Harvard, published what Korn describes as "hateful commentary about Muslims in India" (128). Harvard did not rehire him. For Korn, disciplining Swamy demonstrated "the power to enforce academic justice" (128). She states that the same standard ought to have been applied in 1971 when a Harvard psychologist, Richard Herrnstein, published an essay in support of research on intelligence and heredity that Korn asserts was racist. It should also be applied today to discipline a Harvard government professor, Harvey Mansfield, whose recent book contained comments about rape that Korn characterizes as sexist. Korn argues that "'Academic freedom' might permit such an offensive view of rape to be published; academic justice would not" (129).

Korn implies that the same standard used to punish Swamy ought to apply to faculty like Herrnstein and Mansfield. Korn's argument by precedent is unconvincing. First, she fails to establish that the actions taken again Swamy were fair and just, which is crucial since she presenting an argument in favor of academic "justice." She assumes that Harvard took the correct action in not rehiring Swamy, but does not present any support for or explanation of that assertion. She simply assumes that the justice of Harvard's action is self-evident. However, without establishing that Harvard acted properly and justly with Swamy, no precedent is set to serve as a basis for claiming that Jensen and Mansfield ought to have been dealt with similarly. It could be that in not rehiring Swamy, Harvard acted unjustly, in violation of academic freedom, and does not want to repeat that mistake.

Korn also argues that academic freedom can be curtailed for political reasons because academic freedom is never absolute and academic work is always political in nature. In Korn's view, "no one ever has 'full freedom' in research and publication. Which research proposals receive funding and what papers are accepted for publication are always contingent on political priorities" (128). In other words, research funding and publication are always political decisions. If this is true, then political criteria are used to make these decisions, and adding "academic justice" as one of those criteria is not a significant change. Also for Korn, "no academic question is ever 'free' from political realities" (128). That is, the criteria of academic justice applies not just to what research gets funded and published but also which research questions ought to be asked.

Korn's reasoning in this argument is not convincing. Decisions about what research might get funded or published, could involve politics, but may not be exclusively or predominately political. Other factors may come into play (lack of funds, for example, or fundamental problems with the research methodology or writing). To reduce all issues to politics oversimplifies reality. Korn's assertion that all academic questions are political is tenuous as well. They may, in part, be political, but that does not mean they are exclusively political or that political concerns ought to determine what academic questions are asked. That gives far too much power to one, possible inconsequential, motivation for asking the question. Korn privileges politics to support her argument. If politics rules all academic questions, research, and publication, the pursuit of knowledge at the heart of higher education would be stifled. In fact, Korn contradicts her own argument in the piece. She acknowledges, "It would not do for academics to have their research restricted by the political whims of the moment" (128). Yet this is exactly what would result under Korn's proposal to prioritize political considerations in the name of academic justice.

In fact, the very term "academic justice" poses a major problem for Korn's argument. She asserts that this standard should replace "academic freedom" in higher education, but she does not define what she means by "justice" or indicate who would decide whether particular research questions or publications are just. A few defining criteria are offered: research should be stopped that is oppressive (128), "racist" (128), or "sexist" (128), yet Korn assumes that these terms are not in dispute. Do students or faculty at a university decide? How many students or faculty are must deem a research project "oppressive" for it to be censored? Which students or faculty? If research projects are permitted one year at a university then stopped the next because the student population changes or faculty changed their minds, all research would cease. No faculty would commit to a project that might get him or her fired if someone at some time at the institution deemed it unjust. These questions do no not come into play when research is protected under academic freedom.

Academic freedom does not protect faculty or students at a university from being offended by someone's research. Yet, such offense can be the justifying reason for some research to take place: challenging accepted wisdom, pushing against political constraints, or asking uncomfortable questions is essential to knowledge making mission of a university. Korn states that shifting to a standard of academic justice may result in "frustrating restrictions" (129) for some researchers, but the consequences would be much more serious. In her essay, Korn does not present a convincing argument to abandon academic freedom at universities for academic justice—an ill-defined, ill-conceived restriction on the pursuit of knowledge.

Summary Chart

How to Write a Critique

---

1. **Carefully read and annotate the source text.**
   * *Read and reread the text.*
   * *Identify the author's intent, thesis, and primary assertions or findings.*
   * *Write an informal summary of the piece.*

2. **Analyze and evaluate the reading, breaking it down into its parts and judging the quality of each element.**

   Identify and evaluate the author's logic and reasoning.
   * *Is the thesis clearly stated, and does it direct the development of the text?*
   * *Are the author's primary assertions reasonable and clearly tied to the thesis?*
   * *Are there problems with logical fallacies?*
   * *Are the author's positions or findings logically presented?*

   Identify and evaluate the text's evidence.
   * *Does the author support his or her assertions or findings?*
   * *Is the support offered adequate to convince readers?*
   * *Is the evidence authoritative?*
   * *Is the evidence current?*
   * *Does the author explain how the evidence supports his or her assertions or findings?*
   * *Has the author ignored evidence or alternative hypotheses?*

   Identify and evaluate the text's organization.
   * *Is there a clear connection between the assertions developed in the essay?*
   * *Are the assertions or findings tied to a guiding thesis?*
   * *Does there seem to be a reason for one assertion following another, or do they seem randomly organized?*

   Identify and evaluate the text's style.
   * *Is the author's diction consistently maintained?*
   * *Is the author's word choice clear and effective?*
   * *Is the author's tone consistent and effective?*
   * *Are the author's sentences clear?*

SUMMARY CHART: HOW TO WRITE A CRITIQUE *(CONTINUED)*

3. **Formulate your thesis and choose the criteria you will include in your essay.**
   - *Draft a thesis, a brief statement concerning the overall value or worth of the source text.*
   - *Choose which elements of the reading you will focus on in your critique.*

4. **Write your rough draft.**
   - *Introduce the topic, source text, and your thesis.*
   - *Establish your evaluative criteria and your judgments of them.*
   - *Offer examples to substantiate each of your criteria and judgments.*
   - *Explain your judgments, clarifying how the examples you provide support your assertions.*

5. **Rewrite your critique.**

   Check to make sure your writing is accurate.
   - *Does your writing honestly reflect your judgment?*
   - *Does your writing misrepresent the author?*

   Check to make sure your writing is thorough.
   - *Do you cover all the aspects of the source text you need to cover?*
   - *Do you clearly and thoroughly explain and support your assertions?*

   Check to make sure your writing is organized.
   - *Does your thesis statement guide the development of your essay?*
   - *Have you provided transitional devices to help lead your reader through your work?*

   Check to make sure your writing is clear.
   - *Is your terminology clear?*
   - *Are your sentences clear?*
   - *Are your examples and explanations clear?*

CRITIQUE REVISION CHECKLIST

	Yes	No
1. Have you included the title of the reading and the author's name in your introduction?	_____	_____
2. Does your thesis make clear your overall assessment of the reading?	_____	_____
3. Toward the beginning of your critique, have you provided a brief summary of the reading?	_____	_____
4. In the body of your critique, do you examine only one element of the reading at a time?	_____	_____
5. Do you clearly state a judgment concerning each element of the reading you explore?	_____	_____
6. Do you provide examples from the reading to support and illustrate your judgment of each element you examine?	_____	_____
7. Do you clearly and thoroughly explain your judgments concerning each example you provide from the reading?	_____	_____
8. Have you employed proper evaluative criteria and standards?	_____	_____
9. Have you provided clear transitions between the major sections of your paper?	_____	_____
10. Is there a clear relationship between each section of your paper and your thesis?	_____	_____
11. Have you provided proper documentation for all quoted, paraphrased, and summarized material?	_____	_____
12. Have you revised your paper for accuracy? In other words, does the final draft reflect your honest appraisal of the reading?	_____	_____

Critique Revision Checklist *(continued)*

	Yes	No
13. Have you reviewed the language in your paper to make sure your words adequately capture and communicate your judgments?	_____	_____
14. As you review your work, do your judgments still stand? Do you need to change your thesis or any part of your paper?	_____	_____

Chapter 8

RHETORICAL ANALYSIS OF WRITTEN TEXTS

In this chapter you will learn how to

1. Identify a reading's rhetorical situation

2. Identify a reading's core rhetorical strategies

3. Evaluate a reading in terms of its rhetorical situation and rhetorical strategies

4. Compose an effective rhetorical analysis of a written text

DEFINITION AND PURPOSE

A rhetorical analysis essay is a special form of critique (see Chapter 7). In a critique essay, you determine a source text's overall value or worth by critically examining a set of relevant criteria; in a rhetorical analysis essay, you determine a source text's rhetorical effectiveness by examining how the author employs language and/or visual images to achieve a particular effect on an audience. This chapter addresses how to compose a rhetorical analysis of a written text; the following chapter offers instruction on how to compose a rhetorical analysis of a visual text.

Writing a rhetorical analysis of a reading requires you to answer three related questions:

- What response is the author of the reading trying to elicit from his or her readers?
- How does the author employ language to elicit that response?
- How well does the author succeed in achieving this response?

Composing a rhetorical analysis requires you to examine a source text from the perspective of both a reader and a writer, assessing how well an author achieves certain rhetorical goals in a text.

Rhetorical analysis of print texts is based on certain assumptions about how writers write and the way writing works. First is the assumption that writing is purposeful, that every text is written by someone who directs it toward some audience to achieve some purpose. To accomplish their ends, writers make a series of strategic choices—they choose this approach to the topic instead of that approach, this set of arguments rather than that set of arguments, this evidence instead of that evidence, this thesis rather than that one, this organizational plan in place of another, this word rather than that word. In a rhetorical analysis essay, you critically examine this series of choices, identifying and critiquing the strategies a writer employs to achieve his or her rhetorical goals.

A second assumption is that text and context are intimately connected, that text is fundamentally influenced by the context in which it is written. Writers work within a set of givens, a rhetorical context or situation that includes their reasons for writing the text, their purpose or aim, their audience's needs or interests, and their knowledge of the topic they are addressing. To be effective, writers must adapt their writing to meet the needs of the given rhetorical situation. If they ignore or misconstrue any element of the rhetorical situation, their writing will be less effective than it might otherwise be. Because writers typically want to produce the most effective text possible, they take particular efforts to ensure that their language suits the text's audience, purpose, message, and occasion. Therefore, to evaluate a text's rhetorical effectiveness, you must understand the context in which it was written.

A final assumption is that no rhetorical analysis is definitive. Readers often disagree about a text's purpose, intended audience, rhetorical strategies, and effectiveness. Because readers always bring their own knowledge, experiences, sensitivities, and biases to a text, they will form unique, individualized responses to even the most fundamental questions concerning how a reading communicates its meaning. Consequently, when you write a rhetorical analysis essay, you must explain your conclusions as clearly as you can, supporting them with thorough explanations and specific references to the source text.

THE RHETORICAL SITUATION

When you compose a rhetorical analysis essay of a written text, you must examine how an author uses language to achieve a particular response from readers. However, your task is a little more complicated than it might appear at first. You will actually be examining how an author uses language to achieve a particular response from readers *given the specific context in which the writer produced the text*. This "specific context" is called the text's **rhetorical situation**, which includes the author's audience, subject matter, purpose, and occasion for writing. In your paper, you will assess how the writer manipulates language to meet the needs of the rhetorical situation and achieve his or her goals for the text.

A brief example may help explain why understanding the rhetorical situation of a source text is essential to composing an effective rhetorical analysis essay. Suppose your source text is a set of instructions for installing a new hard drive on a computer. Your task is to evaluate how well the instructions achieve their intended purpose. The first thing you notice is that the instructions are full of undefined technical terms—IDE cables, jumper selectors, drive rails, boot drives. Are the instructions effective? Upon consideration, you would have to conclude that the answer is, "It depends." If the instructions are written for someone who is already well versed in computer technology, they may be fine; if they are written for a novice computer owner, they may not be so effective. Composing an effective rhetorical analysis of the instructions requires that you evaluate the writing in light of its purpose and intended audience, two crucial elements of the text's rhetorical situation.

Because understanding a text's rhetorical situation is so fundamental to writing this type of essay, it is worthwhile to examine each element in isolation. The following section contains definitions of various elements of a text's rhetorical situation and a series of questions writers frequently ask of each element as they prepare to write a rhetorical analysis essay.

ELEMENTS OF THE RHETORICAL SITUATION

Author—the person or people who wrote the text

- Who wrote the piece?
- What is the author's background in terms of race, sex, education, political affiliation, economic status, or religion?
- What are the author's possible or likely biases?
- What perspective does the author bring to the topic?
- How does the author "sound" on the page—angry, detached, confused, funny?
- What has the author written about the topic in the past?

Topic—what the text is about

- What is the person writing about?
- Is the author addressing a particular aspect of the topic or the topic as a whole?
- Which aspects of the topic receive the most attention and which receive the least?
- What, exactly, is the author stating about the topic?
- What have others said about this subject matter?
- What is the relationship between what others have written about the topic and what the author is writing about it?

Audience—whom the writer is addressing

- To whom is the text addressed?
- If the text is not written to a specific person or group of people, what kind of reader did the author seem to have in mind when writing the piece? For example, does the author seem to be assuming he or she is

addressing a friendly audience or a hostile audience? An expert audience or a novice audience? An academic audience or a popular audience?

- What is the audience's likely knowledge of or attitude toward the author and/or subject matter?
- What assumptions does the author make about the audience? Are these assumptions accurate?

Purpose or Aim—what the author is trying to accomplish in writing the text

- If the author states a purpose or aim for the piece, what is it? To inform, persuade, entertain, educate, provoke to action, draw attention, ridicule, shock?
- If it is not stated, what is the author's implied purpose or aim for the text?
- Is there more than one purpose or aim for the text? If so, what are they? Does one purpose seem more dominant than the others? Which one?
- How does the author's purpose influence the text's content, structure, or language?

Occasion—what prompted the writer to write the piece

- Why did the author feel compelled to write this text?
- What is the historical context of the piece?
- Is the author adding to a debate over a particular political issue or social question? Is the author responding to another writer or text? Is the author responding to a particular historical event or cultural phenomenon?

Writing a rhetorical analysis essay usually requires you to examine the complex interrelationships that exist among these elements. For example, how does the author's audience influence what she writes about the topic or the language she employs? What is the relationship between a text's purpose and the time or place it was written? How effective is the author in producing a text that is appropriate for both the audience and the occasion?

RHETORICAL STRATEGIES

After you understand the text's rhetorical situation, you are ready to turn your analysis to the author's rhetorical strategies—the way the author manipulates the text's content, structure, or style to achieve his or her aim. **Content** concerns the material an author includes in the text, **structure** concerns the order in which the author presents that material, and **style** concerns the language and sentence structure an author uses to convey that material. A rhetorical analysis essay is unlikely to address every aspect of a text's content, structure, or style. In fact, it may address just one or two of the author's rhetorical strategies.

As the person writing the analysis, you will determine which strategies you wish to examine. They will likely be the ones that you think are most essential to the author achieving his or her aim.

CONTENT

When composing a rhetorical analysis essay, most writers analyze a text's content in one or two related ways: by examining its arguments, evidence, and reasoning or by examining its persuasive appeals. Because both approaches are closely related, writers will often examine aspects of each in their essays. Both are discussed here.

Arguments, Evidence, and Reasoning

When analyzing a text's rhetorical strategies in terms of its arguments, evidence, and reasoning, you are primarily concerned with examining the claims or assertions a writer makes, the way that writer supports those claims, and the way he or she explains them. You need to ask yourself, given the text's rhetorical situation, why the writer would choose those particular arguments. Are they the best arguments for the writer to make? Why did the writer choose to support those claims the way he or she did? Again, was this the best choice of evidence? How effective were the writer's decisions? Does the writer explain his or her reasoning in the piece, exploring or defending the link between his or her claims and supporting evidence? Are there certain assumptions or leaps of reasoning the writer leaves unstated? Why might the writer have made that choice? Was it a good decision? Following are some questions that can help you analyze and evaluate a text's rhetorical strategies in terms of its arguments, evidence, and reasoning.

Arguments or Assertions

- What arguments or assertions does the author make and how are they related to the rhetorical situation?
- How does the audience, purpose, and occasion of the text influence the author's arguments or assertions?
- Given the audience and purpose of the text, are these the most effective arguments? If so, what makes them effective? If not, why not? What arguments might be more effective?
- What arguments or assertions are emphasized the most? Why did the author decide to emphasize those assertions instead of others?
- What relevant arguments or assertions are ignored or slighted? Why do you think the author chose not to address them?
- How might the intended audience respond to the arguments offered? How well does the author seem to anticipate and perhaps address these likely responses?

Evidence or Examples

- How does the author support his or her assertions? Are they supported by primary or secondary research? By personal experience? By statistics or expert testimony?
- What is the source of the author's evidence for each assertion or argument? Are they particularly effective sources, given the text's rhetorical situation?
- Is the evidence offered appropriate, given the text's rhetorical situation? Does the evidence offered effectively support each claim?
- How might the intended audience respond to the evidence or examples offered? How well does the author seem to anticipate and perhaps address these likely responses?
- Is the presentation balanced or one-sided? In either case, is that choice appropriate given the rhetorical situation?
- How does the author address possible counterarguments or evidence that does not support his or her assertions?
- Are there obvious arguments the author chooses to ignore or gloss over? What are the effects of these omissions? How might they be explained, given the text's rhetorical situation?

Reasoning

- Does the author present a clear and cogent line of reasoning in the text?
- How well does the author move from one assertion to the next?
- How compelling is the connection the author makes among assertions? Between assertions and their supporting evidence?
- Does the text lead logically and convincingly to its conclusion?
- Are there clear connections between the text's thesis and its primary assertions?
- Are there any important assumptions that the author leaves unstated? Does leaving them unstated and undefended make the text any less successful?
- Is the reasoning fair and balanced? Should it be, given the text's rhetorical situation?
- Are there any logical fallacies or flaws in reasoning that might hinder the text's effectiveness, given its audience, purpose, and occasion?

Persuasive Appeals

Another set of strategies authors often employ to achieve their rhetorical goals involves appealing to their readers' rationality (logos) or emotions (pathos) or establishing their own credibility as an authority on the topic (ethos). Though one of the three appeals may dominate a particular reading, most effective persuasive texts use elements of all three. In brief, when authors try to persuade readers by presenting a reasonable series of arguments supported by evidence and examples, they are relying on **logos** to achieve their goal; when they try to persuade readers through emotional language or examples or by appealing to the reader's needs or interests, they are relying on **pathos**; when they try to persuade readers by appearing fair, balanced, and informed or by establishing their own credibility and authority on the subject, they are relying on **ethos**. Below are some questions you can ask about a text's persuasive appeals if you are analyzing its rhetorical effectiveness.

Logos

- How reasonable and appropriate are the author's claims, given the rhetorical situation?
- How clear are the author's claims?
- Are the author's claims broad and sweeping or does the author limit or qualify them?
- How well does the author use facts, statistics, and expert testimony to support his or her claims?
- Are the author's claims adequately explained?
- Does the author avoid lapses in reasoning or logical fallacies?
- Does the author address opposing or alternative viewpoints?
- Are there relevant claims the author fails to address?
- Are the author's claims convincing?

Pathos

- Does the author attempt to convince his or her readers through appeals to their emotions?
- To which emotions is the author appealing? To the readers' personal fears or concerns? To the readers' economic or social self-interests? To the readers' desires for acceptance, love, or beauty? To the readers' sense of justice or social responsibility?
- Does the author appeal to his readers' emotions through his choice of arguments, evidence, language, or some combination of the three?
- How are appeals to emotion balanced with other appeals in the text?
- Does the author try too hard to appeal to readers' emotions? Are the appeals to emotion too clumsy or awkward to be effective?
- Is an appeal to the readers' emotions an effective strategy to employ given the rhetorical situation?

Ethos

- How does the author attempt to establish her credibility or authority?
- What level of expertise does the author demonstrate when writing about the topic of her text?
- Does the author's own experience or expertise lend credibility to the text?
- Does the author demonstrate or document the validity of the source texts used to support her assertions?

- Does the author present a balanced or a one-sided argument? Is that approach appropriate, given the rhetorical situation?
- Does the author demonstrate a sufficient understanding of the topic's complex or controversial nature?
- Does the text's tone or the author's voice contribute to or detract from her credibility?

STRUCTURE

Although many rhetorical strategies are related to a text's content, others involve its structure. After writers decide what information or arguments they will include in their essays, they need to decide the order in which to present them. Structure also involves the way a writer introduces and concludes a text and draws connections among parts of the text. Following are some questions you can ask about a text's structure as you evaluate its rhetorical effectiveness.

- In what order does the author present information or claims?
- What purpose might lie behind this order?
- How might the text's structure influence an audience's response to the author's ideas, findings, or assertions?
- Does the text present a clear and consistent line of reasoning?
- Are there clear connections between the text's stated or implied thesis and its topic sentences?
- Does the text's structure enhance its appeal to logic? Does the author draw clear, logical connections among the text's ideas, findings, or assertions?
- Does the structure of the piece enhance its appeal to emotion, particularly in its introduction or conclusion?
- Does the structure of the piece enhance its appeal to credibility? Does the author seem in control of the writing? Does the text hold together as a whole? Are there any obvious flaws in structure that might damage the author's credibility?

STYLE

Finally, when analyzing an author's rhetorical strategies, consider his or her style. Among other elements of writing, style concerns the text's sentence structure, word choice, punctuation, voice, tone, and diction. Here are some questions that can help you assess how style contributes to a text's rhetorical effectiveness:

- What type of syntax does the author employ? How does the author vary sentence length (long or short) and sentence type (simple, compound, complex, and compound-complex; cumulative, periodic, and balanced)? How is syntax related to the audience, purpose, or occasion of the text?
- What types of figurative language does the author employ (for example, metaphors, similes, or analogies)? Are the choices of figurative language appropriate and effective given the text's rhetorical situation?

- What types of allusions does the author employ? Are they appropriate and effective?
- How appropriate and effective is the author's voice, given the text's rhetorical situation?
- How appropriate and effective is the author's tone, given the text's rhetorical situation?
- How appropriate and effective is the author's diction, given the text's rhetorical situation?

ANALYZING A TEXT'S RHETORICAL STRATEGIES—AN EXAMPLE

To better understand how to analyze a text's rhetorical strategies in terms of its content, structure, and style, carefully read the following speech, Abraham Lincoln's Second Inaugural Address. Lincoln delivered this speech on March 4, 1865, in Washington, D.C. Though the Civil War was not yet over, the struggle had turned in the Union's favor, and the end of the conflict was in sight. In this address, Lincoln acknowledges the price the nation has paid for the war and argues that lasting peace and reconciliation will come only through mercy and forgiveness. Many historians and rhetoricians consider this Lincoln's greatest speech.

Lincoln's Second Inaugural Address

Fellow-Countrymen:

At this second appearing to take the oath of the Presidential office there is less occasion for an extended address than there was at the first. Then a statement somewhat in detail of a course to be pursued seemed fitting and proper. Now, at the expiration of four years, during which public declarations have been constantly called forth on every point and phase of the great contest which still absorbs the attention and engrosses the energies of the nation, little that is new could be presented. The progress of our arms, upon which all else chiefly depends, is as well known to the public as to myself, and it is, I trust, reasonably satisfactory and encouraging to all. With high hope for the future, no prediction in regard to it is ventured.

On the occasion corresponding to this four years ago all thoughts were anxiously directed to an impending civil war. All dreaded it, all sought to avert it. While the inaugural address was being delivered from this place, devoted altogether to *saving* the Union without war, urgent agents were in the city seeking to *destroy* it without war; seeking to dissolve the Union and divide effects by negotiation. Both parties deprecated war, but one of them would *make* war rather than let the nation survive, and the other would *accept* war rather than let it perish, and the war came.

One-eighth of the whole population were colored slaves, not distributed generally over the Union, but localized in the southern part of it. These slaves constituted a peculiar and powerful interest. All knew that this interest was somehow the cause of the war. To strengthen, perpetuate, and extend this interest was the object for which the insurgents would rend the Union even by war, while the Government claimed no right to do more than to restrict the territorial enlargement of it. Neither party expected for the war the magnitude or the duration which it has already attained. Neither anticipated that the *cause* of the conflict might cease with or even before the conflict itself should cease. Each looked for an easier triumph, and a result less fundamental and astounding. Both read the same Bible and pray to the same God, and each invokes His aid against the other. It may seem strange that any men should dare to ask a just God's assistance in wringing their bread from the sweat of other men's faces, but let us judge not, that we be not judged. The prayers of both could not be answered. That of neither has been answered fully. The Almighty has His own purposes. "Woe unto the world because of offenses; for it must needs be that offenses come, but woe to that man by whom the offense cometh." If we shall suppose that American slavery is one of those offenses which, in the providence of God, must needs come, but which, having continued through His appointed time, He now wills to remove, and that He gives to both North and South this terrible war as the woe due to those by whom the offense came, shall we discern therein any departure from those divine attributes which the believers in a living God always ascribe to Him? Fondly do we hope, fervently do we pray, that this mighty scourge of war may speedily pass away. Yet, if God wills that it continue until all the wealth piled by the bondsman's two hundred and fifty years of unrequited toil shall be sunk, and until every drop of blood drawn with the lash shall be paid by another drawn with the sword, as was said three thousand years ago, so still it must be said "the judgments of the Lord are true and righteous altogether."

With malice toward none, with charity for all, with firmness in the right as God gives us to see the right, let us strive on to finish the work we are in, to bind up the nation's wounds, to care for him who shall have borne the battle and for his widow and his orphan, to do all which may achieve and cherish a just and lasting peace among ourselves and with all nations.

A Rhetorical Analysis of Lincoln's Speech

In terms of the speech's content, notice how Lincoln makes several related arguments designed to persuade his audience that after the Civil War ends, the North must treat the South with charity and compassion. He opens his address by asserting that he will not detail the current state of the conflict—clearly everyone in the nation has been and continues to be consumed by the war. Next, Lincoln asserts that the primary cause of the war was slavery. Four years earlier, the Union sought to halt the spread of slavery peacefully. However, the Confederacy, he asserts, would not accept this position and turned to armed conflict instead. Neither side, though, anticipated the duration and ferocity of the war. Although both sides in the conflict call on God for victory, Lincoln questions whether any divine power would support the perpetuation of slavery. Interestingly, he sees *both* sides in the war being chastised for their involvement with slavery and hopes that the suffering all are undergoing can purge their collective guilt and set the stage for a more just nation. Lincoln closes his speech by asserting that reconciliation will only succeed if it is based on mercy, forgiveness, and justice, not revenge and recrimination.

Both Lincoln's position as president and the occasion of the speech lend credibility to his address. However, Lincoln enhances his credibility by articulating the North's perspective on the war's causes, a position most of his audience would presumably endorse. Making numerous references to God and God's will also serves to enhance his ethos but serves as an emotional appeal as well: Lincoln hopes the citizens of the North will be swayed to extend mercy to the South after the war by ascribing such a position to divine will. By speaking mercifully and understandingly about the suffering of the South during the war, Lincoln models the behavior and attitudes he hopes the members of his audience will adopt themselves.

Structurally, Lincoln opens his address by commenting on the previous four years of his presidency and acknowledging the country's current struggle before laying out the North's view of the war's cause. Having articulated a position his audience would accept, Lincoln then changes the direction of the speech. Instead of attacking the Confederacy for its secession from the Union, he speaks about the suffering the war has brought to *all* Americans, how neither side in the conflict accurately anticipated the terrible nature of the war, and how the South has already suffered severely for its actions. Audience members might expect Lincoln to call for revenge against the South; instead, he argues that both sides have suffered enough. At the end of his speech, he urges his audience to treat the South with charity.

Stylistically, the speech is remarkable for its somber tone. Though this is an inaugural speech, Lincoln is not celebrating. Instead, his tone reflects the suffering the nation has endured over the previous four years and the hard work that lies ahead of it. Syntactically, he employs balanced sentences to create memorable phrases—"All dreaded it, all sought to avert it," "Fondly do we hope, fervently do we pray," "With malice toward none, with charity for all"—and to emphasize the balanced view he takes concerning the war's consequences. The North and South have both suffered, and Reconstruction must be based on an understanding of their shared humanity. Lincoln repeatedly employs language from the Old Testament to emphasize his view of the war as a form of divine judgment against the nation for its past offenses. Underlying this argument is the notion that justice lies in the hands of God: if God has scourged the nation for its transgressions, there is no need for humans to further the South's punishment following the war.

This brief rhetorical analysis of Lincoln's speech gives you some idea of how an author can manipulate a text's content, structure, and style to achieve a particular aim.

WRITING A RHETORICAL ANALYSIS ESSAY

STEP 1—CAREFULLY READ THE ASSIGNMENT

As you read the assignment, be sure you understand who *your* audience is for your essay. What can you assume your reader knows about the source text, its author, or the context in which it was written? How much information do you need to provide so your reader will understand your analysis of the text? Also, what can you assume your reader knows about rhetoric? What terms, if any, will you need to define in your essay?

STEP 2—ESTABLISH THE SOURCE TEXT'S RHETORICAL SITUATION

First, establish the rhetorical situation of the source text (see "The Rhetorical Situation" previously). Following are some of the questions you should answer either before or as you carefully read the source text:

- Who is the author?
- What is the writer's message?
- Who is the writer addressing?
- What is the writer's purpose or goal?
- Why is the writer composing this text?
- When was the text produced?
- Where was the text published?

To establish the text's rhetorical situation you might need to do a little research, but writing a rhetorical analysis essay requires that you understand the context in which the text was produced.

STEP 3—DETERMINE THE AUTHOR'S GOAL

In a sentence or two, paraphrase what you think the author is trying to accomplish in the text. What effect does she want to have on the audience? Is the author trying to persuade her readers to adopt a particular position? Does the author want to influence what her readers believe? Is the author trying to elicit a particular emotional response from people who read the text? State the author's purpose or goal, as you understand it, as clearly and specifically as you can.

STEP 4—IDENTIFY AND EVALUATE THE TEXT'S RHETORICAL STRATEGIES

When you have a clear sense of the text's rhetorical situation, read through it again to identify the strategies the author employed to achieve his goal. Examine the text's content, structure, and style in relation to its rhetorical situation. How has the author manipulated various elements of the text to achieve a particular response from his readers? Spend as much time on this step in the process as you need—the ideas and insights you develop now will help you form a thesis for your essay. Remember that in your essay, you will not address every rhetorical strategy the writer employed. Instead, you will focus on the strategies you think most significantly contribute to the text's ability or inability to achieve its rhetorical goal. As you reread the text, make a list of the ways the author employs content, structure, and style to achieve his purpose, noting specific examples of each from the reading. Based on this list, decide which strategies help the writer achieve his goals and which do not, given the text's audience, topic, purpose, and occasion. State in one or two sentences what makes each strategy successful or unsuccessful.

STEP 5—DETERMINE YOUR THESIS

In your thesis, you will state how successful you think the author is in achieving his or her rhetorical goal and indicate which of the author's rhetorical strategies you will examine in your essay. Your thesis may indicate that the author succeeds in achieving his or her rhetorical goals, fails to achieve them, or succeeds in some ways but fails in others. Whatever your assessment, state it clearly in your thesis, along with the rhetorical strategies you will examine to explain and defend your judgment.

Sample Thesis Statement 1: Author succeeds in achieving his or her rhetorical purpose

> Lincoln's Second Inaugural Address effectively establishes the North's moral imperative for successful Reconstruction by making repeated appeals to authority and emotion.

Sample Thesis Statement 2: Author fails to achieve his or her rhetorical purpose

> Lincoln's Second Inaugural Address fails to establish the North's moral imperative for successful Reconstruction because he relies too heavily on religious allusions and does not adequately address the North's desire for revenge after the war.

Sample Thesis Statement 3: Author has mixed success in achieving his or her rhetorical purpose

> Lincoln's attempts to establish the North's moral imperative for successful Reconstruction in his Second Inaugural Address are aided by his repeated appeals to authority, but they are hindered by his overreliance on religious allusions.

Whatever stand you assume, your thesis statement should establish the purpose and focus of your essay.

STEP 6—WRITE YOUR ROUGH DRAFT

Although every rhetorical analysis essay will be structured a little differently, the following outline may help you determine how to organize your paper.

Introductory Section

- Indicate the topic of the source text.
- Introduce the text you are analyzing or evaluating.
- State your thesis.
- Capture reader interest.

In this part of your paper, you need to indicate the topic of your essay, introduce the source text (provide the author's full name and the title of the reading), and state your thesis. One of the real challenges in writing the introductory section of a rhetorical analysis essay is to capture reader interest as well. You may be able to develop reader interest in your essay by opening with a question raised by the source text, starting with an exciting quotation from the reading or providing some interesting information about the reading's author or historical significance.

Summary of Source Text and Overview of the Rhetorical Situation

- Briefly summarize the source text.
- Explain the source text's rhetorical situation.

In one or two paragraphs, summarize the reading and its rhetorical situation. In addition to stating what the author wrote, explain the audience, purpose, and occasion of the piece. Your analysis will depend on readers understanding the source text's rhetorical situation, so explain it carefully in this part of the paper. You will be making frequent reference back to this information in the body of your essay.

Body Paragraphs

- Examine the text one rhetorical strategy at a time (content, structure, or style).
- Cite specific examples from the source text to support any assertion you make.
- Explain the link between the examples you provide and the assertions you make.

As you draft the body of your rhetorical analysis essay, carefully critique the text one rhetorical strategy at a time, explaining whether employing that strategy helps the author achieve his or her rhetorical goal. You will need to illustrate and support your assertions with specific examples from the source text. Generally, each of your body paragraphs will contain (1) an assertion regarding whether a particular rhetorical strategy helps the author achieve his or her rhetorical goal, (2) examples from the source text that illustrate that particular rhetorical strategy, and (3) an explanation of how each example you cite supports your assertion.

Do not make the mistake of thinking that the examples you cite will "speak for themselves"—that you do not need to explain how the examples support your assertion because the link will be obvious to anyone who has read the text. Instead, always explain the link between your evidence and your assertion. In fact, the success of your rhetorical analysis essay often depends on the clarity and logic of this explanation: your readers need to understand how the examples you cite support your assertion.

Conclusion

- Wrap up the essay.
- Remind readers of your thesis.
- Maintain reader interest.

In the conclusion of your rhetorical analysis essay, provide your readers with a sense of closure and remind them of your thesis. The conclusion should flow naturally from the body of your essay and recapture your readers' interest. One strategy you might employ is to echo your paper's introduction. For example, if you open your essay with a question, you might want to come back to it in your conclusion; if you open with a quotation, consider concluding your essay with one. This repetition will help give your essay a sense of balance and closure.

STEP 7—REVISE YOUR ESSAY

When revising your rhetorical analysis essay, make sure your work is accurate, developed, organized, clear, and documented.

- *Accurate*—your essay accurately captures your analysis and accurately represents the source text.
- *Developed*—you thoroughly develop and explain your assertions.
- *Organized*—the assertions in your essay are easy to follow and are interconnected.
- *Clear*—you have provided your readers with the information they need to understand your essay and have presented your ideas using clear, accessible language and sentences.
- *Documented*—all quoted and paraphrased material is documented as needed and your readers can easily discern which information comes from the source texts and which information you provide.

Check the Accuracy of Your Assertions and Examples

As you revise, start by checking your essay's content. First, make sure you have covered everything you intended to cover in your paper and that your essay accurately reflects your views. Second, be sure you have not misrepresented the author of the source text—any material you quote or paraphrase from the source text must accurately capture what the author actually wrote. Finally, be sure you fairly and accurately represent the text's rhetorical situation.

Check the Development of Your Essay

All of your assertions need to be fully explained and supported. Because your rhetorical analysis essay will reflect your individual response to and evaluation of the source text, you have to explain all of your assertions thoroughly. Readers need to know not only what you think but also why you think it. Do not expect readers to draw connections between your assertions and evidence on their own.

Check the Organization

First, be sure your thesis statement offers an accurate overview of your essay. The thesis statement should help guide your reader through your rhetorical analysis, previewing assertions you will develop in the body of your essay. Next, check the topic sentences in the body of your essay. Each topic sentence should relate back to the thesis statement, introduce a new idea, and provide a transition from the previous section of your essay. Be sure that you employ effective transitions within your body paragraphs as well, highlighting the logical relationship of one sentence to the next. Finally, check the opening and closing sections of your essay to be sure each accomplishes what it is supposed to accomplish.

Check for Clarity

Are there any terms that need to be defined? Any references drawn from the source text that need to be explained? Any sentences that could be more clear? Check to see that all quoted and paraphrased material will make sense to someone who has not read the source text and that any technical terms that need to be defined are defined.

Check Your Documentation

Because you are working with a source text, be sure that all quoted and paraphrased material is properly documented.

SAMPLE RHETORICAL ANALYSIS ESSAY

The following is a rhetorical analysis of Lincoln's Second Inaugural Address.

RHETORICAL ANALYSIS OF LINCOLN'S SECOND INAUGURAL ADDRESS

When President Lincoln stepped up to the podium to deliver his second inaugural address, he knew the Civil War was reaching its end. Though victory was not certain, events on the battlefield suggested that Union forces would soon put down the Southern rebellion and reunite the country. Lincoln knew he would soon be presiding over a deeply divided country, with many in the North demanding revenge against the Southern states, including the arrest and execution of the Confederacy's leaders. A close analysis of Lincoln's address makes clear, however, that he envisioned a Reconstruction based on mercy and forgiveness rather than vengeance, a message he forcefully conveys though the somber tone of the speech and its many religious allusions.

Since the Union forces were nearing victory after four years of brutal warfare, one might assume that Lincoln would deliver a joyful second inaugural address. Instead, the speech's tone is somber and reserved. While he states that the war's progress has been "reasonably satisfactory and encouraging to all" (147), Lincoln makes no prediction about its final outcome. He asserts that both sides in the conflict "deprecated" (148) war and that neither "expected for the war the magnitude or duration which it has already obtained" (148). Lincoln claims that "American slavery" (148) was the primary cause of the war, and though he states that the South was at fault for maintaining and spreading the practice, Lincoln claims that God "gives to both North and South this terrible war as the woe due to those by whom the offense came . . ." (148). Instead of celebrating the North's impending victory in the war, Lincoln claims that both the North and the South are paying a terrible price for their moral transgressions.

In his speech, Lincoln soberly assesses the causes and consequences of the war and indicates how the nation should proceed once peace comes. The final paragraph of his speech begins with the famous phrase "With malice toward none, with charity for all" (148), summing up Lincoln's message of mercy and forgiveness. The needed course of action now, Lincoln contends, is "to bind up the nation's wounds, to care for him who shall have borne the battle and for his widow and orphan" (148). This statement embraces both sides in the conflict: the nation's obligation is to care for both Yankee and Rebel soldiers, for all widows and orphans. Such mercy is the only way to obtain "a just and lasting peace among ourselves and with all nations" (148). Again, "ourselves" is inclusive: Lincoln is including the people of both the North and South in this statement, pointing the way to a reunited country. Lincoln's reflective, restrained tone in this speech indicates how he would like every citizen of the United States to respond to war's conclusion: with forgiveness, introspection, and understanding.

Lincoln's message of mercy and forgiveness is also furthered by his many religious allusions. Rather than claiming that the North's coming victory in the war has been ordained by God, Lincoln believes that God is neutral in the conflict, that the North and South are united by a common religious heritage: "Both read the same Bible and pray to the same God . . ." (148). Though Lincoln doubts that any deity would support human slavery, he warns his listeners, "judge not, that we be not judged" (148). Lincoln's repeated invocations of God strike a note of humility, reminding his audience that their fate is not in their own hands, that Providence dictates the course of history. The North has no reason to gloat in its victory or to judge the South severely after the war. Both sides have suffered judgment already; now is the time to act "with firmness in the right as God gives us to see the right . . ." (148).

Lincoln's Second Inaugural Address establishes a somber, reflective tone and employs numerous religious allusions to convey successfully his central message that, in victory, the North must act with mercy, forgiveness, and humility during Reconstruction. Revenge and retaliation is not the path to reestablishing a peaceful, united, just nation. "With malice toward none, with charity for all," the nation could be reunited. Unfortunately, one of those attending the speech that day was John Wilkes Booth, who would soon assassinate the president at Ford's Theater. Lincoln never had the chance to put his philosophy of merciful Reconstruction to the test.

Summary Chart

HOW TO WRITE A RHETORICAL ANALYSIS ESSAY

---

1. **Carefully read the assignment.**
   - *Who is your audience?*
   - *What can you assume your audience knows about the source text and rhetoric?*

2. **Establish the source text's rhetorical situation.**
   - *Who is the source text's author?*
   - *What is the source text's topic?*
   - *Who is the source text's audience?*
   - *What is the source text's purpose?*
   - *What was the occasion for writing the source text?*

3. **Determine the author's goal.**
   - *In a sentence or two, state clearly and specifically what you think the author is trying to accomplish in the source text.*

4. **Identify and evaluate the source text's rhetorical strategies.**
   - *strategies involving the text's content*
   - *use of arguments, evidence, and reasoning*
   - *use of logos, pathos, and ethos*
   - *strategies involving the text's structure*
   - *strategies involving the text's style*

5. **Determine your thesis.**
   - *State how successful the author is in achieving his or her rhetorical goal.*
   - *State which rhetorical strategies you will examine in your essay.*

SUMMARY CHART: HOW TO WRITE A RHETORICAL ANALYSIS ESSAY *(CONTINUED)*

6. Write your rough draft.

- *Write the introductory section of your essay, indicating the topic of the source text, its title and author, and your thesis. Capture reader interest as well.*
- *Summarize the source text and its rhetorical situation.*
- *Draft the body of your essay, examining one rhetorical strategy at a time and supporting your judgment with specific examples from the source text. Explain how each example you cite supports your claim.*
- *Write the concluding section of your essay, reminding readers of your thesis and maintaining reader interest.*

7. Revise your essay.

- *Make sure your writing is developed.*
- *Make sure your essay thoroughly develops and explains your assertions.*
- *Make sure your writing is organized.*
- *Make sure the assertions in your essay are easy to follow.*
- *Make sure the assertions in your essay are connected logically.*
- *Make sure your essay accurately reflects your thesis.*
- *Make sure your writing is clear.*
- *Make sure you have provided your readers with the information they need to understand your essay.*
- *Make sure you have checked to be sure all of your sentences are clear.*
- *Make sure your essay accurately represents the source text.*
- *Make sure all of the material in your essay that needs to be documented is documented.*
- *Make sure readers can tell which information in your essay came from your source text and which information comes from you.*

Rhetorical Analysis of Written Texts Revision Checklist

	Yes	No
1. Have you analyzed the assignment to determine who *your* audience is?	_____	_____
2. Have you established the source text's rhetorical situation?	_____	_____
3. Have you paraphrased the author's goal?	_____	_____
4. Have you evaluated the author's rhetorical strategies in light of his or her goal?	_____	_____
5. Have you determined which of the author's rhetorical strategies you will evaluate in your essay?	_____	_____
6. Check the introductory section of your essay. Do you:		
• introduce the topic of your source text?	_____	_____
• introduce your source text?	_____	_____
• capture reader interest?	_____	_____
7. Examine the wording of your thesis. Do you:		
• state whether the author successfully achieves his or her goal?	_____	_____
• indicate which rhetorical strategies you will examine in your essay?	_____	_____
8. Do you summarize the source text and describe its rhetorical situation?	_____	_____
9. Check each section in the body of your essay. Do you:		
• examine one rhetorical strategy at a time?	_____	_____
• support your judgments with specific examples from the source text?	_____	_____
• explain the link between your assertions and their supporting evidence?	_____	_____

RHETORICAL ANALYSIS OF WRITTEN TEXTS REVISION CHECKLIST *(CONTINUED)*

	Yes	No
10. Have your revised your essay for:		
• accuracy?	_____	_____
• development?	_____	_____
• organization?	_____	_____
• clarity?	_____	_____
• documentation?	_____	_____

Chapter 9

RHETORICAL ANALYSIS OF VISUAL TEXTS

In this chapter you will learn how to

1. Identify the rhetorical situation of visual texts

2. Identify a visual text's rhetorical strategies

3. Evaluate a visual text in terms of its rhetorical situation and rhetorical strategies

4. Compose an effective rhetorical analysis of a visual text

DEFINITION AND PURPOSE

Consider for a moment the power of images—how photographs, drawings, or graphics affect the way you experience texts. Images can add emotional punch to a reading, illustrate an assertion, or make a text more entertaining. Images can even make an argument, either alone or in combination with written text. In our daily lives, we are constantly surrounded by visual images. Which ones grab your attention? How do writers manipulate the visual aspects of a text to achieve their desired effects? By analyzing these images, what lessons can you learn about effectively using visual images in your own texts?

The ability to critically read and rhetorically analyze visual texts is becoming an increasingly important skill. Although visual texts have long been a part of human communication (think about the prehistoric cave drawings found throughout the world), they have become more central to communication over the last century. Since the advent of television, our culture has become more centered on visual images, and advances in computer technology have made it increasingly possible for students to incorporate visual images in their own texts. In fact, at some schools, visual presentations—films, streaming video, PowerPoint presentations, and posters—have replaced traditional print-based assignments like term papers and reports. In many majors, students are expected to develop the same kind of fluency in manipulating visual images as they are in manipulating the written word.

This chapter offers advice and instruction on how to read, interpret, and rhetorically analyze different types of visual texts. Although you may not have had much experience thinking about visual texts the way you will be instructed to do in this chapter, remember that the processes you will employ and the types of questions you will ask closely resemble those you commonly use to read, analyze, and interpret written texts.

READING VISUAL TEXTS CRITICALLY

You might find it odd to consider how you "read" visual texts like photographs, drawings, cartoons, or advertisements. People often draw a distinction between written and visual texts: they "read" words, not pictures. However, as discussed in Chapter 1, reading a text—any text—involves understanding, analyzing, and interpreting it. Similar processes apply to both written and visual texts.

Following are a series of questions you can consider to help you read visual texts critically. Answering them will give you a clearer sense of a visual text's content, creator, purpose, and audience, as well as your response to the image.

QUESTIONS CONCERNING THE VISUAL TEXT ITSELF

- What image does the visual represent?
- What are the various parts of the visual?
- What written text, if any, accompanies the visual?

As with written texts, start your reading of a visual text by forming a clear understanding of its literal meaning—what is it in and of itself, what are its parts, and what is its relationship to any accompanying written text? Although this first step may sound easy, it can actually be difficult to examine a visual text objectively, to identify its constituent parts, and to find language that accurately describes what you see. Your first step is to summarize and paraphrase the visual text: state in your own words what you think the visual is depicting. At this point, you are not concerned with the visual's intention or purpose, only with its literal meaning. Pay particular attention to the details of the image. Your eye may immediately be drawn to only one or two aspects of the visual text, but don't stop your analysis there. Examine every aspect of the image—note what is in the background and in the foreground, in light and in shadow, in color and in black and white.

Next, identify the various parts of the visual text. When analyzing a written text, you may discuss its thesis, claims, examples, explanations, structure, and so forth. When analyzing a visual text, you will focus your attention on elements such as these:

Images: What images are contained in the visual? How many are there in the text? Which ones seem to command the most attention? Are there images of people in the text?

If so, who? What are they doing? Are particular objects included in the text? Which ones? What type of setting is depicted in the text: interior or exterior, urban or natural, realistic or fantastic?

Layout:

How are the images arranged in the visual? How are they grouped? Which aspects of the images are emphasized in the layout? Which aspects are deemphasized? If there are people in the image, where do they appear in relation to the other images in the text? What appears in the foreground, and what appears in the background? What appears in light, and what appears in shadows?

Color:

How is color used in the visual text? What colors are used? What is highlighted by the text's use of color, and what is not? If you are examining a black-and-white image, how is shading used to highlight or emphasize particular elements? If there is written text, what color is it? How does color influence the way you respond to the writing?

Appeals:

What elements of the visual text are intended to appeal to the reader's emotions, values, or needs? How does the author of the text manipulate its content and/or layout to elicit a particular emotional response from readers? What elements of the text are included to appeal to the reader's intellect or reason? Which elements, if any, are intended to establish the author's credibility or authority?

Note: Carefully examine any written text included in the visual. What does the text say? What is the relationship between the written and visual elements of the text? For example, does the text comment on the images or draw the reader's attention to particular visual elements of the text? How is the writing placed in the text, and where does it appear? Is the placement of the written text significant? Does it impact how you read the visual text?

QUESTIONS CONCERNING THE VISUAL TEXT'S CREATOR OR SOURCE

- Who created the visual text?
- What is the source of the visual text?
- In what publication or website does the visual appear?
- Toward what readership is the publication or website aimed?
- What, generally, is the editorial stance of that publication or website?

Although finding answers to these questions might prove difficult, you should try. As with written texts, identifying the authorship of a visual text is central to understanding and evaluating it. Authorial bias can affect visual texts just as it can written texts. If possible, identify who created the visual text. Who was the artist or photographer? What can you learn about that person's previous work and his or her credentials or affiliations? Approach visual texts as skeptically as you would written texts. We tend to trust visual texts more readily than we do written texts. After all, who hasn't heard the saying, "Pictures don't lie"? Of course, we know that pictures can lie—visual texts can be manipulated as easily as written texts. Visual texts can communicate truths, untruths, or half-truths. Understanding who created a visual text can help you establish its credibility.

Also consider the visual text's source. In what periodical did it appear? On what website? On what television show? In what film? In what advertisement? You need to understand the agenda of the visual text's source. What is the publication or website attempting to accomplish through its use of this particular visual text? Is its intention to inform, persuade, or entertain readers? What biases or agendas might influence the types of visuals a source employs or how it uses those sources? As noted in the chapter on critical reading (Chapter 1), if you are investigating the topic of abortion rights, it would be important to note whether a visual text you are examining was published by the National Abortion Rights Action League or by Operation Life. Each group has its own agenda on this issue, which may well influence how each designs and employs visual texts in its publications or on its website. Again, the possible bias does not disqualify or discredit a visual text. You simply need to take that bias into account when you read, analyze, or evaluate the text.

To better understand a publication's or website's general editorial stance, read some of the articles it publishes or posts and examine other visual texts it provides. Although you may not be able to conclude definitively that the particular visual text you are examining reflects the publication's or website's general editorial stance, you will be in a better position to read that material in context. You will be able to conclude whether the particular visual text you are examining is typical of that publication or website.

QUESTIONS CONCERNING THE VISUAL TEXT'S PURPOSE

- What is the intended purpose of the visual?
- How does the creator attempt to achieve that purpose?

Purpose can be difficult to determine when analyzing a text—visual or written—because any text may be serving multiple purposes. Broadly speaking, a visual text may be attempting to inform, persuade, or entertain readers. Although it may be difficult to determine a visual text's exact intent, making an effort to do so is important. You can misread a visual text if you fail to understand its intended purpose.

For example, imagine an advertisement placed in a news magazine by the Sierra Club, one of the nation's largest environmental groups. The full-page ad consists of a black-and-white picture of a mountainside recently cleared of trees by a logging company. All that is left is a seemingly endless string of stumps, charred tree limbs, and muddy pits. In the lower left-hand corner of the page is a single message, printed in white type against the gray background: "The Sierra Club: *www.sierraclub.org*." What is the purpose of this advertisement? Is it informative, persuasive, or both? Is it trying to inform readers about the Sierra Club's work, encourage them to find out more about the organization, or persuade them to join? While the picture itself may be striking, is the intention of the advertisement to entertain? How do you know? What if the text were different; that is, what if it read: "Help Us Fight Homelessness, *www .sierraclub.org*"? How would this new text change your interpretation of the advertisement's purpose?

Students sometimes run into problems when they read persuasive visual texts as if the texts were merely informative. We tend to read informative texts as if they were objective and factual; after all, that's what makes them different from persuasive texts. From experience, we know we need to read persuasive texts more skeptically than we do informative texts, because the author is actively attempting to sway our opinion about something or move us to act in a particular way. Our defenses are up when we read texts that we believe are persuasive in ways they are not when we read texts we think are primarily informative. In other words, our interpretation of a text's purpose influences how we read that text, how open we are to its message, and how critical we are as readers. Clarifying the purpose of the visual texts you read can help you read them more effectively and accurately.

QUESTIONS CONCERNING THE VISUAL TEXT'S AUDIENCE

- What audience is the visual text's creator trying to reach?
- How has the creator manipulated the visual text to successfully reach that audience?
- How does your understanding of the visual text's intended audience influence the way you read that text?

When you read a visual text, consider the type of reader its author or creator is attempting to reach. Sometimes you can base your conclusion on the publication in which the visual text appears: certain publications cater to certain types of readers. The general readership of *Inside Wrestling* magazine is likely different from the general readership of *Opera Aficionado* (although there may well be people who subscribe to both). Consider the interests and backgrounds of the people who would likely read the periodical or visit the website in which the visual text appeared. How might the author's interest in appealing to that type of reader influence the visual text he or she creates?

Another approach to analyzing audience is to consider the elements of the visual text itself: how did the author's view of his or her audience influence the way he or she constructed the visual text? Put another way, if you did not know the publication or website in which the visual text appeared, how could you determine the writer's or creator's sense of audience by carefully analyzing various elements of the text itself? Consider these questions:

- What types of images are included in the text? Would they appeal to a wide range of readers or to just certain types of readers?
- What examples are included in the text? Would they appeal to a popular or to a specialized audience?
- If there are human models in the text, who are they? What types of people are they? Who might identify with these models? Who might not?
- If there is written text, how formal is it? What cultural references does the written text include? What types of figurative language does it employ? Which readers would likely understand and appreciate this use of language?

Forming an understanding of the visual text's intended audience is important because it will guide the way you analyze that text. Central to analysis is a deceivingly simple question: why did the author/creator construct the text this way? Assuming a rhetorical intent for all texts—that they are produced to have a particular effect on a particular audience—identifying the intended audience can guide the way you analyze the text itself. In other words, your analysis of the text will be based on your understanding of its intended audience.

QUESTIONS CONCERNING YOUR RESPONSE TO THE VISUAL TEXT

- What is my response to the visual text?
- Which aspects of the visual text elicit that response?
- What are the sources of my response?
- How does my response influence my understanding of the text?

Authors often incorporate visuals into their texts because they know readers are likely to respond to them in ways they will not respond to words alone. Visuals can stir our imagination, move us to anger or sympathy, attract us or alienate us, and cause us to laugh or to cringe. However, we often don't stop to consider our responses to visual texts: we are so wrapped up in responding to them that we don't consider the nature or cause of the response itself. The first step, then, is to recognize and articulate your reaction to a visual text. How does it make you feel? What is your response? Although it might prove difficult, find language that captures your reaction.

Next, identify which elements of the text evoke those responses. People looking at the same visual text may have very different emotional reactions to it, even if they are focusing on the exact same elements. Likewise, two people may have the same emotional response to a text even if they are focusing on different elements: one may be responding to a particular image included in the text and another to the text's layout. As you consider your response to a visual text, try to identify the specific elements that give rise to it. Encountering that text, you felt a particular way—what was in the text, exactly, that gave rise to your response?

Finally, consider why you respond to particular elements of the text the way you do. What knowledge, experience, or values do you have that cause you to react that way? Examining this link can be difficult, but doing so is extremely important, especially if you are going to discuss your response with someone else. For example, you and a classmate may have similar reactions to the same elements of a visual, but why you respond to those elements in a certain way may be very different. Articulating the link between the elements of the text and your responses can help you more fully understand your reactions and how they differ from the responses of others.

READING A VISUAL TEXT—AN EXAMPLE

The following example of a visual text (see the next page) is an advertisement produced by the National Center for Family Literacy and published in the April 2008 edition of *Black Enterprise* magazine. Take a few minutes to carefully study the advertisement, then answer the following questions to get a better sense of how you are reading the visuals and text.

QUESTIONS CONCERNING THE VISUAL TEXT

- What images does the advertisement contain? How would you describe them?
- What do you assume is the relationship between the two people photographed in the advertisement? Why do you assume that? How does the photograph lead you to that conclusion?
- What else does the advertisement contain besides a photograph of the two people? For example, there's copy, but what else is there?
- What does the copy say? What words or ideas stand out in the copy? Why?
- Notice the National Center for Family Literacy name and logo at the bottom of the advertisement. Why are they included? What copy appears below the logo?
- Examine how the images and words on the page are arranged. What purpose might their arrangement serve?
- Notice how the copy employs two shades of gray. What purpose does that alternation serve?
- Which words stand out because they are flush with the margin? Which stand out because they are in dark type?
- What emotional appeals is the advertisement making? Examine how the people are posed for the picture. What appeal is the photographer making? Read the copy carefully. Point out instances in which particular words or phrases are included to appeal to readers in specific ways.

Because I can read,
    I can understand. I can write a letter.
    I can fill out a job application.
    I can finally get off welfare.

Because I can read,
    I can learn. I can help my daughter
    with her homework.
    I can inspire her to be better.
    I can be a role model.

Because I can read,
    I can succeed, I can
    contribute. I can live
    my life without fear,
    without shame.
    I can be whatever
    I want to be.

Because I can read.

 National Center for Family Literacy

Literacy can make the difference between poverty and progress.
Visit **www.famlit.org** to help us write more success stories.

©2005 Photographer: Marvin Young

Source: National Center for Family Literacy

QUESTIONS CONCERNING THE VISUAL TEXT'S CREATOR OR SOURCE

- This advertisement appeared in *Black Enterprise* magazine. What do you assume or know about this publication?
- The advertisement was placed by the National Center for Family Literacy. What do you assume or know about this organization?
- Which types of people are likely to read *Black Enterprise*? What can you assume about their backgrounds and interests?
- How has the National Center for Family Literacy used images and copy to appeal to this type of reader?
- Why does the advertisement include copy like the following:

  - "Because I can read, I can understand. I can write a letter. I can fill out a job application. I can finally get off welfare."
  - "Because I can read, I can succeed, I can contribute."
  - "Literacy can make the difference between poverty and progress."

QUESTIONS CONCERNING THE VISUAL TEXT'S PURPOSE

- What is the advertisement's intended purpose? How do you know?
- Is the advertisement primarily a call to action ("Visit www.famlit.org to help us write more success stories"), or does it serve other purposes as well? If it serves other purposes, what are they?
- How has the National Center for Family Literacy attempted to achieve their purpose with this advertisement? How are their efforts related to the publication in which the advertisement appears?
- If the goal of the advertisement is primarily to inform readers, what do its creators intend for them to learn? How does the advertisement attempt to do this?
- If the advertisement is primarily a call to action, what is the action its creators want readers to take? How do they attempt to convince or move readers to act in this way?

QUESTIONS CONCERNING THE VISUAL TEXT'S AUDIENCE

- What audience is this advertisement attempting to reach?
- If the advertisement is a call to action, who is supposed to act? How do you know?
- How has the National Center for Family Literacy attempted to reach its intended audience? How has it manipulated the elements of the advertisement—for example, images, copy, layout, color—to reach its audience?
- Who do you assume is the speaker in the advertisement? Who is the first-person narrator? How do you know this? Why might the advertisement be written this way?

- What are the race, gender, and age of the people shown in the advertisement? Why do you think they were chosen as models for this advertisement? How might that choice be related to the intended audience?

QUESTIONS CONCERNING YOUR RESPONSE TO THE VISUAL TEXT

- How do you respond to the advertisement?
- Do you find it interesting? If so, why? If not, why not?
- Are you moved to take any action as a result of reading the advertisement? If so, what action and why? If not, why not?
- Do you respond one way to the photograph of the people and another way to the copy? Why?
- What personal experience or knowledge might influence the way you respond to this advertisement? What is the link between that experience or knowledge and your response?

WRITING A RHETORICAL ANALYSIS OF A VISUAL TEXT

Although on occasion you may be asked to write essays in which you just describe visual texts, you will more commonly be required to analyze and evaluate them rhetorically as well. When you write this type of essay, you will identify how the text's author attempts to achieve a particular rhetorical goal and assess his or her success.

STEP 1—CAREFULLY READ THE ASSIGNMENT

As always, be sure you understand the assignment's intent and requirements. The words *analysis* or *evaluation* may never appear in the assignment. Instead, you might be asked to "assess" or "critique" the text, to decide "how effective" it is, or to argue "how well" it achieves its goal. If you have any questions regarding the goals of the essay you are being asked to write, talk to your teacher.

Also be sure you understand whether you will be evaluating a visual text you locate on your own or if you will be working with an assigned text. If you are free to choose your own visual text for rhetorical analysis, clarify whether there are any restrictions on your choice. For example, does your teacher want you to work with a particular type of visual text (i.e., an advertisement, a political cartoon, a photograph, a sign, or a painting)? Are particular types of visual texts excluded from the analysis? Finally, if the choice of source texts is up to you, have your teacher approve your selection before you begin to write your essay.

STEP 2—ANALYZE AND DESCRIBE THE TEXT

Although this step sounds simple, in some ways it is the most difficult. You need to carefully and objectively examine the text, finding language to describe exactly what you see and read. In several chapters, this textbook discusses the issue of bias when it comes to writing and reading texts—readers need to understand and take into account possible authorial bias when they read texts and acknowledge the biases they themselves bring to the texts they read and write. The same concerns hold true for visual texts as well.

Although you need to consider the biases that may have influenced the visual text's creation, you also need to be aware of any biases that could cloud or color your reading of it. Bias can lead you to misinterpret a visual image or actually fail to "see" what is on the page or computer screen because you are not looking for it. Therefore, when you analyze and describe a visual text, try to put aside as best you can any prejudices or assumptions you have concerning the text's content, message, creator, or source. Just as when you write a summary of a print text, your goal here is to be as objective as possible. Try to describe the visual text as objectively and accurately as you can, using language that is neutral and clear.

STEP 3—ESTABLISH THE TEXT'S RHETORICAL SITUATION

To establish the visual text's rhetorical situation, consider your answers to the following questions. Be sure to draw on the insights you gained through your earlier critical reading of the text:

- Who is the text's author or creator?
- Where was the text published, or where does it appear?
- What is the text's message? If there is more than one message, what are they? Does one message dominate?
- Who is the text's intended audience?
- How does the text want to affect that audience? What is the text's purpose?

If you have a hard time answering any of these questions, consider asking someone else—a classmate, roommate, parent, or friend—to examine the text and discuss it with them. Sometimes talking about a visual text with someone is the best way of determining its rhetorical situation.

STEP 4—DETERMINE HOW THE TEXT ATTEMPTS TO ACHIEVE ITS RHETORICAL GOALS

After you have determined the text's rhetorical goals, identify how its creator manipulates its images and/or text to achieve those ends. Here you would examine how the various elements of the text you identified earlier work separately and together to achieve the text's purpose. Your goal is to find language to describe how the visual text "works," how it communicates its message, and how it accomplishes its goals. The various elements of the text you focus on at this stage in the writing process are the ones you will likely write about in your essay.

STEP 5—DETERMINE YOUR THESIS

Your thesis statement can be either open or closed. An open thesis statement would indicate how successfully you believe the visual text achieved its rhetorical goal. Using the National Center for Family Literacy ad on page 168, an open thesis statement may read something like this:

> The National Center for Family Literacy produced an advertisement that successfully encourages readers to support their organization.

This thesis identifies what the writer believes to be the advertisement's goal or purpose (to encourage readers to support the sponsoring organization) and asserts a judgment concerning its success.

A closed thesis statement would indicate both your judgment of how well the visual text achieved its goals and the elements of the text you will examine to support your conclusion. Again, using the ad presented on page 168, a closed thesis statement could resemble this:

> Through its copy and its depiction of a mother and her daughter, the National Center for Family Literacy advertisement successfully encourages readers to support their organization.

This thesis still indicates the writer's judgment concerning how successfully the advertisement achieves its goal but also indicates how she will support her claim (by examining the advertisement's use of copy and its portrayal of a mother and her daughter).

STEP 6—WRITE A ROUGH DRAFT

Although the content and structure of the essays you write will vary by the type of visual text you are analyzing and evaluating, the following guidelines will help you write an effective rough draft.

Introductory Section
- Introduce the topic of your essay.
- Introduce the source text you will be working with.
- State your thesis.
- Capture reader interest.

You might consider opening your essay by introducing the topic that the visual text addresses, discussing the specific genre of visual text you will be working with (for example, an advertisement or a web page), or paraphrasing the assignment you've been given. Next, introduce the specific visual text you will be working with in your essay, indicating its authorship, source, and perhaps its date of publication. You should also include your thesis statement, typically placed toward the end of your introduction.

Description of the Visual Text and Overview of the Rhetorical Situation

- Describe the visual text.
- Explain the text's rhetorical situation.

In this section of your essay, describe and summarize the visual text you will be working with. Students sometimes understandably question why this section of the paper is needed, especially if the visual text is going to accompany the essay they write: why describe the text when readers will have access to it? Keep in mind that your description is preparing your readers for the argument you are going to make concerning the text's effectiveness. Through your description, you will bring to your readers' attention the aspects and elements of the text you will discuss in the body of your essay. You will introduce those aspects and elements in this section of your essay and evaluate them later.

The same advice holds true for explaining the visual text's rhetorical situation. You need to tell your reader where and in what context the visual text appeared, who created it, when it was created, and why it was produced. Identify what you believe to be the text's intended audience and purpose. If you believe your readers might interpret the text's purpose differently than you do in your essay, address those concerns here, acknowledging them and defending your own interpretation. The more clearly you explain the text's rhetorical situation in this part of your essay, the easier it will be to write a convincing argument in the body of your paper.

Body Paragraphs

- Develop your thesis one criterion or one example at a time.
- Cite specific examples from the visual text to support your assertions.
- Explain how those examples support the assertions you are making.
- Address possible objections or alternatives to your interpretations, as needed.

As you explain and develop the assertion(s) you put forward in your thesis, examine one evaluative criterion or example from the visual text at a time. For example, if you are basing your evaluation of a text on its use of color, examine one use of color in the text at a time, explaining how it supports the assertion you are making. Afterward, move on to your next example. If you are basing your evaluation on the text's use of color and layout, don't jump back and forth between the two—develop one criterion at a time.

Also, do not assume that the examples you cite speak for themselves or that your readers will understand on their own how the examples you draw from the visual text support the assertion you are making. Instead, carefully explain the link as you see it, and explain how each example lends credibility to your assertion.

Finally, be aware that any conclusions you have reached regarding the visual text are based on your interpretation of that text. Your judgments reflect the way you have interpreted and responded to the images and/or writing. Other readers could legitimately interpret the text differently. As you develop and explain your particular interpretation, note likely objections to your assertions or viable alternative interpretations, when necessary. Acknowledging and addressing these objections or alternatives increases your credibility as a writer and strengthens your assertions.

Conclusion

- Wrap up your essay in an interesting way.
- Remind readers of your thesis.

As with other types of source-based essays, you want to wrap up your analysis/ evaluation of a visual text in a way that reminds readers of the primary assertions you've made and that maintains interest. One way to reassert your primary claims is to simply restate your thesis; however, this approach does little to sustain reader interest. Instead, consider closing your essay with an interesting question or provocative assertion, to either challenge other readers' interpretations of the visual text or to predict the future, perhaps speculating on how successful the visual text will be in achieving its desired goals.

STEP 7—REVISE YOUR ESSAY

When revising your analysis/evaluation of a visual text, make sure your writing is clear, developed, and well organized.

- *Clear*—your readers understand the assertions you are making and the link between your evaluations and the source text.
- *Developed*—you have thoroughly explained your assertions and have examined alternative interpretations when needed.
- *Organized*—your assertions are logically connected, and your evaluation is guided by an overarching thesis.

Check for Clarity

When you revise your essay, at some point try to switch roles: you are no longer the author of your paper but someone reading it for the first time. Are there any assertions a reader might have a difficult time understanding? Are there any terms that need to be more clearly defined? Is the connection between your analysis/evaluation and the source text itself always clear? In other words, would readers understand exactly what aspects or elements of the source text you are analyzing, evaluating, or responding to? Have you explained your assertions thoroughly? Revise your essay as necessary to improve clarity.

Check the Development of Your Essay

Have you supported each of your assertions with references to the source text? Have you explained the connection between your assertions and the source text? The examples you cite from the source text cannot speak for themselves; do not expect your readers to understand the link between your assertions and the evidence you cite. Instead, clearly explain your reasoning.

Check the Organization

First, check your thesis statement. Does it accurately reflect and predict your essay's content and structure? If not, revise it. Second, check your topic sentences. Does each one introduce a new idea, provide a transition from the previous section of your essay, and, in some way, echo your thesis statement? Check the quality of the opening and closing sections of your essay—do they accomplish their intended goals? Finally, add transitions within paragraphs where needed to help guide your readers through your essay.

SAMPLE RHETORICAL ANALYSIS OF A VISUAL TEXT

The following sample essay analyzes and evaluates the National Center for Family Literacy advertisement on page 168.

AN EFFECTIVE ADVERTISEMENT FOR LITERACY SUPPORT

The idea of an organization devoted to the promotion of literacy paying for a magazine advertisement may seem odd. After all, if people can read the ad, they are already literate and have no need of the organization's services. If they are illiterate, they cannot read the ad at all. So what would be the purpose of such an advertisement? Judging by the ad placed by the National Center for Family Literacy in the April 2008 edition of *Black Enterprise* magazine, the purpose would be to garner support for the organization's programs and services. Through its use of copy, layout, and models, the National Center for Family Literacy demonstrates just how effective such an ad can be.

Unlike many other advertisements in *Black Enterprise*, the one sponsored by the National Center for Family Literacy is simple—using shades of black and white rather than color. Most of the ad consists of copy printed on a white background with two models—seemingly a mother and her daughter—appearing in the bottom right-hand corner. The bottom left-hand corner contains the National Center for Family Literacy name and logo, the message "Literacy can make the difference between poverty and progress," and an appeal to "Visit www.famlit.org to help us write more success stories."

The copy consists of the phrase "Because I can read" repeated four times in boldface print. Below three of these phrases—which serve as headings—are first-person statements (presumably from the mother in the ad) printed in a lighter typeface to finish the sentence. Under the first heading, the copy explains how becoming literate helped her find a job and get off welfare. Under the second heading, the copy focuses on how becoming literate helped her become a better mother and role model for her daughter. Under the third, the copy explains how being able to read has enabled the mother to live without fear and shame, allowing her to achieve economic success.

One reason this advertisement works well is that its copy appeals to the type of person likely to read *Black Enterprise* magazine. *Black Enterprise* is aimed primarily at African-American businesspeople, entrepreneurs, and philanthropists, people who have established or work for successful companies, who are looking for business opportunities, or who seek charitable opportunities. Those who read this magazine are aware of how important it is to have a trained, literate workforce and may have a greater understanding of and sympathy for people who must overcome obstacles to succeed.

Consequently, the copy under the first heading reads, "Because I can read, I can understand. I can write a letter. I can fill out a job application. I can finally get off welfare." Many readers of *Black Enterprise* would want to support an organization that helps potential workers learn how to fill out a job application, join the workforce, and move off of welfare. The copy under the second heading appeals to the readers' emotions. Supporting the work of the National Center for Family Literacy will improve the life of the family pictured in the ad—thanks to the organization, the mother can now "help my daughter with her homework," "inspire her to be better," and be a better "role model." Supporting the National Center for Family Literacy is not just in the economic interest of those who read *Black Enterprise*, it is also a humanitarian act.

The copy under the third heading combines elements of the first two. It opens with an echo of the first: "Because I can read, I can succeed. I can contribute." The copy indicates that the National Center for Family Literacy can help women like the one in the advertisement enter the workforce and achieve economic success. The next two statements, however, return to emotional appeals: "I can live my life without fear, without shame. I can be whatever I want to be." The copy is designed to build a bridge between the readers' experiences and the National Center's mission by stressing the need to help people overcome fears and obstacles and by working hard, to succeed.

Also making the National Center for Family Literacy's ad effective is its use of layout—how the copy and visuals are arranged on the page. The phrase "Because I can read," is repeated four times, printed in boldface along the left-hand margin of the page. Because of their placement and appearance, these words catch the reader's eye first. This repeated phrase dominates the ad, leading the reader's eye down the page to the National Center for Family Literacy's logo. The lighter-colored text underneath each heading catches the reader's eye because of its appearance and the repetition of "I": nine of the thirteen lines under the headings begin with "I." The use of first person in these lines makes the advertisement's copy personal, encouraging readers to identify with the mother and daughter pictured in the lower right-hand corner. People are more likely to support a charitable organization if they can identify and empathize with those who will be receiving the aid.

In fact, the depiction of the people in the advertisement also makes it effective. The copy surrounds and frames the two people, a mother and her child. Reading the headings left to right leads the reader's eye directly toward them. The mother is squatting down and her daughter is standing behind her, leaning in, a hand on each of her mother's shoulders. The mother's right hand is on her knee; her left hand rests on top of her daughter's right hand. The mother has a slight, proud grin on her face, while the daughter shows a full-toothed smile. These are average people—the mother appears to be wearing a sweatsuit of some sort and the daughter a polo shirt. The mother and her daughter are quite ordinary people, people whom the readers of *Black Enterprise* might know or see every day on the street. The message of the ad is clear: the National Center for Family Literacy helps average families like this one.

Finally, the facial expressions and race of the mother and daughter are crucial elements of the advertisement. The daughter seems overjoyed with the fact that her mother can now read, while the mother is brimming with confidence. Who wouldn't want to support an organization that would improve the life of such a cute little girl? Significant, too, is the fact that the mother is white while her daughter is biracial. Although *Black Enterprise* magazine primarily attracts African-American readers, the advertisement makes clear that the National Center for Family Literacy works to improve the lives of all people, regardless of race.

The National Center for Family Literacy advertisement that appeared in *Black Enterprise* magazine is not aimed at recruiting people who need the center's services. Instead, it is intended to attract possible donors and supporters. Beneath the center's logo at the bottom of the ad is copy that reads, "Literacy can make the difference between poverty and progress," and an appeal to "Visit www.famlit.org to help us write more success stories." Readers with a charitable heart may well consider supporting the organization after reading this successful ad.

Summary Chart

HOW TO WRITE A RHETORICAL ANALYSIS OF A VISUAL TEXT

1. **Carefully read the assignment.**
   - *Clarify your purpose.*
   - *Clarify the degree of freedom you have to select a visual text to evaluate.*

2. **Analyze and describe the text.**
   - *Examine every aspect of the text.*
   - *Attempt to put aside any biases you bring to the text.*

3. **Establish the text's rhetorical situation.**
   - *Who is the text's author or creator?*
   - *Where was the text published or where does it appear?*
   - *What is the text's message?*
   - *Who is the text's intended audience?*
   - *What is the text's purpose?*

4. **Determine how the text attempts to achieve its rhetorical goals.**
   - *How do the various elements of the text work separately and together to achieve the text's purpose or goal?*

5. **Determine your thesis.**
   - *Identify what you think the text's goal is and assert a judgment concerning how well it succeeds in achieving that goal.*
   - *Decide if you will use an open or closed thesis.*
   - *If you use a closed thesis, indicate which elements of the text you will examine in your essay.*

6. **Write a rough draft.**
   - *Write the introductory section of your essay, indicating the topic of your essay, identifying the source text you will be working with, stating your thesis, and capturing reader interest.*
   - *Provide a brief but thorough description of the text and explain its rhetorical situation.*
   - *Draft the body of your evaluation in a manner that is consistent with your thesis, examining one element at a time of the visual text, citing specific examples from the text to support any assertions you make, explaining how those examples support your claims, and addressing possible objections to or questions concerning your interpretation.*
   - *Write the concluding section of your essay, writing up your evaluation, reminding readers of your thesis, and maintaining reader interest.*

7. **Revise your essay.**
   - *Make sure your writing is clear.*
   - *Make sure your writing is well developed.*
   - *Make sure your writing is organized.*

RHETORICAL ANALYSIS OF A VISUAL TEXT REVISION CHECKLIST

	Yes	No
1. Have you carefully analyzed the assignment to determine whether you are supposed to describe, analyze, and/or evaluate the text?	_____	_____
2. Have you carefully examined every aspect of the source text?	_____	_____
3. Have you established the visual text's rhetorical situation?	_____	_____
4. Have you established how the creators of the visual text attempt to achieve their rhetorical goal?	_____	_____
5. Have you determined how well they achieve their goal?	_____	_____
6. Have you expressed your findings in a clear thesis statement that can guide the development of your essay?	_____	_____
7. In the introductory section of your essay, do you:		
• introduce the topic?	_____	_____
• introduce the source text?	_____	_____
• state your thesis?	_____	_____
• attempt to capture reader interest?	_____	_____
8. In the body of your essay, do you:		
• provide an overview or description of the visual text?	_____	_____
• develop your essay one criterion at a time?	_____	_____
• cite specific examples from the text to support your claims?	_____	_____
• explain how those examples support your assertions?	_____	_____
• address possible objections to your interpretation?	_____	_____

	Yes	No
9. In the concluding section of your essay, do you:		
• wrap up your essay in an interesting way?	_____	_____
• remind readers of your thesis?	_____	_____
10. Have you revised your essay for:		
• clarity?	_____	_____
• development?	_____	_____
• organization?	_____	_____
11. Have you proofread your essay?	_____	_____

Chapter 10

INFORMATIVE
SYNTHESIS

In this chapter you will learn how to

1. Read critically to identify similarities and differences among texts

2. Combine information from multiple readings

3. Develop an effective thesis and organizational plan

4. Support assertions with appropriate evidence and examples

5. Document multi-source informative essays

DEFINITION AND PURPOSE

In a synthesis, you combine information from two or more readings to support a position of your own. Your aim in the paper can be expository (to convey information) or argumentative (to convince readers that your thesis concerning the readings is correct). In either case, when writing a synthesis, you combine material from two or more readings with your own knowledge and reasoning to explain or support your thesis.

College writing assignments often require you to synthesize material. In some courses the assignment will be direct and clear: "Compare what author A and author B have to say about topic X. How are their views alike and how are they different?" Other times the assignment might be more subtle: "Authors A, B, and C all address topic X. Which do you find most convincing?" Completing either assignment would require you to form and defend a thesis by drawing information from two or more readings.

To write a synthesis, you first need to sort through the readings to find information you can use in your paper. Being able to annotate readings thoroughly is essential. Second, you need to find the best way to organize this material around your own thesis and the demands of the assignment. Third, you need to find a place in the essay for your own ideas, findings, or arguments. Composing a synthesis usually involves more than just stringing together quoted and paraphrased material from other writers. Fourth, as you write your paper, you need to keep straight who receives credit for which ideas. Through proper documentation, you need to clarify for your readers when you are drawing on the work of a particular author and when you are developing material yourself. Finally, as you revise your work, you need to keep clearly in mind the rhetorical situation of the assignment. In your efforts to work with other people's ideas, you cannot afford to lose sight of your readers' needs and the purpose of the assignment.

TYPES OF SYNTHESIS ESSAYS

Synthesis essays can assume many different forms in college, some rather specialized and sophisticated. One way to begin sorting through all this variety is to recognize that for the most part the assignments you receive will ask you to compose either an **informative** or an **argumentative** synthesis (see Chapter 11).

The goal of an informative synthesis is to clearly and efficiently communicate the information you have gathered from two or more readings. You do not defend a position of your own or critique the source texts in this type of paper. Your primary aim is to summarize the material in the readings and convey the information to your readers in a clear, concise, organized fashion, often comparing and contrasting the texts. In contrast, the goal of an argumentative synthesis is to convince your reader to accept an argument you are presenting on either the quality of the readings or the topic they address. You use the material in the source texts to support your thesis, sometimes summarizing the readings and sometimes critiquing them.

Either type of synthesis can be organized in a variety of ways. Often writers will choose to employ either a **block** or an **alternating** format. When you use a block format to structure your synthesis, you discuss only one source text at a time. With an alternating format, you switch back and forth between readings as you develop your thesis point by point.

Before examining each type of synthesis in more detail, read the following arguments concerning the relationship between television viewing and childhood violence. What is each author's stance on the topic? What aspects of the topic most capture the author's interest? How convincing is each author's argument?

Humanity 2.0?

Enhancement, Evolution and the Possible Futures of Humanity

Sarah Chan

Sarah Chan is a Research Fellow at the Institute for Science, Ethics, and Innovation at the University of Manchester, UK.

Particular concern about human enhancement often seems to focus on genetic manipulation and the undesirability of using it to enhance our children or ourselves. As I have argued . . . there is nothing wrong with enhancement *per se*. Opponents of genetic enhancements, therefore, must show that there is something particular about the use of genetic technologies that renders these enhancements unacceptable, whereas the use of chemical or mechanical enhancements is not.

Genetic manipulation might be perceived as less acceptable because it is a relatively new procedure—at least when applied to human beings—and therefore carries the possibility of unforeseen risks. Gene therapy, in particular, has received bad press after a few cases in which potential dangers did manifest. Examples include the gene-therapy trials to treat severe defects of the immune system that resulted in leukaemia (Cavazzana-Calvo et al., 2000) and the death of Jesse Gelsinger, who suffered an adverse reaction to the virus used as a vector in gene therapy against ornithine transcarbamylase deficiency (Savulescu, 2001).

The presence of risk is not a factor unique to genetic enhancement—it is also likely that other types of enhancement technology have risks associated with their application, as do current drug therapeutics. Every new treatment involves some amount of risk; this, in itself, does not render it unethical. If we were to avoid every activity that carried any amount of risk, no matter how small, then we would never drive motor cars, cross the road or even get out of bed in the morning. The most ethical course of action in the face of risk is to evaluate the balance of risk and benefit, and attempt to minimize the risks where they must be faced. This might not be an easy thing to do in the case of new technologies, but it is better done than not.

So is there anything intrinsically wrong with genetic manipulation? There certainly cannot be a moral proscription against modifying the somatic genome: we are at liberty to make changes to our physical bodies in terms of their appearance, condition or health, and DNA is simply a part of that—in fact, somatic mutation occurs all the time.

Arguments against human genetic modification have therefore concentrated in particular on the ethical unacceptability of germ-line gene therapy. The distinguishing feature of germ-line genetic modification—as opposed to somatic genetic modification—is that any changes made to the genome will be heritable and therefore affect not only the individuals treated, but also their descendants—and by extension, the future human race as a whole.

The argument invoked is that it is wrong to make genetic choices for our descendants. One reason given for this is sometimes expressed in terms of the "right to an open future" (Feinberg, 1980): that is, by predetermining the genes of our children, we are somehow limiting their own right to choose. Choosing the genes of our children, so the argument goes, deprives them of the right to make their own choices about their lives and thereby infringes their autonomy (Buchanan et al., 2000; Davis, 2001; Habermas, 2003; Mameli, 2007).

Yet children can never exert a choice over the genes that they are born with, regardless of whether their parents do. Those who believe in genetic determinism must realize that abandoning our children to the mercy of the 'genetic lottery' does not free them from the tyranny of their genes, rather, it merely removes any element of choice on the part of anyone as to what those genes are. Those of us, by contrast, who look beyond genetic determinism to see that it is far more than genes that determine the future of our children, will probably also realize that—to the extent that genes do determine some aspects of our lives, in particular our health and associated quality of life—it is surely far better to have a predisposition to a healthy life than to risk a higher chance of suffering and disease.

The corollary to the above argument is that parents themselves should not seek to make such choices and that attempting to enhance children represents "a kind of hyperagency—a Promethean aspiration to remake nature, including human nature, to serve our purposes and satisfy our desires" (Sandel, 2004, 2007). According to this argument, parental virtue requires acceptance rather than control and an "openness to the unbidden", rather than the "hubris [of] an excess of mastery"—that is, an appreciation of the 'gifted' nature of human achievement, rather than an aspiration to increase these achievements. Choosing to enhance is therefore wrong both because it violates the principles of good parenting and because of the negative social consequences that will follow the abandonment of such principles.

In each case, however, it is not clear whether the availability or use of genetic enhancements will result in the predicted disintegration of social values, or if allowing parents to make choices about their children contravenes the requirements of parental responsibility. It is true that the use of genetic-enhancement technologies will involve parents making decisions about the genetic heritage of their children. However, once the technology exists and has been proven to be safe, to refrain from using it is likewise to make a decision about the genetic inheritance of our descendants— specifically: that they will not receive such enhancements and will be denied the consequent benefits. If we were to have the choice of eradicating a serious disease for future generations and decided against doing so, I doubt that our descendants would thank us for it. Abdicating choice is not the action of a responsible parent; exercising choice wisely is.

Of course, this applies equally to both genetic and non-genetic interventions. Every parent wants to have a healthy child and there is nothing wrong with this. Indeed, we might look askance at a parent who did not claim to want the best for their children. Yet what do we mean by healthy? The only logical answer to this question is 'as healthy as possible'. For example, we know that certain maternal behaviours during pregnancy can have adverse consequences for child health: the use of alcohol and tobacco increase the risk of low birth weight and associated developmental delay, and poor maternal diet can increase the chances of developing type 2 diabetes in later life. We encourage mothers-to-be to improve the health of their children by avoiding these things; indeed, we consider them to be irresponsible if they fail to do so. Similarly, we advocate folate supplements as a positive measure to decrease the risk of spina bifida. Therefore, we see it as a strong obligation on parents to use the available knowledge and medical technology to maximize the health of their children. We also encourage the use of vaccination and other choices for children that protect and benefit them.

Surely, then, this argument also applies to genetic enhancement. If we could, with safety and certainty, engineer our children to have immunity to viral infection, protection from heart disease and reduced susceptibility to cancer, we should do so. In other words, not only is genetic enhancement morally acceptable, but, if and when it becomes safe and affordable, there will be a moral imperative to use it for the benefit of future generations (Chan & Harris, 2007).

More general concerns about genetic manipulations focus on the consequences of genetic enhancement for the future of the human race. These concerns include worries about the loss of genetic diversity: that we will become a race of clones—either literally, through the use of reproductive cloning to create armies of identical beings, or because our uniform desire for enhancements will result in overall genetic uniformity. Others seem to have the opposite fear: that changing our genome and creating genetic differences will lead to the fragmentation and destruction of the human race. The American bioethicist George Annas, for example, has described genetic engineers as "potential bioterrorists" because of the possibility of genocide based on engineered genetic differences (Annas, 2001). The United Nations Educational, Scientific and Cultural Organization (UNESCO) Universal

Declaration on the Human Genome states that, "the human genome must be preserved as the common heritage of humanity" (UNESCO, 1997). However, the only way to eradicate all genetic differences that might lead to genocide, and the only way to preserve the human genome exactly as it is today, is universal human reproductive cloning—a course of action that neither Annas nor UNESCO would be likely to favour.

These arguments, then, are confusing and contradictory, yet they strike a note of concern with many. Even if this concern is misplaced or misdirected, we might well wonder what the consequences of enhancement will be for humanity as a whole.

We are familiar with the idea of Darwinian evolution: natural selection acting on genetic variation to produce long-term changes in our genetic make-up. There is also a sense in which human society and culture can be said to undergo evolution, as ideas that are more successful—whether because they are correct or intuitively attractive or both—will propagate themselves: a process known as meme evolution. This, of course, includes the progression of technological ideas.

It is reasonable to say that the relationship between humans and technology has probably influenced the course of our genetic and cultural evolution in the past. For example, it seems likely that the technological developments since pre-history have changed the selection pressures acting on human beings—one can plausibly suppose, for example, that the transition from hunter–gatherer to agricultural societies would have altered the environment to allow different genes to be favoured. Moreover, technology has undeniably influenced the course of social development.

It is often said, with reference to the human race, that we have halted evolution by doing away with natural selection. It is true that modern medicine allows many individuals to survive and reproduce when they might not otherwise have done so; yet, we must remember that the marked reductions in infant mortality, deaths from disease and so on are only a product of the past century or so—a mere few generations. In the context of the roughly three billion year history of life on Earth, it seems to be a little premature to declare victory over natural selection—although we are probably the first and only species that understands evolution and might be in a position to influence its course deliberately.

Even if we were to remove the influence of natural selection entirely, it would not necessarily mean the end of evolution—if by evolution we mean social change or cultural evolution—or the end of genetic change. In fact, although the collective human genome is not changing appreciably faster than it has in the past, the development of human society as a whole—that is, evolution in the cultural sense—is progressing faster than ever, and is constantly accelerating. What we want to do and what we dream of doing is rapidly outpacing what we can do with the genomes and the bodies that we are presently born with. Hans Moravec, who is a robotics expert at Carnegie Mellon University (Pittsburgh, PA, USA), has expressed this as, "the drag of the flesh on the spirit . . . the problem is that cultural development proceeds much faster than biological evolution" (Moravec, 1989). Interestingly, he noted this in the context of artificial intelligence and wondered whether machines might overcome the "drag of the flesh" from which humans suffer. With the new biological technologies offered to us, we might be able to overcome the drag in our own bodies.

Modifying the human genome might be one way of doing this. Some see it as tampering with the process of natural evolution that produced the human genome in its current form. True enough, our present genome is, by definition, a successful one: it is still around today. However, evolution so far has operated somewhat in the dark. The happenstance of natural evolution has also bequeathed us a legacy of genetic failings: susceptibility to disease, cancer and the depredations of old age, to name but a few. We are, as the British evolutionary scientist Richard Dawkins might put it, stranded on our own particular peak of 'Mount Improbable' (Dawkins, 1996), lumbered with all the genetic encumbrances of our evolutionary history, good and bad.

We have, almost within our reach, the power to transcend this situation: to change our genotypes, much as we can already change our phenotypes to improve health and quality of life. There might be no guarantee of success; however, in comparison to natural evolution, any genetic modifications aimed at improving the human condition will at least be evidence-based rather than random, and unless blind watch-making is to be the new gold standard in scientific research, that is as good as it gets with current technology (Chan & Harris, 2006).

How will this new "enhancement evolution" (Harris, 2007) be mediated? The prospect of genetic enhancement is always haunted by the spectre of eugenics—the state-coerced use of technology to change us whether we will or no. To this point, we should emphasize once again the importance of individual choice. Yet, enhancements might also limit individual choices through the so-called genetic arms race, in which everyone is forced to use enhancements to 'keep up with the Joneses'. Is this a bad thing? Evolution, again, has always been a genetic arms race: we are designed to compete. The end point in this case, however, is not the threat of mutually assured destruction, but rather the survival of our species. Of course, we should have the option not to participate, to refuse enhancements. Yet why would we want to? If the ultimate result of these technologies is better lives for all humans, then their use is probably a good thing. Put another way, we currently engage in a type of educational arms race of enhancements. Reading and writing was once the province of a few privileged scholars; now it is almost mandatory to equip children with these skills, if they are to keep up with their peers. The result of this educational arms race has been almost ubiquitous literacy—surely a benefit?

Even these sort of claims, however, really only apply to the developed and industrialized world. The 'ubiquitous' benefits that we enjoy are often not readily available to those in developing nations—and in this sense, enhancements raise crucial questions of justice. Will the ultimate result of human enhancement be better lives for everyone, or will it be better lives for a few at the expense of the disadvantaged many?

The issue of how to address the aims of justice with respect to enhancement technologies is a complex one, and I have scope only to note two brief points here. The first is that concerns about justice do not warrant turning our backs entirely on enhancement technologies—"it is doubtful ethics to deny a benefit to some unless and until it can be provided to all" (Harris, 2007). Certainly, that is not the position we take on most new technologies. Allowing access to expensive technologies to those who can afford them will, in all likelihood, speed their development to become more readily available to everyone. The second point is that this process might need a helping hand: if we see injustice, we should move to address it in a positive way, to 'level up', so that the same opportunities are available to all, rather than 'levelling down' and reducing everyone to the same level.

A few last words, then, on what enhancement might mean for humanity. Enhancement technologies, provided their application is correctly managed, will ultimately be of benefit to humankind and, as such, we have good moral reasons to pursue them. They will not, as some fear, destroy humanity by turning us into something other—something more—than what we are. We have always wanted—and will probably always want—to be more than we are. Yet by the same token, we will always remain 'what we are'—in the sense of that which really matters to us, that which makes us human. Surely, being human and the definition of 'humanness' should not depend arbitrarily on a particular combination of abilities and limitations—to run no faster than 25 miles per hour, to live no longer than a century. Indeed, logically it cannot depend on such limitations, or we would be forced to admit that we ourselves are no longer human compared to our predecessors who had more limited abilities and life spans.

Instead, what make us human are our aspirations, our awareness of ourselves as beings in the world (including our limitations), our ability for self-contemplation and reflection, and the desire to attempt to change what we see. We are not designed to remain "passive, inert players in the game of life" (Chan & Harris, 2007). What makes us uniquely human is the ability to shape our own destinies according to our desires—and genetic and other enhancement technologies provide further means for us to do so. In this sense, enhancements and the desire to avail ourselves of them are an expression of our essential humanity.

The advent of new forms of human enhancement on our technological horizon does not therefore signify, as some have warned, the end of humanity. Rather, it is just the next step in a continuing process: that of human evolution, which stretches far back into the dim past and, we might hope, will continue into the future for many thousands of years to come.

References

Annas G (2001) Genism, racism and the prospect of genetic genocide. Presentation at UNESCO 21st Century Talks: World Conference Against Racism, Racial Discrimination, Xenophobia and Related Intolerance in Durban, South Africa, September 3rd. www.thehumanfuture.org

Buchanan A, Brock DW, Daniels N, Wikler D (2000) *From Chance to Choice: Genetics and Justice.* Cambridge, UK: Cambridge University Press

Cavazzana-Calvo M et al. (2000) Gene therapy of human severe combined immunodeficiency (SCID)-X1 disease. *Science* **288**: 669–672

Chan S, Harris J (2006) The ethics of gene therapy. *Curr Opin Mol Ther* **8**: 377–383

Chan S, Harris J (2007) In support of enhancement. *Studies in Ethics Law and Technology* 1: Article 10

Davis DS (2001) *Genetic Dilemmas.* New York, NY, USA: Routledge

Dawkins R (1996) *Climbing Mount Improbable.* London, UK: Penguin Books

Feinberg J (1980) The child's right to an open future. In *Whose Child? Children's Rights, Parental Authority and State Power,* W Aiken, H LaFollette (eds), pp 124–153. Totowa, NJ, USA: Rowman and Litlefield

Habermas J (2003) *The Future of Human Nature.* Cambridge, UK: Polity

Harris J (2007) *Enhancing Evolution.* Princeton, NJ, USA: Princeton University Press

Mameli M (2007) Reproductive cloning, genetic engineering and the autonomy of the child: the moral agent and the open future. *J Med Ethics* **33**: 87–93

Moravec H (1989) Human culture: A genetic takeover underway. In *Artificial Life,* CG Langton (ed). Indianapolis, IN, USA: Addison-Wesley

Sandel MJ (2004) The case against perfection: What's wrong with designer children, bionic athletes, and genetic engineering. *Atl Mon* **292**: 50–54, 56–60, 62

Sandel MJ (2007) *The Case Against Perfection: Ethics in the Age of Genetic Engineering.* Cambridge, MA, USA: Belknap

Savulescu J (2001) Harm, ethics committees and the gene therapy death. *J Med Ethics* **27**: 148–150

UNESCO (1997) *Universal Declaration on the Human Genome and Human Rights.* Paris, France: UNESCO

On Designer Babies: Genetic Enhancement of Human Embryos Is Not a Practice for Civil Societies

Sheldon Krimsky

Sheldon Krimsky is Lenore Stern Professor of Humanities and Social Sciences at Tufts University.

You may remember a short period in the 1990s when a broad consensus emerged among biologists about the ethics of human genetic engineering. Somatic cell gene therapy was considered an acceptable biomedical research program, whereas germ line genetic modification was treated as unethical. By the new millennium, that moral boundary had eroded.

A recent debate in New York City in which I was a participant highlighted the cultural change. Our topic: "Babies Should Not Be Genetically Engineered." I argued in support of the proposition to prohibit the genetic modification of human reproductive cells prior to gestation in the womb.

Two compelling reasons to genetically alter human reproductive cells in preparation for childbirth, I argued, are for curing or preventing a disease or for the "enhancement" of a child. With respect to the former, there are safer and more dependable methods for preventing the birth of a child with a severe genetic abnormality than by genetic modification of the germ cells. The use of prenatal screening or preimplantation embryo diagnosis will suffice in most cases to prevent the birth of a genetically abnormal embryo.

Accordingly, the only remaining rationale for engaging in the genetic modification of human reproductive cells is for enhancement of the child to achieve such traits as heightened intelligence, resistance to disease, muscle strength, appealing personality or longevity, to cite a few common examples. I believe that pursuit of this goal represents the greatest scientific folly and moral failure.

First, for whatever enhancement is sought, the only method for determining efficacy is to engage in a clinical trial with a few dozen fertilized human eggs or embryos, where half would be genetically modified, all would be carried to term, and the development of the children would be followed throughout their lives to determine whether the genetic modification worked and worked safely. No animal studies can answer these questions.

It is unimaginable that any humane society would permit such a trial where the potential risks so outweigh the social benefits.

The second reason to shun genetic enhancement is that it makes no sense from a biological and developmental perspective. The human traits typically cited for enhancement, such as intelligence, personality or musicianship, are complex and not only involve dozens if not hundreds of genes, but are the result of a complex mix of determinants, including nutrition, social and environmental factors, gene-to-gene interactions and epigenetic switches that are outside the reductive chemistry of the DNA code.

Even for height, one of the most heritable traits known, scientists have discovered at least 50 genes that can account for 2 to 3 percent of the variance in the samples. There could be hundreds of genes associated with height. If you want a tall child, then marry tall.

Finally, the idea of genetic enhancement grows out of a eugenics ideology that human perfection can be directed by genetics. I am all for human enhancement, but it must start after an egg is fertilized beginning in utero—by protecting the fetus from neurotoxins and other endocrine-disrupting substances and continuing after birth with nutritional and cognitive enrichment and moral education, for example.

The greatest danger of a belief in genetics engineering lies in its likely social impact. Eugenics will inevitably be used by those with wealth and power to make others believe that to be prenatally genetically modified makes you better. This would be as much a myth as believing that the sperm from Nobel Laureates will produce a genius child.

A Moderate Approach to Enhancement

Michael Selgelid

Michael Selgelid is Director of the Centre for Human Bioethics at Monash University in Melbourne.

Revolutionary developments in biomedical science, particularly in genetics, may lead to new cures or preventative therapies for a wide variety of human diseases. Just about everyone agrees that this would be a good thing.

However, the very same kinds of developments that may be used to combat disease might also be used for the purpose of human enhancement—that is, to make people "better than well".

Consider genetic testing, for example. Genetic testing of embryos produced by *in vitro* fertilization (IVF) can allow us to detect genetic sequences known to be associated with a wide variety of diseases before embryos are implanted in the mother's uterus. Couples can thus increase the likelihood of having healthy offspring by choosing to implant only those embryos that test negative for genetic diseases. As knowledge about the relationship between genes and human traits increases, we will be able to detect genetic sequences associated with a wide variety of positively desired characteristics too. Many parents might then want to select *for* traits such as increased height, intelligence, strength, beauty, and so on, with the aim of giving their children higher-quality lives. The limits would depend on the extent to which a genetic basis for such traits is eventually demonstrated by genetic science. We can imagine a future where each embryo produced via IVF receives a "genetic report card", indicating predispositions to a large number of advantageous as well as disadvantageous human traits.

Similar possibilities may arise via genetic engineering. When diseases are caused by an individual lacking an important genetic sequence, or having a disease-causing genetic sequence, it might eventually become possible to insert the missing sequence, or replace the pathogenic sequence with a normal sequence, via "genetic therapy". If and when such procedures are perfected, it might also be possible to alter an individual's genome purely for enhancement purposes. Genetic sequences associated with normal stature, for example, might be replaced by those associated with greater than average, or even exceptional, height; genetic sequences associated with normal cognitive capacity might be replaced by those associated with greater than average, or even exceptional, cognitive capacity, and so on. The limits will depend again on the extent to which relationships between genes and human traits are eventually demonstrated by genetic science, and in this case, also on the extent to which it becomes technically possible to make precise changes to human genomes.

This of course raises questions about whether or not non-therapeutic enhancement-oriented genetic interventions are morally permissible, and whether or not they should be permitted legally. Most people agree that using such procedures to reduce disease would be relatively non-problematic, at least if these procedures can be shown to be safe and effective. On the other hand, many object to the idea of using biomedical technology for the purpose of enhancement. But why should this be so?

The Good of Individuals Versus the Good of Society

Advocates of enhancement often point out that enhancement is, by definition, a good thing. "To enhance" *means* "to make better". So when we are talking about true enhancements, we are necessarily talking about making people better off than they otherwise would have been in terms of their overall wellbeing. In the case of genetic screening in the context of IVF, we are talking about parents choosing embryos that, based on the best available information, they expect to have the healthiest or happiest lives. What, one wonders, could possibly be wrong with that?

The best objection to true human enhancement appeals to potential adverse social consequences. In other words, it might be good for enhanced individuals, but bad for society as a whole. In particular, the practice of human enhancement would be expected to lead to increased social inequality. If the kinds of genetic technologies discussed above are indeed developed, then they will presumably only be available to those with the money to pay for them. It is hard to imagine that they would be made freely available to all via universal healthcare systems, which, due to resource constraints, are often unable to provide even medically necessary services to all who need them. So the relatively wealthy will then be able to enhance themselves and their children while the relatively poor and their children will remain unenhanced, or at least less enhanced. The (more) enhanced richfolk will then have even greater competitive advantages than previously. The divide between the haves and have-nots will inevitably increase, and become more intractable. Or so the argument goes.

This kind of appeal to equality is routinely made by those opposed to genetic enhancement. Advocates of genetic enhancement routinely reply by pointing out that we already tolerate a wide variety of inequality-promoting non-genetic enhancements. The wealthy send their children to special schools, sports camps, music lessons, and so on—and these things increase the advantages of those children who are already advantaged in other ways. What, genetic enhancement advocates ask, could be so different about genetic enhancements that they would be wrong, while other non-genetic kinds of enhancements are perfectly acceptable? Given that it is hard to imagine what could be so special and different about (true, safe and effective) genetic enhancement *per se,* they conclude that genetic enhancement must be acceptable too. They often appear to think this should be an argument stopper.

However, this argument in defense of enhancement is not altogether convincing. It might be true that there is no inherent moral difference between genetic enhancement and the other kinds of enhancements enumerated above. But there could very well turn out to be important *differences in scale.* If enough genetic enhancements become available, their use becomes sufficiently widespread, and they turn out to be especially powerful in their effects on people's capacities, then *the extent of their impact on equality* could turn out to be much greater than that which results from currently available non-genetic means of enhancement. According to some authors, the threat to equality posed by genetic enhancement may be unprecedented. Existing kinds of enhancements might be tolerable because we value the liberty of individuals to pursue them, and because the inequalities that result are not bad enough to justify our infringing on this liberty. On the other hand, if the consequences of the inequalities were bad enough, then liberty considerations might be outweighed by equality considerations.

In addition to being unjust, deep inequality can compromise democracy and social stability. Severe inequality can thus make everyone significantly worse off. And the use of genetic enhancements could have adverse effects on society in other ways. One less frequently discussed concern about the social consequences of enhancement is that if it becomes especially profitable to develop and offer genetic enhancement services, then this will drain medical research and healthcare provision resources away from disease treatment and prevention.

We are already faced with a situation known as the "10/90 divide": 90 per cent of medical research resources focus on diseases that account for 10 per cent of the global burden of disease. This is because the majority of medical research focuses on developing the drugs and other interventions expected to make the most profits, rather than those that are most important from a global public health perspective. We can imagine that this situation will only be exacerbated if the provision of genetic enhancement services turns out to be highly profitable. If a drain of resources thus occurs, the quality of life improvements *overall* made by enhancement may turn out to be less than would have been achieved if those resources had instead focused on disease reduction and the prevention of suffering.

Conflicting Values

Questions about the ethics of genetic enhancement thus turn both on unresolved empirical questions and on unresolved philosophical questions.

There are unresolved empirical questions about (1) the extent of inequality that would likely result from an unrestricted practice of human enhancement, and (2) the overall impact that an unrestricted practice of human enhancement would have on human wellbeing. We cannot predict such consequences with certainty, of course, but interdisciplinary social science research, including sophisticated modeling and so on, could shed some light on the potential impact of genetic enhancement under various scenarios—that is, depending on the kinds of genetic enhancements projected to become possible. In the meantime, it is surprising and unfortunate that so many philosophers have spilt so much ink on speculative discussion about what the social consequences of genetic enhancement are likely to be—telling just-so stories about why the impact of genetic enhancement on social equality or welfare will or won't turn out to be problematic. These philosophers should more often admit that questions about the likely impact of enhancement ultimately require empirical research by those with the appropriate expertise for conducting it. They should refrain from pretending that these empirical questions are really philosophical questions.

The spectre of genetic enhancement does, however, also raise important and difficult philosophical questions—but these have received insufficient attention, being only very rarely explicitly addressed in the burgeoning literature. The key unresolved philosophical questions concern how the value of personal liberty should be weighed against social equality and welfare in cases where these values conflict.

Liberty is an important value, and there are widely-accepted presumptions in favour of its protection unless there are very good reasons for interfering with it. Liberty is rightly considered especially important in the context of reproduction in particular. Insofar as we place an especially high value on reproductive liberty, we should be reluctant to restrict parents' choices regarding the genetic enhancement of their offspring.

However, liberty should not be thought to have absolute priority over all other values. Liberty, equality and welfare all matter, so none should have absolute priority over the others. Thus if the social costs of the unrestricted practice of genetic enhancement are sufficiently great (i.e., disastrous) for welfare or equality, then the importance of individual liberty might be outweighed by the importance of these other values. The unresolved philosophical question is thus: How socially damaging would enhancement need to be in order for personal liberty to be justly overridden? This points to a need for theoretical development in the fields of ethics and political philosophy.

At present there are three main approaches on the table. First, utilitarians argue that aggregate benefit is the only thing that ultimately matters to society, and so "utility", the greatest benefit for the greatest number of people, should always be promoted, even at the expense of liberty and equality. By contrast, egalitarians often place extreme weight on the value of equality; and libertarians place extreme weight on the value of liberty. Each of these perspectives gets something right, because the values they respectively emphasize each matter. But they each arguably get something wrong too, insofar as they each tend to place absolute or overriding weight on the values they emphasize. In this latter respect they are out of line with commonsense ethical thinking and what is generally considered to be good policy-making. To resolve questions about genetic enhancement, and many other difficult issues in practical ethics, we need a fourth approach that provides a principled way of striking a balance or making trade-offs between liberty, equality, and utility in cases of conflict. Development of a "moderate pluralist" theory such as this would be necessary to determine how great the costs of enhancement would need to be for us to be justified in denying people the freedom to enhance themselves and their offspring, and to what extent.

INFORMATIVE SYNTHESIS

Definition

Your goal in writing an informative synthesis is to combine material on some topic you have gathered from two or more readings into a clear, organized essay. After finishing your essay, a reader should have a better understanding of the topic and should know the position of the various authors whose work you include. You are not trying to show how one author is correct in what she says and another is wrong. Neither are you trying to advocate a position of your own on the topic. Instead, you are trying to present other people's ideas or findings as clearly and concisely as you can, highlighting key similarities and differences. Teachers also commonly refer to these papers as "reports" or "comparison-contrast essays."

For example, if you were writing an informative synthesis of the essays included in this chapter, you would want to summarize what each writer had to say about the genetic enhancement of human beings. In fact, a good way to write this paper would be to isolate for examination certain aspects of the topic that all of the writers address—that way you could draw direct comparisons among the pieces. As you point out for your reader important similarities or differences you see in the various essays, you would not argue that one author is correct in his or her position on the topic and that the others are misguided, nor would you comment on the quality of the writing or argument in any particular essay.

To compose an informative synthesis, you employ many of the same skills needed to write summaries. As with writing summaries, you may encounter a number of problems when composing an informative synthesis:

1. Because of their content, language, or structure, the source texts themselves might be hard for you to understand. Because you need to form a clear understanding of the readings before you write about them, you need strong critical reading skills to write a successful synthesis.

2. You will often be looking for subtle differences among readings—not just different arguments or findings that the authors put forward, but slightly different interpretations of data, slightly different uses of terminology, slightly different emphases. Because a synthesis involves multiple source texts, when you examine a reading you plan to use in your paper, you also have to keep in mind the material contained in the readings you have already read. The more readings you are working with, the harder it is to keep track of the material contained in each and the easier it is to overlook the subtle differences between them.

3. You need to stay as objective as possible when examining the source texts and writing your essay. You do not editorialize in an informative synthesis: your goal is *not* to comment on the topic of the readings or on the quality of their writing. Instead, you need to be open-minded when reading them,

to pull out from them material relevant to your thesis, and to present that material as clearly, concisely, and fairly as possible. As when you are writing a summary, remaining neutral can be difficult, especially when you feel strongly about a topic and must include in your informative synthesis ideas that disturb or anger you.

4. Organizing an informative synthesis can also be challenging. You need to decide how to construct your thesis so it adequately guides your reader through your work, how to order the information you include in your paper, and how to employ transitions within the body of your essay.

5. Supplying proper documentation in an informative synthesis can be problematic. One paragraph of your paper may contain information you have drawn from several different authors. Learning how to document such passages properly can be trying; remembering to do it is crucial. Improper documentation can lead to problems with clarity and plagiarism.

WRITING AN INFORMATIVE SYNTHESIS

Because writing an informative synthesis can be challenging, it is best to break the process down into a series of more manageable steps:

1. Analyze the assignment.
2. Review and annotate the readings.
3. Formulate a thesis and organizational plan.
4. Write your rough draft.
5. Revise your draft.
6. Check your quotations and documentation.

Remember that this method of writing a synthesis will not work for everybody. We all have our preferred way of writing papers, which can vary according to the type of essay we are composing and the time we have to complete the assignment. For example, some writers like to complete a rough draft before they write their thesis, while others must have a thesis in hand before they begin to write; some will rewrite a paper several times before they turn it in for a grade, while others revise very little. Use these directions as a rough guide for writing an informative synthesis. The important principle to keep in mind is to complete your paper in a series of steps, no matter the nature or order of those steps.

Step 1—Analyze the Assignment

Read the assignment carefully to make sure your instructor is asking you to write an informative rather than an argumentative synthesis. If you have any doubt, ask your teacher to clarify the assignment. Make sure you understand how many sources you are required to consult when researching the topic or to include when writing your paper. Also, check on the type of source texts your teacher expects you to use if you are required to collect the readings yourself. Some instructors will want you to use only "academic" sources—material written by experts in the field.

Step 2—Review and Annotate the Readings

After you have assembled the readings that will serve as the basis of your synthesis, read through them several times with your assignment in mind. In most cases, you will look for specific information in each reading, passages that address the topic of your paper. Thoroughly annotate the reading and then summarize it. As you work with the material, remember to be fair and open-minded. Consider how the author's perspective on the topic is similar to or different from what other authors have written and decide whether you think it should be included in your essay.

Step 3—Formulate a Thesis and an Organizational Plan

Your thesis in an informative synthesis serves an important function. More likely than not, it will indicate the topic of your essay and indicate how you will structure your synthesis—what you will discuss and in what order you will discuss it. Always keep in mind the rhetorical function of your thesis statement. When people read your paper, they need to know early on what you will be discussing and will look to your thesis as a guide.

Your thesis for an informative synthesis can be either open or closed. In an open thesis you indicate the topic and general structure of your paper:

> Chan, Krimsky, and Selgelid offer a range of opinions on the ethics of human genetic enhancement.

or

> While both Chan and Selgelid support human genetic enhancement, Krimsky disagrees.

With a closed thesis you list the specific issues you will address in your essay. However, you have to be careful not to put too much information in your thesis—doing so will only lead to cluttered prose. A possible closed thesis statement for the paper described above might read something like this:

> Chan, Krimsky, and Selgelid offer a range of opinions on the ethics of human genetic enhancement, primarily focusing on how it might impact social stability and individual liberty.

Either type of thesis can be effective, but in general, the longer your paper will be, the more likely you are to use an open thesis.

When writing an informative synthesis, you can employ either a block or alternating format to organize your essay. With a **block format,** you discuss what one source says about the topic in relation to your thesis before moving on to what the next source says. However, instead of just summarizing each source text, you also compare and contrast them, pointing out their key similarities and differences. Suppose, for example, that you are writing an essay with the thesis, "Chan, Krimsky, and Selgelid offer a range of opinions on the ethics of human genetic enhancement." In outline form, your paper might look something like this:

Opening Section

> Introduce the topic of your essay
>
> Give your thesis

Section on Chan Essay

> Summarize Chan's position on the topic
>
> Discuss its relationship to the other two readings

Section on Krimsky Essay

> Summarize Krimsky's position on the topic
>
> Discuss its relationship to the other two readings

Section on Selgelid Essay

> Summarize Selgelid's position on the topic
>
> Discuss its relationship to the other two readings

Conclusion

You might, though, choose to use an **alternating format** to organize your essay, especially if you use a closed thesis. Remember that with a closed thesis, you list the specific issues you will address in your essay. Using an alternating format allows you to discuss what each source says about these specific issues in order. For example, suppose you are writing an essay with this thesis: "Chan, Krimsky, and Selgelid offer a range of opinions on the ethics of human genetic enhancement, primarily focusing on how it might impact social stability and individual liberty." Using an alternating format, your paper might be organized like this:

Opening Section

> Introduce the topic of your essay
>
> Give your thesis

Effect of Human Genetic Enhancement on Social Stability

> Chan's views and their relation to the other authors' views
>
> Krimsky's views and their relation to the other authors' views
>
> Selgelid's views and their relation to the other authors' views

Effect of Human Genetic Enhancement on Individual Liberty

Chan's views and their relation to the other authors' views

Krimsky's views and their relation to the other authors' views

Selgelid's views and their relation to the other authors' views

Conclusion

Of course, you could write the same paper using a block format. If you did, it might be organized like this:

Opening Section

Introduce the topic of your essay

Give your thesis

Chan Essay

Her views on how human genetic enhancement might impact social stability and how they are similar to and/or different from the views of the other authors on the topic

Her views on how human genetic enhancement might impact individual liberty and how they are similar to and/or different from the views of the other authors

Krimsky Essay

His views on how human genetic enhancement might impact social stability and how they are similar to and/or different from the views of the other authors on the topic

His views on how human genetic enhancement might impact individual liberty and how they are similar to and/or different from the views of the other authors

Selgelid Essay

His views on how human genetic enhancement might impact social stability and how they are similar to and/or different from the views of the other authors on the topic

His views on how human genetic enhancement might impact individual liberty and how they are similar to and/or different from the views of the other authors

Conclusion

Alternating and block formats have their particular strengths and weaknesses. The alternating format allows you to compare and contrast the views of different writers fairly easily. In this paper, for example, you would be able to present each author's position on how human genetic enhance-ment might impact social stability in its own section of your own essay before moving on to discuss its impact on individual liberty. If you were using a block format, you might discuss Chan's views on page one of your paper and might not get to Selgelid's views until page six or seven. Your reader might have a hard time remembering Chan's views by the time you reached Selgelid's views. Using a block format, however, allows you to give your readers a good sense of the general argument presented by each author in sequential order. Yet the block format often results in repetitive prose and frequently discourages students from discussing similarities and differences among the readings, simply summarizing each author's views instead.

Regardless of the structure you employ, your job in writing an informative synthesis involves more than summarizing what each critic has to say. In writ-ing this paper, you would not be arguing a position of your own concerning the effects of human genetic enhancement. Instead, you would point out for your readers important similarities and differences among the views advanced by the source texts' authors.

After you have designed your thesis, you need to go back through the read-ings, consult your annotations, and locate material you want to include in your essay. Preparing an informal outline can be quite helpful at this point. In your outline, indicate the focus for each part of your paper, the material you will draw from the readings to develop that section of the essay, and the ideas you will contribute.

Step 4—Write Your Rough Draft

The introductory section of an informative thesis should, first, capture your readers' interest. You might consider opening your paper with an interesting anecdote, a case history, an important statistic, or a telling quotation from one of the readings. Writing an effective opening gives you the chance to be imagi-native and creative. A second goal of the opening section of your synthesis is to introduce the topic of your essay. The title of the synthesis should give your readers some indication of your essay's topic, but you want to be sure to clarify the topic in your opening section. Finally, the introduction to your essay should contain your thesis statement. Whether your thesis is open or closed, you need to include it in your introduction to serve as a guide to the rest of your synthesis.

In the body of your essay, you will follow the structure supplied by your thesis, explaining ideas one author or issue at a time. If you were writing an informative synthesis using the three articles on human genetic enhancement as your source texts, in the body of your paper you would summarize, para-phrase, and quote what each author has to say about the topic, including in your essay material that best captures each writer's views and illustrates your thesis. However, not all the material in your informative synthesis will come from the readings. You have significant contributions to make, too. Besides quoting, paraphrasing, and summarizing what various authors have to say, you will contribute transitions, elaborations, clarifications, and connections.

For example, in one paragraph of your essay, you may introduce the issue to be discussed, introduce a reading by giving the author's name and qualifications as well as the title of the article, quote a relevant passage from the piece, restate the author's ideas in your own words to clarify them, point out how the author's stance differs from the author you discussed in the previous paragraph, and provide a transition to your next paragraph. If you devote a sentence to each of these tasks, your paragraph will be six sentences long, with only one sentence coming directly from the reading. The rest of the material in the paragraph comes from you.

When concluding your informative synthesis, you want to reiterate the main issues or findings you have covered in the body of your essay and give your work a sense of closure. You might want to look back at your opening strategy and reemploy it in your conclusion, if possible. For example, if you opened your paper with a quotation, consider ending it with a quotation. If you began with a question, conclude with the same question, perhaps answering it this time. If you began with a story, come back to the story in your conclusion.

Step 5—Revise Your Draft

Revising a synthesis takes time. In fact, it is probably best to revise your paper in several stages. Initially, you might check the **content** of your essay. Here you have two concerns. First, reread what you have written to make sure you are being true to your own intentions. You might ask the following questions of your manuscript:

- Does my thesis accurately reflect my understanding of the readings?
- Have I said in my paper what I wanted to say?
- Have I covered all of the material I hoped to cover when annotating the readings?
- Have I covered the ideas I discovered as I wrote the essay, ideas I did not plan on addressing but developed as I wrote?

A related goal is to review the content of your essay in light of the assignment. Here the questions you ask might include:

- Have I met the demands of the assignment?
- Have I adequately covered the ideas contained in the reading?
- Have I avoided editorializing or arguing a particular position?
- Have I kept my reader in mind? Would this essay make sense to someone who knows little or nothing about the readings? Do any ideas need more development or explanation?

Next, you might review the **organization** of your essay. Here you are concerned with the quality of your thesis statement, topic sentences, and transitions. These are some of the questions you should be asking:

- Does my thesis guide the development of the essay? Put another way, does my essay follow the format suggested or outlined by my thesis?
- Do I have clearly stated topic sentences introducing the major sections of my essay? Are these topic sentences tied to the thesis?
- Have I supplied enough transitional devices to guide my reader through my synthesis, especially when I move from discussing one author to discussing another?

Finally, revise with an eye toward **accuracy** and **clarity.** Here your concerns are word choice, sentence structure, and documentation. Again, you need to ask yourself a series of questions as you review your work, making needed changes when any of your answers are no:

- In choosing words, have I remained as fair and objective as possible?
- Have I successfully avoided jargon and highly technical terms when such language would not be appropriate for my audience?
- Are my sentences easy to read?
- Have I varied the type and length of my sentences?
- Have I quoted material accurately and properly?
- Have I paraphrased material accurately, properly, and fairly?
- Have I documented material thoroughly and properly?

You may need to revise your informative synthesis several times to address all of these concerns adequately.

Step 6—Check Quotations and Documentation

Before you turn in your final draft for a grade, be sure to check the accuracy of your quotations and documentation. Take the time to check any material you quoted against the source text to be sure you have accurately transcribed the information. Pay special attention to any passages in which you have added language to or taken language out of a quotation: these changes should not alter the meaning of the source text. Also, check to be sure that you have documented all of the material in your paper that needs to be documented and that you have employed the proper form of documentation in each instance. Remember that all paraphrased and quoted material in your paper should be documented. Because you are combining information from two or more sources in your synthesis, be sure it is always clear to your reader which source text you are referring to in your documentation.

SAMPLE INFORMATIVE SYNTHESIS

Following is a sample informative synthesis of the three articles on genetic enhancement provided earlier in this chapter. Notice how the writer structures the essay and employs material from the readings.

The Ethical Debate over Human Enhancement and Designer Babies

Advances in modern genetics have been astounding. What used to be dreamed of only in science fiction is becoming reality today. Scientists have discovered how to manipulate human genes to help eradicate disease and will soon be able to alter embryonic genes to enhance certain traits, such as a person's height, intelligence, or musical ability. All of these advances, however, raise serious ethical questions: Is it right to alter a person's genetic makeup? Are treatments to prevent disease more acceptable than those to enhance personal characteristics? Not surprisingly, scientists and philosophers addressing these questions have yet to reach consensus.

An important distinction in the debate is the difference between therapeutic and non-therapeutic genetic modification—whether the manipulation is undertaken to prevent disease or deformity (therapeutic) or whether its aim is to enhance certain desirable physical traits or abilities (non-therapeutic). Currently, when *in vitro* fertilization methods are used to have children, embryos can be tested for a range of genetic disorders or illnesses and parents can choose to implant only healthy embryos, a process known as genetic screening. To a growing degree, though, doctors are able to alter the genetic makeup of the embryo to correct the disorder or cure the illness prior to implantation—a process known as genetic therapy. Sarah Chan, a Research Fellow at the Institute for Science, Ethics, and Innovation at England's University of Manchester, argues that genetic therapy is a moral imperative: "If we could, with safety and certainly, engineer our children to have immunity to viral infection, protection from heart disease and reduced susceptibility to cancer, we should do so. . . . there would be a moral imperative to use it for the benefit of future generations" (187).

Michael Selgelid, a professor of human bioethics, generally agrees with at least part of Chan's argument. In "A Moderate Approach to Enhancement," Selgelid notes that current genetic screening enables parents to implant only healthy embryos, a process he also believes is morally acceptable: "Most people agree that using such procedures to reduce disease would be relatively non-problematic, at least if these procedures can be shown to be safe and effective" (194). Selgelid does not take up the issue of genetic therapy.

However, in his essay "On Designer Babies: Genetic Enhancement of Human Embryos Is Not a Practice for Civil Societies," Sheldon Krimsky does address the issue of genetic therapy and strongly disagrees with Chan. Krimsky argues that "the genetic modification of human reproductive cells prior to gestation in the womb" (192) is immoral because "there are safer and more dependable methods for preventing the birth of a child with a severe genetic abnormality" (192), namely, genetic selection.

The greatest disagreement among these authors concerns the question of non-therapeutic genetic enhancement. Selgelid summarizes what will soon be possible:

> As knowledge about the relationship between genes and human traits increases, we will be able to detect genetic sequences associated with a wide variety of positively desired characteristics too. Many parents might then want to select *for* traits such as increased height, intelligence, strength, beauty, and so on, with the aim of giving their children higher-quality lives. (194)

Selgelid then addresses a major objection to non-therapeutic genetic enhancement: the procedures might promote greater social inequality. Those with enough money to pay for enhancement will be greatly advantaged over those who cannot pay for them. If genetic enhancement becomes widespread and limited to the rich, equality and democracy may be threatened. As a result, the right to choose enhancement may need to be curtailed due to the adverse social consequences.

Krimsky unambiguously opposes non-therapeutic genetic modification, stating that the "pursuit of this goal represents the greatest scientific folly and moral failure" (192). First, Krimsky argues that even testing whether such genetic engineering can work is immoral: in a clinical trial, scientists would have to enhance some embryos and not others, then study the resulting children for the rest of their lives to determine whether the procedure worked and whether unforeseen negative consequences resulted. Society would not accept using children as lab rats in this way. Second, the characteristics parents may seek to enhance in their children are only moderately determined by genetics—attempting to make a child more musical through genetic manipulation, for example, fails to account for the environment the child is raised in, the child's exposure to music, the impact of teachers and peers, and so on. In addition, no single gene accounts for a particular human characteristic. According to Krimsky, "Even for height, one of the most heritable traits known, scientists have discovered at least 50 genes that can account for 2 to 3 percent of the variance in the sample" (193). Attempting to identify and alter all of the genes involved "makes no sense from a biological and developmental perspective" (193). Finally, Krimsky raises the same objection Selgelid noted: non-therapeutic gene therapy will favor the wealthy over the poor, promoting social inequality.

Chan, who supports non-therapeutic genetic enhancement, addresses many of the concerns Selgelid and Krimsky raise. First, Chan believes in the primary importance of people being able to lead good lives. Diseases inhibit one's ability to lead a good life; therefore, genetic therapy is acceptable: "to the extent that genes do determine some aspects of our lives, in particular our health and associated quality of life—it is surely far better to have a predisposition to a healthy life than to risk a higher chance of suffering and disease" (186).

Yet, leading a good life goes beyond just being free of illness. Human lives can actually be enhanced through genetic engineering—children can be made stronger, taller, faster, smarter, more beautiful, more musical, and so on (Chan 190; Krimsky 192; Selgelid 194). What's more, these traits will be passed along to future generations (Chan 186). In fact, Chan argues that genetically enhancing one's children would be an act of responsible parenting:

> . . . once the technology exists and has been proven to be safe, to refrain from using it is likewise to make a decision about the genetic inheritance of our descendants—specifically: that they will not receive such enhancements and will be denied the consequent benefits. . . . Abdicating choice is not the action of a responsible parent; exercising choice wisely is. (187)

In other words, as this technology becomes more widely available and safe, the question will become how parents choose to enhance their children genetically, not whether they will.

Chan largely discounts the social impact of genetic enhancement, believing that although at first the technology will be expensive, over time it will become available to all (190). She also maintains that once humans start to become enhanced, justice will dictate that everyone should have the opportunity to "level up" (190). In the conflict between individual liberty and social obligation that Selgelid discussed, Chan comes down firmly on the side of the individual. She states that all decisions about enhancement should be based on "individual choice" (189).

Human enhancement is already here: sports stars use steroids to get bigger and stronger, college student drink coffee to help them study, children get vaccinated, people with mental or physical illnesses take medications to improve the quality of their lives. Of course, these types of enhancements influence only the individual; they are not passed on to future generations through genetic manipulation. Together, Chan, Selgelid, and Krimsky offer a glimpse of the benefits genetic enhancement can offer but also raise serious ethical questions that at some point humans will have to answer.

Summary Chart

HOW TO WRITE AN INFORMATIVE SYNTHESIS

---

1. **Analyze the assignment.**
   - *Determine whether you are being asked to write an informative or argumentative synthesis.*
   - *Determine the number and types of readings you are expected to use in your paper.*

2. **Review and annotate the readings.**
   - *Review the readings with your assignment in mind, looking for and marking information related to the topic of your paper.*
   - *Briefly summarize each reading.*

3. **Formulate a thesis and organizational plan.**
   - *Determine what stance you will assume in your essay.*
   - *Determine whether you will use an open or closed thesis statement.*
   - *Decide how you will order the ideas you will develop in your essay.*
   - *Decide whether you will present your ideas using a block or alternating format.*

4. **Write your rough draft.**
   - *Follow the organization plan implied or stated by your thesis.*
   - *Summarize and combine (synthesize) material from the source texts to support your thesis.*
   - *Both paraphrase and quote material as necessary.*
   - *Add transitions, elaborations, clarifications, and connections where needed.*
   - *Include a concluding paragraph.*

SUMMARY CHART: HOW TO WRITE AN INFORMATIVE SYNTHESIS *(CONTINUED)*

---

5. **Revise your draft.**

   Revise to improve the content of your essay.
   - *Does your thesis accurately reflect your position and intention?*
   - *Have you communicated in your paper what you want to communicate?*
   - *Will your paper give your reader a thorough understanding of the source texts and your thesis?*
   - *Have you avoided editorializing in your paper?*
   - *Would your essay make sense to someone who has not read the source texts?*

   Revise to improve the organization of your essay.
   - *Does your thesis guide the development of your essay?*
   - *Do you provide topic sentences to introduce major sections of your essay?*
   - *Have you provided transitions that help lead your reader through your paper?*

   Revise to improve the accuracy and clarity of your essay.
   - *Have you used language that is as fair and impartial as possible?*
   - *Have you avoided jargon and overly technical language when they would not be appropriate?*
   - *Have you checked for sentence variety and clarity?*
   - *Have you proofread for spelling, punctuation, and usage errors?*

---

6. **Check your quotations and documentation.**
   - *Have you quoted and paraphrased material properly, accurately, and fairly?*
   - *Have you documented all the material that needs to be documented?*
   - *Have you documented material employing the proper format?*

INFORMATIVE SYNTHESIS REVISION CHECKLIST

	Yes	No
1. Have you checked your assignment to be sure you have written the proper kind of synthesis essay: informative or argumentative?	____	____
2. In your introduction do you:		
• introduce the topic of the paper?	____	____
• offer your thesis?	____	____
• capture your readers' interest?	____	____
3. Examine the wording of your thesis. Does it clearly indicate what stance you will assume in your essay?	____	____
4. Examine the structure of your essay. Does it follow the organizational plan indicated by your thesis?	____	____
5. Check each section in the body of your essay. Do you:		
• examine just one issue at a time?	____	____
• combine information from your source texts?	____	____
• explain the link between the examples you cite and the assertion you are making?	____	____
• make clear the relationship you see among your source texts?	____	____
6. Examine your transitions. Have you provided adequate signals to help guide your readers through your work?	____	____
7. The first time you introduce a source text, do you give the full title of the piece and the author's full name?	____	____
8. Have you properly documented all quoted, summarized, and paraphrased material?	____	____

INFORMATIVE SYNTHESIS REVISION CHECKLIST *(CONTINUED)*

	Yes	No
9. Have you reviewed your quotations for accuracy and variety?	——	——
10. Is your works cited or reference list correct?	——	——
11. Have you reviewed your essay to be sure the content accurately communicates your position and intention?	——	——
12. Have you reviewed your word choice for clarity and accuracy?	——	——

Chapter 11

ARGUMENTATIVE SYNTHESIS

In this chapter you will learn how to

1. Recognize the elements of argument and persuasion in readings
2. Compare readings in terms of the arguments they present
3. Develop and state an argumentative thesis
3. Employ material from readings to support an argument
4. Document multi-source argumentative essays

DEFINITION AND PURPOSE

In an argumentative synthesis, you use material from various readings to support and illustrate an argument of your own, usually concerning the quality of writing in the source texts or an issue they address. If your argument centers on the quality of the readings, you might argue that one text is better written or more convincing than the others. If, however, your teacher asks you to present an argument on the issue the readings address, you will draw on the material in the readings to support your thesis.

For a number of reasons, writing an argumentative synthesis can be challenging:

1. As with the informative synthesis, the sources you consult when gathering information for this type of essay can be difficult to read. They will often present complex arguments themselves or employ terminology or research methodologies new to you. Being able to read this material critically is essential if you hope to write a successful argumentative synthesis.
2. As you read these source texts, you will need to critique them. For example, if you are arguing that one is better written than another, you will have to critique both to determine the relative strengths and weaknesses of each. If you are using the readings to develop an argument of your own on the topic they address, again you will have to critique the source texts to determine the quality of the arguments and information in each. You want to base your argument on the best available material.

3. When you compose your argumentative synthesis, you have to be concerned, first, with the content and quality of *your* argument. You need to decide if the material you are including in your paper will achieve the desired effect on your reader—will your audience be convinced by your argument? At the same time, since you are working with source texts, you have to pay close attention to the way you are using other people's findings or arguments to be sure you are fairly representing their work.

4. Part of composing an argumentative synthesis is deciding how best to order the claims, evidence, findings, or arguments you present. You need to decide which ideas or arguments you will present in which order and to provide effective transitions between and within the major sections of your argument.

5. In supporting your argument with source material, you will need to quote, summarize, and paraphrase other people's ideas, arguments, and findings. As a result, documentation becomes a challenge. You will need to be explicit and clear in acknowledging the source of the information you use to support your assertions.

THE ELEMENTS OF ARGUMENT

As you develop, draft, and revise your argumentative synthesis, pay particular attention to the three basic elements of any argument: **claims**, **grounds**, and **warrants**. According to British philosopher Stephen Toulmin in *The Uses of Argument* (Cambridge University Press, 1958), every argument involves an assertion (claim) that is supported by evidence (grounds) and rests on a particular set of assumptions or line of reasoning (warrant). Effective arguments employ clear, limited claims; reliable, appropriate grounds; and fully developed, explicit warrants. Understanding each of these elements can help you compose more effective argumentative synthesis essays.

CLAIMS

A **claim** is an assertion that you want your readers to accept. In an argumentative synthesis essay, your thesis statement is a claim, one you will develop and support with other claims in the body of your essay. Suppose, for example, you are writing an argumentative synthesis using the articles on human genetic enhancement in Chapter 10 and decide on the following thesis: "Due to her analogies, examples, and reasoning, Chan's argument that human genetic enhancement is ethical proves more persuasive than Krimsky's argument that it is not ethical." Your thesis is a claim: Chan's argument is stronger than Krimsky's argument. You will support this assertion with three other claims or "because" statements: Chan's argument is stronger because she employs more effective analogies, better examples, and a clearer line of reasoning. In the body of your essay you will develop these three claims with valid grounds and warrants if you want readers to accept your thesis.

When you compose an essay from source texts, most of your claims will be based on what you read and can include:

- claims concerning the source text's topic;
- claims concerning the source text's content, organization, or style;
- claims concerning the quality of the source text's writing; and
- claims concerning your response or reaction to the source texts.

Your teacher may give you several readings to study or require you to collect material on your own outside of class. In either case, you will be expected to critique the readings, form an argumentative thesis or claim, and explain or defend that assertion in your essay.

Well-written claims are **accurate**, **clear**, and **limited**. Any claim you make about a reading should be accurate: you should not misrepresent what an author writes. Claims should also be clear and unambiguous. "There are several good things about Chan's argument" is not a clear claim. What does the writer mean by "good" or by "things"? When forming claims, be as specific as you can, using language that precisely captures the assertion you want to make. Also, avoid broad, unlimited claims because such assertions are usually inaccurate and difficult to support. Claims like "Chan's essay is the best piece of writing ever produced" or "There is absolutely no value at all to Chan's argument" are not sufficiently limited. In writing limited claims, you may find yourself using words like "most" instead of "all," "often" instead of "always," or "likely" instead of "certainly." Limited claims (including limited thesis statements) are easier to explain and defend than unlimited, sweeping claims.

GROUNDS

Grounds is another name for the evidence you use to support a claim. As with claims, when you compose a source-based argumentative synthesis essay, you will draw most of your grounds from readings, though many teachers will allow you to use relevant personal experience to support a claim as well. Source-based grounds can include facts, statistics, testimony, and opinions. Each type of evidence has its own strengths and limitations. When deciding how to employ each in support of a claim, consider the questions that follow. Remember: the quality of your essay often depends on the quality of the grounds you employ to support your claims. If you rely on weak, questionable, or irrelevant grounds to support your claims, your writing is unlikely to convince thoughtful readers.

Facts: information the author of the source text presents as verifiably true

- Is the information up to date?
- Does the information come from a reliable source?

- Is the information documented?
- Is the information clear and unambiguous in its meaning?
- Is the information relevant to the claim you are making?
- Is the information consistent with your understanding, knowledge, or experience?
- Is the information consistent with what other source texts contend?

Examples: illustrations drawn from the source text to support your claim

- Are the examples relevant to the claim you are making?
- How much background information do you need to provide so that your reader will understand the examples you incorporate from the source text?
- Are the examples true or fictional? Is either acceptable given your assignment?
- Do the examples come from a reliable source?
- Are the examples timely?
- Are the examples representative and typical or limited and unique?

Statistics: data the author of the source text employs to support his or her claims

- Do you understand the statistics, what they mean, and their limitations?
- Do the statistics come from a reliable, trustworthy source?
- What are the possible biases of the source text? How might those biases affect the statistics offered in the piece?
- How do the statistics compare with evidence found in other source texts?
- Does the author of the source text acknowledge the limitations of the statistics?
- Are the statistics relevant to the claim you are trying to support in your essay?
- Can you adequately explain the link between the statistics you cite and the claim you are supporting?

Testimony: personal experiences offered by the author of the source text in support of his or her claims

- Does the testimony come from a reliable, qualified source?
- Is the testimony firsthand or secondhand?
- How is the testimony relevant to the claim you are trying to support?
- What background information from the source text will you need to provide so that your reader will understand the meaning and nature of the testimony?
- Does the author of the source text acknowledge the limitations of the testimony?
- How does the testimony complement (or contradict) other grounds provided in the essay?

THE ELEMENTS OF ARGUMENT

Opinions: what the author of a source text believes to be true

- Is this the opinion of the source text's author or is the author offering someone else's opinion?
- Is the person sufficiently qualified to offer an opinion worth citing in your essay?
- How will you make clear in the body of your essay that this opinion comes from a reliable source?
- Does the author sufficiently explain and clarify his or her opinion?
- Does the author support that opinion with evidence?
- Is the opinion sufficiently qualified?
- Is the opinion supported by other types of evidence in the source text or by evidence you have gathered from other sources?

Whatever grounds you employ in your essay, be sure they are **relevant**, **reliable**, and **appropriate**. As you defend or illustrate a claim, first be sure the evidence you use is relevant to the assertion you are making. Writing an argumentative synthesis can be confusing because you are working with multiple texts and multiple claims. As you select the grounds you will use to support a particular claim, be sure they clearly relate to that claim and not to some other assertion you are making in your essay. Also, be sure the grounds are reliable—examine the credentials and possible biases of the source text's author, the publication's or website's credibility, and the date of publication. Finally, be sure your grounds are appropriate for the assignment and audience. As you write papers in classes across the curriculum, you will discover that what counts as valid grounds in one class may not count as valid grounds in another. Learning what grounds are appropriate for arguments in a field of study is part of learning how to reason like a member of that discipline. Analyze the texts you read in class to determine the kinds of evidence successful authors in that field of study utilize in their arguments and ask your instructor for help if you have doubts about the appropriateness of evidence you plan to use in any essay.

One final note about grounds: most writers know that they can support a claim in an argumentative synthesis essay by quoting, paraphrasing, or otherwise alluding to the work of authors who agree with the position they are advancing. Citing authorities who support the claims you make improves your work's credibility. However, there are other ways to use source material to support an argument. For example, consider citing authorities who *disagree* with the claim you are making. Incorporating counterexamples into your argumentative synthesis can be effective if you employ them correctly. First, acknowledging alternative positions increases your credibility as a writer. It demonstrates your knowledge of the subject matter, your fairness, and the confidence you have in your own position. However, citing counterexamples alone will not help you achieve these benefits; instead, you must integrate them into your essay by refuting them, conceding to them, or accommodating them.

When you **refute** counterexamples, you offer a fair summary of the opposing view, then demonstrate how that position is wrong, problematic, or otherwise flawed. You can then explain how your position is better. When you **concede** to an opposing view, you acknowledge how and when the opposition might be right in its assertions. However, you then demonstrate how that fact does not seriously damage your own position or thesis. Finally, when you **accommodate** an opposing view, you explain how that position and your own may be equally correct and how, by combining them, one might gain a better, more comprehensive understanding of the issue. In short, be imaginative in your use of source material as grounds in an argumentative synthesis. Just be sure the grounds you use are linked to your claims with strong warrants.

WARRANTS

Warrants are a little harder to understand than claims or grounds because they tend to be more abstract. Simply stated, though, a warrant is a line of reasoning, a set of assumptions, or an explanation that links a claim to its grounds. When writing an argumentative synthesis, remember that in most cases the grounds will not speak for themselves: you need to explain how they support the claim you are making. For instance, suppose you wrote the following passage, a claim supported by an example:

> Chan's argument is stronger than Krimsky's, in part, due to the analogies she employs to support and illustrate many of her claims. For example, she compares human genetic enhancement to the widely accepted practice of vaccinating children for diseases or providing children the best possible education after they are born.

Are you ready to move on to your next claim now? Have you sufficiently supported your claim by citing an example or two from the text? No. What's missing here is your warrant—before you move on to your next claim, you have to *explain how* the analogies you cite make Chan's argument more convincing than Krimsky's. What is it about citing statistics or citing *these* analogies that makes Chan's argument more convincing? Why might readers be more convinced by Chan's argument than the one put forth by Krimsky because Chan includes these analogies in her essay? As you explain the link between your assertion and the evidence you provide for it, you are articulating your warrant.

When you draft and revise your argumentative synthesis, you need to ask yourself a series of questions concerning the nature and effectiveness of your warrants.

1. **Is my warrant stated or unstated? If unstated, will the link between my claims and my grounds be sufficiently clear for my readers?**
   In everyday conversation, many warrants go unstated: the link between a claim and its grounds is so clear or so readily accepted that no warrant is needed. In academic writing, however, warrants usually need to be stated and explained. The aim of an academic argument is to let your reader know where you stand on an issue (your claim), to convince your reader

to accept this position as reasonable or correct by supporting it with evidence (your grounds), and to explain how this evidence makes the case for the claim (your warrant). Two writers may make the same assertion in their papers and may even support those assertions with similar evidence, but how they explain the link they see between the evidence and the claim will likely differ. In academic writing, warrants can help make your essay distinctive. Therefore, examine your essay for any unstated warrants and decide whether they need to be made explicit. If you think there is any chance your readers may question the link between a claim and its grounds, state your warrant.

2. **Is my warrant logical and reasonable?**
   How *do* the grounds you employ actually support your claim? What assumptions are you making about the link between your grounds and claims? Are you assuming that your readers will recognize and accept the connection you see between your claims and grounds? Is the connection you see between them logical and reasonable? Will your readers see the connection as logical and reasonable?

3. **Is my warrant clear, fully explained, and supported?**
   Underdeveloped warrants are a common problem with argumentative synthesis essays: writers, understanding that they need to state their warrants, simply fail to explain them adequately. Clear, well-developed warrants are crucial to successful arguments, especially if you believe your audience will question the validity of your claim or grounds. In these cases, you may need to explain your warrant at length, perhaps even acknowledging alternative readings of your grounds as you clarify your own interpretation. Determining whether your warrants are sufficiently explained and supported can be difficult, which is why you should have other people read and critique drafts of your writing. Specifically ask them to read your essay skeptically; to question the validity of your claims, grounds, and warrants; and to indicate any weaknesses they note or questions they have. Sometimes the warrants themselves rest on unstated assumptions that need to be explained and defended.

ARGUMENT AND PERSUASION

Rhetoricians often draw a distinction between argument and persuasion. Argument, they maintain, involves demonstrating the credibility of a position; persuasion involves moving readers to accept or act on that position. The most commonly acknowledged agents of persuasion are logos (logic), pathos (emotion), and ethos (character): writers can often persuade readers to accept or act on an argument by appealing to the readers' logic or emotions or by sufficiently establishing their own credibility or character (see Chapter 8 for a further discussion of logos, pathos, and ethos).

APPEALS BASED ON REASON

In an argumentative synthesis, successful appeals to **logos** largely depend on the quality of your claims, grounds, and warrants. Clear, qualified claims supported by valid grounds and clear, reasonable warrants will go a long way toward persuading a reader that your position is reasonable enough to accept and act on. Such writing, however, rarely happens by accident. It results from careful, critical drafting and revision. Here are a few steps you can take to improve the logical appeal of your argumentative synthesis essay:

1. **Make clear, limited claims.**
   Be sure all of your claims are clear, reasonable, and limited. Vague claims will not be convincing and neither will unreasonable assertions or sweeping generalizations. The claims you make—including your thesis—form the framework around which you will build your argumentative synthesis. If your claims are unclear, unreasonable, or unconnected to one another, the logical appeal of your essay will be diminished.

2. **Employ grounds that are relevant, credible, and timely.**
   As you decide what evidence or examples to offer in support of a claim, choose the material that is most relevant to your assertion. First, avoid using grounds that are only tangentially related to your claim. Second, be sure the grounds you employ come from credible sources. If you use reliable sources in your essay, readers are more likely to see your assertions as reasonable. Basing your paper on material drawn from questionable sources will bring into question the legitimacy of your own assertions. Finally, be sure the material you use in your paper is timely. As a rule, draw on the most recent research you can find when writing your paper—employing out-of-date source texts may hamper your efforts to sway readers' opinions.

3. **Explain your reasoning process.**
   One of the best ways to improve the logical appeal of your essay is to explain your reasoning process on the page. Lay bare for your readers the reasoning process that led you to your conclusions: elaborate on the meaning of your claims, explain connections among your assertions, explore alternative arguments, and discuss the links you see between your claims and their grounds. Most academic audiences will expect to find this type of discussion and explanation in your essay.

APPEALS BASED ON EMOTION

Successful persuasive appeals to **pathos** can be difficult to achieve but can also be very effective. Employing pathos to persuade readers is tricky because it can have the opposite effect if used incorrectly or clumsily. Pathos can quickly turn into bathos, or unintentionally comic appeals to emotion. However, when used sparingly and appropriately, emotionally charged grounds or language can prove very persuasive. Here are a few suggestions on how to employ pathos effectively in an argumentative synthesis essay.

1. **Include in your essay material that might appeal to your readers' interests.**

   Although it is often difficult to know with any degree of certainty what material might appeal to your readers' interests, it may be possible to make some educated guesses. For example, what might interest them given their economic, political, educational, or religious backgrounds? What can you assume they know or may want to know about the topic of your essay? What aspects of the topic interest you? How similar are you to your audience—can you assume they might have similar interests? Though it is very difficult to make completely accurate assessments of what material might interest your readers, the closer you come to hitting the mark, the more likely you are to obtain a positive emotional response to your writing.

2. **Include in your essay material that might appeal to your readers' needs or fears.**

   As you consider what material to include in your argumentative synthesis, can you identify examples, arguments, testimonials, statistics, or other material that might appeal to your readers' needs or address their concerns? Your goal is not to play on your readers' emotions. Instead, you want to connect emotionally with readers, to construct a bridge between your essay and reader needs or concerns, thus helping them see the relevancy of your essay to their lives. Is there material, for example, that might appeal to your readers' concerns about their physical, psychological, or financial safety; need for self-affirmation; or desires for joy or happiness? Successfully employing this type of material in your argumentative synthesis greatly increases the chances that readers will find your essay persuasive.

3. **Employ language that is evocative or captivating.**

   Another way to improve the emotional appeal of your argumentative synthesis is to use especially evocative or captivating language. Words have both denotative (literal) and connotative (emotional) meanings. You will often face instances when you can choose among words that have roughly the same denotative meaning but vary widely in their connotative implications. In these cases, consider using language that more effectively appeals to your reader's emotions. Also consider your use of figurative language. Although most academic writers employ extended metaphors sparingly, the use of analogies, allusions, and other figurative language is more common. Your goal is not to produce flowery prose. Instead, your aim is to employ language that persuades readers to accept or act on your arguments by developing in them an emotional understanding of your topic.

APPEALS BASED ON CHARACTER AND CREDIBILITY

In one sense, **ethos** is closely linked to logos because it has to do with the credibility of the claims, grounds, and warrants that you employ in your essay. Ethos involves trust and character: do you demonstrate through the quality of the claims, grounds, and warrants you employ in your writing that you are a trustworthy, knowledgeable, fair-minded individual? If you do, then you may persuade some readers to accept your position through your own ethos as a writer. Ethos, though, also has to do with the quality of your own prose. Even if you compose a synthesis with strong claims, grounds, and warrants, you will lose credibility if your prose is marred by misspellings, grammatical problems, typos, or other surface errors. Readers may feel that they cannot trust authors who are careless with their writing; if an author is so sloppy with word choice, syntax, spelling, or punctuation, how sloppy has the author been with his or her research, reasoning, and documentation? Persuasion depends on trust, and you may lose the trust of your readers—and your credibility as a writer—if your writing is full of easily correctable errors. Here are a few steps you can take to improve ethos in your argumentative synthesis:

1. **Present informed, balanced arguments.**

   You will enhance your credibility as a writer if you present a balanced argument in your essay, examining the strengths and weaknesses of your assertions and exploring alternative points of view. Presenting a balanced argument requires you to research and consider a range of perspectives on your essay's topic. Examining this range of perspectives in your essay increases the likelihood of readers seeing you as a knowledgeable, fair-minded writer, and readers are more likely to consider and perhaps adopt arguments presented by writers they perceive as informed and fair.

2. **Demonstrate the credibility of your source texts.**

   Another way to enhance your ethos is by demonstrating the credibility of the source texts you use in your essay. Readers are more likely to accept or act on your arguments if they perceive that your claims are supported by authoritative sources. In-text documentation is one way to demonstrate that your arguments are supported by credible sources. You can also establish the authority of your source texts by including in your essay the full name of the person who wrote the text and a summary of his or her credentials when you first quote or paraphrase material from him or her.

3. **Employ fair, balanced language.**

   Just as you want the content of your argumentative synthesis to be fair and balanced, you also want to avoid language that might make you appear narrow-minded or uninformed. Although on occasion you will want to employ emotionally evocative language (see the discussion of pathos earlier in this chapter), consistently employing words that make you sound shrill, sarcastic, or hostile will usually hinder your efforts to persuade readers to consider or accept your arguments, especially if you are addressing a neutral or possibly antagonistic audience. In these cases, you might be better served using language that is more judicious and fair.

4. **Proofread your work carefully.**

   Finally, remember that the quality of your own prose influences whether your readers perceive you as a credible authority. Argumentative synthesis essays that are full of surface-level errors are unlikely to persuade many readers. Rightly or wrongly, most readers will judge the quality of your argument by the quality of your prose: in their minds, error-laden writing is likely to reflect error-laden thinking. You can help ensure that your writing is persuasive simply by proofreading your essay thoroughly before you submit your final draft for review.

WRITING AN ARGUMENTATIVE SYNTHESIS

Because argumentative syntheses are so complex, writing them in a number of steps or stages is often helpful. Here are some of the steps you might consider following when writing an argumentative synthesis:

1. Analyze the assignment.
2. Annotate and critique the readings.
3. Formulate a thesis.
4. Choose an organizational plan.
5. Write your rough draft.
6. Revise your draft.
7. Check quotations and documentation.

STEP 1—ANALYZE THE ASSIGNMENT

Some teachers will not specify the type of argument they want you to present in your synthesis. If this is the case, you will need to decide for yourself whether you want to focus on the quality of the writing in the readings or on the issue they address. However, if a teacher specifically asks you to focus your argument on the quality of the source texts, his assignment might include directions such as these:

> Review the readings in Chapter 6 of the textbook. Which author do you believe presents the most convincing case? Why?

* * * * *

> Review the readings in Chapter 6 of the textbook. Which piece is better written? How so?

In the first assignment, the teacher wants you to analyze, evaluate, then compare the **arguments** presented by the various writers, arguing that one presents the best case. In the second assignment, the teacher wants you to analyze, evaluate, then compare the **styles** of the various writers, arguing that one produces the best-written text.

However, when a teacher wants you to take a stand on the topic the readings address, her directions may read something like this:

> Review the readings in Chapter 6 of the textbook. Where do you stand on the issue? Present an argument in favor of your position using the readings for support.

Here the teacher wants you to read the articles, think about the arguments presented by each author, reflect on your own knowledge and feelings concerning the topic, and then present an argument in which you assume and defend a position of your own on the issue.

After you have determined the type of argument the teacher wants you to write, check the assignment to determine the number and types of sources the teacher wants you to use in your paper. Sometimes instructors specify a certain number of readings you must use in your paper, asking you, for example, to base your paper on four to six sources. Other times teachers specify the types of readings you have to use: those provided in class, those you find on your own in the library, academic sources only, and so on. If you have any questions about the number or type of readings you need to use in your synthesis, be sure to check with your instructor.

STEP 2—ANNOTATE AND CRITIQUE THE READINGS

As you begin to collect the readings you plan to use when writing your argumentative synthesis, you need to annotate and critique them (see Chapter 7 for advice on critiquing readings). First, annotate each reading, identifying its thesis, primary assertions, and evidence. Next, analyze and critique the content and structure of each reading. If you base your argument on other authors' faulty writing or reasoning, your essay will likely reflect their weaknesses; likewise, if you base your argument on solid, well-written sources, your argument will likely be stronger. The questions you want to ask of a reading include:

- What, exactly, is the main point of this reading?
- How has the author supported his ideas, arguments, or findings?
- How well has the author explained or supported his ideas, arguments, or findings?
- Do I find the reading convincing? Why or why not?
- How have the structure and tone of the piece influenced my reaction?
- What is the quality of the writing?
- How do the author's ideas, arguments, or findings compare with those found in the other sources I have read?

Place your annotations in the margins of the reading, on sheets of paper, or on index cards. If you use paper or index cards, be sure you copy all the bibliographic information you will need to complete a reference list entry on the source, in case you use any of that material in your paper.

In an argumentative synthesis, all quoted, paraphrased, or summarized material needs to be documented.

STEP 3—FORMULATE A THESIS

Formulating a clear thesis statement is an essential step in writing a successful argumentative synthesis. Your thesis statement tells your readers the position you plan to advance in your paper and will likely indicate the structure of your essay. Put another way, your thesis statement establishes in your readers' minds certain expectations concerning the content and form of your paper. When you satisfy those expectations, your readers will have an easier time following your argument; if you do not, however, readers may feel your work is confusing and disorganized. So you need to spend some time forming and refining your thesis statement.

In an argumentative synthesis you advance a position of your own concerning the quality and/or topic of the readings. If you are focusing on the quality of the readings themselves, you can assume a number of different positions. For example, suppose you are writing an argumentative synthesis using the readings on genetic human enhancement in Chapter 10. You may argue that one essay is more convincing than another:

> While both Chan and Selgelid argue that human genetic enhancement is ethical, Chan offers the more persuasive argument.

Or you may argue that one work is better written than another:

> While both Chan and Selgelid argue that human genetic enhancement is ethical, Chan's essay is more clearly written.

In either case, the thesis sets out the position you will be developing in your paper.

As with other types of essays, thesis statements for argumentative syntheses can be either open or closed. Although both of the examples above are open thesis statements, they could easily be modified to give the reader a better indication of what exactly will be covered in the paper:

> While both Chan and Selgelid argue that human genetic enhancement is ethical, Chan offers the more persuasive argument through her use of analogies and compelling examples.

* * * * *

> While both Chan and Selgelid argue that human genetic enhancement is ethical, Chan's essay is more clearly written because she avoids unnecessary jargon and employs a more casual style of writing.

If, however, your goal in composing an argumentative synthesis is to assert a position of your own on the topic of the readings, your thesis will read a little differently, something like this (employing an open thesis):

> Although philosophers and scientists offer varying assessments and positions, human genetic enhancement is ethical.

Or perhaps this (employing a closed thesis):

> Although philosophers and scientists offer varying assessments and positions, human genetic enhancement is ethical because it helps to prevent disabilities, secures individual liberty, and promotes the general welfare of society.

STEP 4—CHOOSE AN ORGANIZATIONAL PLAN

If you use a **block format** to organize your essay, you would critique in turn what each author has to say about the topic, and then advance your own position. Suppose you were working with this thesis: "Although philosophers and scientists offer varying assessments and positions, human genetic enhancement is ethical because it helps to prevent disabilities, secures individual liberty, and promotes the general welfare of society." In outline form, your paper might look like this:

Argumentative Synthesis—Block Format

Opening Section

Capture reader interest

Introduce the topic

Give your thesis

Discussion of Chan Article

Introduce the article—title, author, publication information

Summarize the article—Chan's argument

Critique the article—strengths and weaknesses of her argument

Tie criticisms to specific passages in the article

Fully explain or defend your criticism

Draw links with other source texts

Discussion of Krimsky Article

Introduce the article—title, author, publication information

Summarize the article—Krimsky's argument

Critique the article—strengths and weaknesses of his argument

Tie criticisms to specific passages in the article

Fully explain or defend your criticism

Draw links with other source texts

Discussion of Selgelid Article

Introduce the article—title, author, publication information

Summarize the article—Selgelid's argument

Critique the article—strengths and weaknesses of his argument

    Tie criticisms to specific passages in the article

    Fully explain or defend your criticism

    Draw links with other source texts

Your Argument Concerning the Ethics of Human Genetic Enhancement

How human genetic enhancement helps to prevent disabilities

    Tie arguments to specific examples from the articles

    Fully explain and defend your assertions

    Refer back to other authors' opinions to bolster your position

How human genetic enhancement secures individual liberty

    Tie arguments to specific examples from the articles

    Fully explain and defend your assertions

    Refer back to other authors' opinions to bolster your position

How human genetic enhancement promotes the general welfare of society

    Tie arguments to specific examples from the articles

    Fully explain and defend your assertions

    Refer back to other authors' opinions to bolster your position

Conclusion

In the opening section of your paper, you would introduce the topic of your essay, capture reader interest, and offer your thesis. In the body of your paper, you would critique the arguments offered by each of your source texts, focusing your attention on what they have to say about the ethics of human genetic enhancement. Finally, you would present your own argument, supporting your position with specific references to the source texts to help support or explain your thesis.

If you prefer, you could organize the paper using an **alternating format**, structuring your essay around the aspects of the topic you have chosen as your focus rather than each source text. In this case, your paper might be organized like this:

Argumentative Synthesis—Alternating Format

Opening Section

Capture reader interest

Introduce the topic

Give your thesis

Discuss how human genetic enhancement prevents disabilities

Explain your assertion

Support your argument with convincing grounds, including material from the source texts

Explain how your position differs from the positions presented in the source texts

Discuss how human genetic enhancement secures individual liberty

Explain your assertion

Support your argument with convincing grounds, including material from the source texts

Explain how your position differs from the positions presented in the source texts

Discuss how human genetic enhancement promotes the general welfare of society

Explain your assertion

Support your argument with convincing grounds, including material from the source texts

Explain how your position differs from the positions presented in the source texts

Conclusion

In the opening of your paper, you would again introduce the topic of your essay, capture reader interest, and state your thesis. In the body of your essay, you would argue, in order, that human genetic enhancement helps to prevent disabilities, secures individual liberty, and promotes the general welfare of society. In developing your argument, you would explain your claims or assertions, support them with grounds (e.g., evidence, examples, reasons) and include material from the source texts when appropriate, and discuss how your position differs from the ones presented in those texts.

After you have drafted at least a preliminary thesis for your paper and have some sense of the assertions that will serve as the focus of your synthesis, you will need to return to the readings to locate material to include in your essay. Remember that the focus of an argumentative synthesis should be the argument you are advancing, not the material from the readings. In other words, your first responsibility is to develop a sound argument; the source material serves to illustrate or support *your* assertions.

Step 5—Write Your Rough Draft

When you feel you are ready to begin writing your rough draft, be sure you have in front of you all of your source texts and notes. Some students like to begin writing immediately—they need to see some of their ideas in writing before they can decide on a final thesis or organize their paper. Other students have to begin with a clear thesis and outline in hand. Follow the method of composing that is most comfortable and successful for you.

When writing your essay, you will support your argument with material from the readings. You can use source material to give your readers background information on the topic (quote or paraphrase material you think your reader needs to know to understand your argument), to support your assertions (quote or paraphrase material that substantiates or illustrates your claims), or to acknowledge opposing views (quote or paraphrase material that calls into question your assertions; you then must decide whether to refute, accommodate, or concede to these different perspectives).

Step 6—Revise Your Draft

Revising your argumentative synthesis to make it ready for others to read is a time-consuming process again best approached in a series of steps. First, revise to improve the **content** of your paper, focusing on the quality and clarity of the argument you are advancing. Here are some questions you might ask about your draft as you revise to improve its content:

- Have I clearly indicated the point I want to prove?
- Have I clearly indicated the reasons I believe others should accept my position?
- Have I supported each of those reasons with expert testimony, statistics, or some other means of support as well as with clear explanations?
- Have I acknowledged opposing views in my paper when necessary? Have I found ways of refuting, accommodating, or conceding to them?

Next, review the **organization** of your essay, asking these questions:

- Is the thesis statement clearly worded, and does it control the structure of the essay?
- Have I provided clear transitions between the major sections of my essay?
- Are there clear connections between the material I draw from the readings and my own elaborations and explanations?

Finally, when checking the **accuracy** and **clarity** of your work, ask yourself:

- Have I chosen words that are clear yet contribute to the effect I wanted to elicit from my readers?
- Are my sentences clearly structured with adequate variety?
- Have I quoted and paraphrased material accurately and properly?

- When incorporating quoted or paraphrased material in my synthesis, have I supplied enough background information on the source text so the material makes sense to my readers?
- Have I defined all the terms I need to define?
- Have I documented all the material that needs to be documented?

STEP 7—CHECK QUOTATIONS AND DOCUMENTATION

Before you turn in your final draft for a grade, set aside time to check the accuracy of your quotations and documentation. First, make sure that you have quoted material accurately by comparing your text against the source text. Second, be sure that you have documented all of the material in your paper that needs to be documented, including all paraphrased information. Because you are combining information from several source texts in your synthesis and presenting your own argument as well, be sure your readers can always tell through your documentation the source of the material you include in your paper.

SAMPLE ARGUMENTATIVE SYNTHESIS

Following is an argumentative synthesis essay drawing on the readings found in Chapter 10. As you read the essay, consider how it is structured, how it uses material from the source texts, and how the writer develops the paper's argument.

MAKE HUMAN ENHANCEMENT AVAILABLE TO ALL

Thanks to groundbreaking work in genetics, the definition of what it means to be human has come into question. As the twenty-first century unfolds, scientists will gain a better understanding of and ability to manipulate the genes that dictate not only our height and weight, the color of our eyes and hair, but also our sex, our susceptibility to certain diseases, and perhaps even our intelligence and emotional disposition. Genetic research has undoubtedly improved the lives of countless people by helping them avoid disease and birth defects, but the next stage of research is more troubling. Genetic engineering makes human enhancement possible, real, and affordable. Parents may soon be able to "design" their future children—manipulating their children's genes to insure they grow up to be strong or smart, tall or musical, assertive or beautiful. These advances have the potential to improve the human condition, but they raise serious ethical questions that must be addressed before the technology is made available to everyone.

The current debate over human enhancement centers around embryonic genetic manipulation and involves only children born through *in vitro* fertilization (IVF). With IVF, numerous embryos are created and several implanted in the mother's uterus. Currently, these embryos can undergo genetic testing before implantation to determine if any of them have genetic abnormalities that could lead to conditions like Down syndrome or to diseases like cancer. Parents can choose to have implanted only those embryos shown to have no genetic problems. This process is termed "genetic screening" and is widely employed (Krimsky 192).

Scientists will soon have the ability to take this process one step further and perfect genetic engineering. With genetic engineering, scientists change the genetic makeup of an embryo prior to implantation to help insure that the resulting child possesses certain physical characteristics (such as height), skills (such as music ability), or dispositions (such as patience), all according to the parents' wishes. As scientists discover which genes control which characteristics, they can modify them prior to implantation. Michael Selgelid, Director of the Centre for Human Bioethics at Monash University, puts it this way:

> As knowledge about the relationship between genes and human traits increases, we will be able to detect genetic sequences associated with a wide variety of positively desired characteristics . . . Many parents might then want to select *for* traits such as increased height, intelligence, strength, beauty, and so on, with the aim of giving their children higher-quality lives. The limits would depend on the extent to which a genetic basis for such traits is eventually demonstrated by genetic science. (194)

Non-therapeutic genetic enhancement—or the creation of "designer babies"—is controversial. It raises some serious ethical concerns that need to be addressed. However, it can also greatly enhance human potential and happiness and must be made available to everyone, not just a select few.

Some argue that embryonic enhancement techniques should never be employed because they interfere with nature: human reproduction should not be tampered with, and parents must love and accept their children no matter what problems or limitations accompany them at birth. In "Humanity 2.0? Enhancement, Evolution and the Possible Futures of Humanity," Professor Sarah Chan offers a different perspective. She acknowledges that genetic engineering technologies challenge natural selection and current conceptions of human evolution. However, in the past, evolution "operated somewhat in the dark" (189) but can be guided by reason. Science, not random luck, can guide the genetic fate of children: "in comparison to natural evolution, any genetic modifications aimed at improving the human condition will at least be evidence-based rather than random . . . " (189).

Sheldon Krimsky, Lenore Stern Professor of Humanities and Social Sciences at Tufts University, believes that genetic enhancement is never morally acceptable. In fact, he believes that the "pursuit of this goal represents the greatest scientific folly and moral failure" (192). Krimsky argues that holding clinical tests of human enhancement technologies are inherently immoral—some embryos must be altered and others not and the results tracked over time. In such a case, the children are laboratory rats bred to serve scientific investigation, fundamentally demeaning their humanity. In his view, human enhancement should take place after the embryo is implanted and take the form of proper nutrition, protection from harm, and moral education following birth.

Krimsky's arguments are logical—clinical testing as he describes it raises serious moral questions—but that is not, in fact, how the technology is progressing. Krimsky is arguing against a procedure that is not being employed and likely will not be. Instead, as genetic engineering becomes increasingly common, no clinical trials will be run—the technology will simply be used, for better or worse.

More serious objections to genetic engineering focus on its societal implications. First, these therapies are expensive. The wealthy in any society are more likely to have access to this type of medical care than are the poor—rich people will be able to enhance their children's lives in ways the poor simply cannot. As Michael Selgelid explains in "A Modest Approach to Enhancement," genetic therapy could lead to "increased social inequality" (195) because the "enhanced richfolk will then have even greater competitive advantages than previously" (195). The rich could afford treatments to help ensure that their children are stronger, smarter, and more competitive than children born without such enhancements, giving them even greater social advantages beyond the wealth they will inherit. If there is not equal access to these therapies, then their use cannot be just, yet it is hard to imagine how universal health care plans will pay for treatments like these when these plans have a hard time covering basic health needs.

Arguments over the ethics of genetic engineering may come down to the balance between society's needs and individual liberty. Selgelid argues that unequal access to these treatments could lead to social instability and even threaten democracy (196) if a wide gulf develops between the genetic haves and the genetic have-nots. As Krimsky notes, genetic engineering "will inevitably be used by those with wealth and power to make others believe that to be prenatally genetically modified makes you better" (193).

Yet social concerns need to be balanced by respect for individual liberty: "The key unresolved philosophical questions concern how the value of personal liberty should be weighed against social equality and welfare in cases where these values conflict" (Selgelid 197). Individual liberty would dictate that people have the right to make decisions concerning their genetic makeup or that of their children. Society ought not interfere with a person's desire to ensure that his or her children are free of genetic abnormalities and possess traits that will help them be happy and successful. For Sarah Chan, the ultimate questions surrounding genetic engineering involve matters of individual choice: "What makes us uniquely human is the ability to shape our destinies according to our desires—and genetic and other enhancement technologies provide further means for us to do so" (190). For Michael Selgelid, the ultimate question genetic engineering must face is this: "How socially damaging would enhancement need to be in order for personal liberty to be justly overridden" (197).

To override personal liberty, the social damage caused by genetic engineering would have to be substantial and real, not just theoretical. Scientists know with growing certainty that genetic engineering can enhance the quality of human life; ethicists can only speculate about possible negative social consequences. Yet this type of philosophical questioning is valuable. Knowing what social consequences might arise from genetic engineering increases the chances that they can be avoided.

Another objection to genetic engineering seems more well founded—the procedures will be expensive and will, initially, be limited to those who can afford them. However, there is every reason to believe that in terms of cost and availability, genetic engineering will follow the same path as other scientific breakthroughs like laser eye surgery or cardiac stents. Initially medical treatments like these are rare and expensive, but over time they become more accessible and affordable. Genetic engineering procedures will undergo the same transformation. "Allowing access to expensive technologies to those who can afford them will, in all likelihood, speed their development to become more readily available to everyone" (Chan 190).

If genetic engineering has the potential to improve human health and well-being, protect people from disease, and improve the general welfare of society by producing more intelligent and more caring children, then policies must be implemented to make it available to everyone. Reserving this technology for only those who can afford it is unjust, unethical, and, as Selgelid argues, could have devastating social consequences. The technologies of human enhancement must be available to all humans and likely will be over time.

Additional Readings

A New Definition of Leadership

Josh Misner

Josh Misner holds a doctorate degree in communication and leadership studies.

Sheryl Sandberg, the chief operating officer of Facebook, recently proposed that we ban the word "bossy." Her reasoning?

> When a little boy asserts himself, he's called a "leader." Yet when a little girl does the same, she risks being branded "bossy." Words like bossy send a message: don't raise your hand or speak up. By middle school, girls are less interested in leading than boys—a trend that continues into adulthood.

A little over a month ago, I posted a quote from Sandberg on my website's Facebook page: "I want every little girl who is told she is bossy to be told she has leadership skills." The post ignited a firestorm of commentary. However, my reasoning behind the post was for my daughters. I want them to grow up in a world that values their leadership skills, especially considering the level of time and effort I am investing in teaching them these skills. As a professor whose doctorate is in leadership studies, it was only a matter of time before I waded into the issue.

In the four weeks that followed my post, and Sandberg's movement to ban the word, the media backlash has been stunning. Most of this backlash states the same thing: that we should call out bossiness for what it is, and leadership for what it is.

I, for one, agree—with BOTH!

In a day and age when we are mostly told to pick a side and that we have to lean one way or another, I propose a new definition of leadership, but one that clearly takes the best of both worlds, without compromising each other.

Let me begin with Sandberg's ideas. She wants to break down the barriers preventing women from having leadership roles, as well as pave the way for women leaders of tomorrow, and rightfully so.

According to catalyst.org, women comprise slightly less than 15 percent of the executive leadership of the Fortune 500, a number that has become stagnant and unchanging over the last four years. Women hold a mere 17 percent of the seats in both houses of Congress. Throughout the U.S., men continue to hold 82 percent of leadership positions, across all sectors.

This is the world in which we live, men and women alike, and it is the world from which Sandberg writes. There is clearly a problem somewhere, and I don't fault Sandberg one bit for trying to do something about it.

Perhaps she's right, at least, to an extent. She cites research that states, between elementary school and high school, girls' self-esteem drops an average of 3.5 times more than boys' self-esteem. Being the father of one teenage girl and one preteen girl, I can vouch for this, on a gut level. Is it because young girls are taught that being assertive is "bossy" or inappropriate behavior for a young lady? When we take a look at the b-word that "bossy" is eventually replaced with once girls become women, we can intuitively see this phenomenon for ourselves being evident in b-words that are both used for the same purpose.

However, we also need to look at the other side of the argument.

There are times when bossy means bossy, whether for a boy or a girl. There are certainly times when authoritative crosses the line into authoritarian, and a child, regardless of gender, needs to be taught the art of leadership. Looking deeper into this point, we can see that "banning bossy" could create myriad problems for future generations.

This is where I propose a new conception of leadership.

The English language, as most of us know, borrows words from many other cultures, and from these cultures, there are many choices we could use to describe leadership. We could use the French "*chief,*" meaning the ruler or head of something. We could use the Dutch "*baas,*" meaning master. We could use the Italian "*maneggiare,*" meaning to control.

But we don't.

Instead, we use the Old English word "*leader,*" which is derived from "*laedan,*" meaning to guide.

Why guide? Deep down in our hearts, we know that to lead **is** to guide, which implies a symbiotic, side-by-side, mutual relationship in which leader and follower benefit equally.

To equate qualities like "bossiness" or assertiveness with being the hallmark of great leaders is a categorical mistake, and this is where I think Sandberg gets it wrong. If a boy or a girl is acting in accordance with words like chief, boss or manager, trying to suppress others' opinions and make decisions in a vacuum, decisions that affect everyone without their input— a.k.a. being bossy—then they should be corrected.

After all, do we want to raise a future generation of managers by allowing such behavior to continue unchecked? Or, would we rather raise a generation of leaders by teaching them to know the difference?

Sandberg's heart is in the right place, and although her critics are now trying to silence her, what they need to realize is the value in what she is trying to accomplish. To raise up a generation of leaders, we cannot continue defining leadership solely from a traditionally male perspective. We need to embrace a new definition of leadership that combines the best of all possible worlds.

Traditionally, an annual performance review at any given U.S. organization will assess an employee based on some or all of the following criteria: *Activities, tasks, objectives, goals, initiative, time and stress management, etc.*

These criteria are what we consider to be task-oriented, and are easily quantified, which coincides with the positivist movement of the Industrial Revolution. This movement was sparked by thinkers such as Max Weber and Henri Fayol, people who saw humans as cogs in a machine and eventually started treating them as such. This movement was responsible for much of the stark, emotionless landscape of the American workplace that existed for many generations beyond the industrial era.

These criteria are also inherently associated with masculinity, which should come as no surprise, because when the idea of performance reviews first emerged, the workplace was dominated by men, so the measure of success was set up by men, for men. As women began flooding the workplace, these women quickly learned that what would help them succeed was to reprogram themselves to live up to inherently male standards.

This was a benign practice five decades ago, but today, with more than half of our workforce comprised of women, it is profoundly wrong.

Leadership for tomorrow must be infused with a new set of qualities—qualities that are traditionally associated with the feminine, and are often too abstract to be measured. These qualities include:

- **Empathy**—The ability to become aware of the thoughts, opinions and feelings of others, as well as to be able to identify with them.
- **Vulnerability**—The ability to remain accountable, accurately assess one's limits and seek out help when needed.
- **Humility**—The drive to serve others through leadership and to offer up credit to others when credit is due.
- **Work-Life Balance**—While giving one's life to work was once admirable, today we know that maintaining a solid work-life balance is critical to mental and emotional well-being.
- **Inclusiveness**—The desire to gain others' perspectives and to make decisions based on the good of the group, rather than the individual alone.
- **Patience**—The greatest leaders do not need it all, nor do they need it now. They are visionary and willing to invest time and energy to achieve a long-term set of goals.

Unlike the assessment criteria for leaders from last century, these are not easily quantified. There are no reliable assessments to assign numerical values to these qualities, so how can we recognize when somebody exhibits leadership as defined by this new perspective?

The answer to this is simple. We need not quantify everything. For the quantifiable, traditionally masculine characteristics of leadership, let's run a report and assess it.

But that must not be the end of the leader's assessment.

For the abstract, relationally based characteristics of leadership that we need to promote as beneficial, let us be more observant and take note. While these qualities are not necessarily measurable, they are most definitely *felt,* so when someone exhibits these qualities, let us nurture them, let us promote them, and most importantly, let us encourage them in all aspects of the new leadership.

Qualities of leadership can no longer continue to be gendered as feminine vs. masculine. These are now necessary to balance leadership. More importantly, these qualities, when taken together as a whole, are needed to take leadership from being a *managerial* conception to that which more closely resembles the *guidance* from which leadership derives its namesake.

To Sandberg and her critics: I will be raising my children as leaders, but not according to a narrow, traditional view of leadership. The problem this leadership professor has with "Ban Bossy" is not the view of leadership where girls are called bossy whenever they assert themselves. The problem I have is with the view of leadership where boys who are bossy are used to define what it means to lead.

My children—both sons *and* daughters—will be raised with balance, knowing how to temper ambition and drive with compassion, and when to pause to listen to others for the good of the group, rather than push forward for their own sake.

Understanding Your Leadership Balance

Lee Ellis

Lee Ellis is president of Leadership Forum, a leadership and team development company.

Abraham Lincoln is frequently cited as our most popular president, probably because he achieved great results in the face of incredibly difficult circumstances. Did you ever stop to think, how did he do it? What was his secret and what are the keys to success for great leadership? I have a good idea after posing this question to hundreds of managers and supervisors. A survey I conducted while facilitating leadership development at several large corporations revealed more than 120 attributes of great leaders.

These attributes fell into four areas: trust, relationships, results, and emotional intelligence. The best leaders exhibit qualities from all levels; however, results and relationship behaviors were mentioned more often than all others. Relationship-oriented and results-oriented attributes correlate very closely with our naturally motivated behaviors (personalities). These behaviors are absolutely critical to success, and they are excellent areas for potential growth in almost all leaders.

After working with thousands of people over the years, I have discovered a natural seesaw effect between relationships and results; that is, most people tend to be good at (and inclined toward) one and struggle with (neglect or avoid) the other. If, therefore, you are naturally good at setting standards and holding people accountable (results oriented), you are likely to struggle with relationship-oriented behaviors like listening, encouraging, and showing empathy. If you are relationship oriented, then the opposite is likely to be true.

Results-oriented Behaviors

Results-oriented behaviors typically garner a great deal of attention because they are obviously necessary for success. Without them, you can't achieve goals or stay in business. It's only natural that organizations have very sophisticated ways of keeping score on how effective leaders are at achieving results. In most companies, there seems to be a constant mantra coming from the top that "results count." Results-oriented behaviors begin with vision and include the energy and drive to challenge people to do their best.

Shown below are the top ranked results-oriented behaviors in my survey on attributes of great leaders:

- Big picture, visionary, strategic
- Straightforward, sets clear expectations
- Strong focus on tasks
- Good problem solver
- Decisive, gives direction, firm (but flexible)
- High standards/goals for self and others

It was interesting to note that of the people surveyed, regardless of whether they were results oriented or relationship oriented, both types valued leaders who set and enforced high standards. Furthermore, they wanted clear expectations, accountability, decisiveness, and challenging work.

President Lincoln experienced great frustration early in the Civil War because there was little action and not many results on the battlefield. His top generals would not initiate the fight, delaying action to "recruit more soldiers," or "get more training," or "rest the horses." He kindly and patiently tried to encourage them, but with little success. Ultimately, he had to fire three successive generals before discovering Ulysses S. Grant, a leader who took the initiative and achieved results.

Relationship-oriented Behaviors

The ability to build good relationships is one of the most powerful leadership assets. Believing that someone else—especially your leader—cares about you and believes in you is a potent motivator. That's why the following relationship-oriented behaviors are so powerful for leading, managing, mentoring, and coaching.

Pause for a moment and reflect on your greatest leader. No matter how results oriented you may be, it's likely that the relationship attributes listed next were evident in that leader's style and played a key role in your personal development and success:

- Good listener
- Cared, concerned about me
- Encouraging, gave positive feedback
- Trusted me to do the job

- Supportive, lent a helping hand
- Respected others and me

The Dilemma of the Relationships—Results Seesaw

Leaders must achieve results to stay in business and be competitive, but they also must build relationships because it's people (with motivations and emotions) who do the work. Both, therefore, are essential to good leadership, but the dilemma is that most leaders are good at one and struggle with the other.

The struggle comes because these attributes are highly correlated to a person's "go to" behavioral style. By nature, some people are relationship oriented and some are results oriented. Typically, one is easy and one is a struggle. The side of the seesaw that's a struggle may not be a weakness, but it will require a conscious (and usually stretching) effort to carry out those behaviors. They are a struggle because it goes against the grain of our natural behaviors.

As already noted, organizational survival and success logically dictate a strong push for results. Consequently, companies are more likely to select results-oriented people for leadership roles. In most organizations, therefore, it's the relationship side of the seesaw that is light and not in balance.

Results Count, and Relationship Behaviors Enhance Results

The good news is that good relationships get better results. Twenty years of research by the Gallup Organization indicates that good relationships improve productivity and retention. This body of evidence provided the central theme for the highly popular business book, *First, Break All the Rules: What the World's Greatest Managers Do Differently*. In it, the authors point out that "The talented employee may join a company because of its charismatic leaders, its generous benefits, and its world-class training programs, but how long that employee stays and how productive he is while he is there is determined by his relationship with his immediate supervisor."[1]

Exit interviews conducted by corporations typically provide similar evidence—that talented people leave because of poor relationships with their immediate boss.

Leading through relationship behaviors is often a challenge for results-oriented people because it "feels" soft. Also, it's not natural for them to think or operate this way. As one highly results-oriented leader said, "It doesn't occur to me to encourage people because I don't need it. I can just look at the numbers and see how we are doing. That's enough for me."

He was missing that many of his people were starving for positive feedback—especially his more extroverted people who needed a regular dose of approval to stay at their peak. In reality, everyone needs encouragement and even the "tough" leaders admit that they admired the leaders who listened to them, supported them, and communicated high regard for their talents and efforts.

What Can You Do to Become a Better Leader?

Results-oriented Leader

Slow down, listen, and soften your tone. Realize that your natural inclination is probably to avoid the relationship behaviors because on the surface they do not appear to contribute to results. Also, since those "people" behaviors may not "feel" natural, you will need to push yourself to stretch and adapt behaviors outside of your comfort zone.

Adapting your normal behavioral style will be easier if you remind yourself frequently of two things:

- It is your responsibility as a leader to take a genuine interest in the growth and development of your people.
- When you value (care about) people you increase their confidence and inspire them to perform at a higher level and, therefore, produce better results with less turnover.

Of course, when your people are feeling better about their relationship with you, they are more confident and thus empowered to be better leaders and teammates themselves. Your investment has a positive multiplier effect that cascades down through the organization. Furthermore, you are modeling the very behaviors you need to coach.

Relationship-oriented Leader

Tighten up, toughen up, and deal proactively with necessary conflict. If you are naturally amiable and people oriented, acknowledge that your desire for harmony has its down side, too. Delaying unpopular decisions and avoiding creative conflict does not help the cause on either side of the leadership seesaw. Resolve to stand up for your beliefs and deal with difficult issues regardless of how it feels to you.

Remember that people want a leader who leads, so initiate, make decisions, and direct others to get results. Set and enforce reasonable boundaries, holding people accountable in a caring but firm way. Doing so will bring you into balance and win the respect of those on both sides of this seesaw. The normally amiable Lincoln succeeded because he adapted his behaviors to the needs of the situation.

In *Presidential Temperament*, the authors say Lincoln "was predisposed to restrain himself . . . But when he was faced with Southern secession, he acted boldly and vigorously . . . When the crisis of the Civil War finally broke . . . the non-directive, rational Lincoln became ceaselessly active and persistently commanding."[2]

The secret of great leaders like Lincoln and so many others is their ability to do what needs to be done even when it doesn't "feel" natural.

Psychologist William James has remarked that it's difficult to feel our way into a new way of acting, so we have to act our way into a new way of feeling. This is the test of true courage—will a person do what is appropriate for the situation, even when it feels unnatural and uncomfortable?

For some, it will take courage to coach themselves into becoming an empathic listener. For others, it will take courage to confront individuals and hold them accountable. Regardless of your tilt, the question is, "Do you have the courage to adapt your behaviors as needed?" Although adapting to new and unnatural behaviors is not the same as attacking a machine gun nest or going into a burning building to rescue someone, it does take emotional courage, and that is an essential quality of great leadership.

The bottom line is that regardless of where we are in our leadership balance we all can improve by developing some of those areas we would rather ignore. To be a great leader, it's not an option to be either results oriented or relationships oriented—we need skills for both. Lincoln learned to do both, and we can, too.

References

1. Marcus and Curt Coffman, *First, Break All the Rules*, Gallup Organization, 1999, pp. 11–12.
2. Ray Choiniere, David Keirsey, *Presidential Temperament*, Promethus Nemesis, 1992.

A Question of Leadership

Gene Klann and Talula Cartwright

Gene Klann and **Talula Cartwright** are both senior program associates at the Center for Creative Leadership.

Gene Klann

Traditionally, management has been viewed as a science because it encompasses rules and principles that appear to be consistent in all situations. Leadership, however, has traditionally been viewed as an art, the reasoning being that it does not have fixed principles and requires greater creativity in its practical application than management does—primarily because no two leadership situations are the same.

But the notion that leadership can also be a science deserves a closer look. Having lived and led in seven countries on four continents, I believe a case can be made that leadership is a science, with rules and principles that can apply to every situation.

One principle to follow is that each person is unique and the population as a whole is diverse. Consequently leaders, to maximize the potential of the people they lead, must deal with each person as a distinct and exclusive personality.

Second, despite this uniqueness and diversity, there is also an element of uniformity and consistency among people. They all have emotions and feelings such as love, hate, fear, anger, joy, and grief. These emotions might be expressed in different ways in different cultures, but the fact remains that they exist in all individuals everywhere. In view of this, leaders should always take the emotional response of their followers into consideration. This is particularly important in difficult, stressful, or crisis situations. Emotions drive behaviors, and leaders should lead in a way that ensures negative emotions are relieved anpd their harmful effects are reduced.

A third principle is that most people want to be treated with respect, trust, and dignity. No normal person wants to be abused, marginalized, or disrespected. This is why systems such as serfdom, slavery, and fascism have never succeeded over the long term—the human spirit has not allowed it. The concept of treating others as you want to be treated is universal, found in every major religion. People also have a strong need for communication, so they want their leaders to give them timely, accurate, and complete information about things that affect them. They also want their leaders to listen to and respond their ideas.

A fourth scientific principle of leadership is that character matters. People want their leaders to tell the truth, to do what they say they will do, and to be consistent in their words and actions. Leaders' willingness and ability to fulfill these desires largely determines their level of moral authority—an important attribute for effective leadership.

So leadership is really a combination of science and art. It is a science because it encompasses universal, consistent rules and principles. However, these rules and principles must be creatively applied to the leadership situation at hand, making leadership a form of art.

Talula Cartwright

Merriam-Webster's Collegiate Dictionary offers some interesting insights into the meanings of the words *art* and *science*. Among the definitions of *art* are "skill acquired by experience, study, or observation"; "an occupation requiring knowledge or skill"; and "the conscious use of skill and creative imagination esp. in the production of aesthetic objects." According to the dictionary the term *skill* stresses technical knowledge and proficiency, whereas *art* implies a personal, unanalyzable creative power.

This is quite different from what the dictionary has to say about *science*, including "knowledge or a system of knowledge covering general truths or the operation of general laws esp. as obtained and tested through scientific method," and "a system or method reconciling practical ends with scientific laws."

So which of these definitions—of art or of science—applies more to leadership?

Leaders may look for general and universal laws that affect specific actions and decisions. People count on their leaders to know how some of these broad principles will bear on leadership actions and decisions so that the organization will not be caught by detrimental surprises as a natural result of those actions and decisions. This aspect of leadership appears to be scientific. Leaders try to apply universal patterns to their specific, local situations, thereby avoiding huge, costly errors. For instance, a leader in the United States who learns of an environment-damaging error by a leader in a different industry and a different country can draw on that experience to avoid making a similar misstep.

Leadership becomes an art, however, when leaders are able to benchmark not only against the lessons drawn from other organizations but also against the many other models leaders have in their lives—childhood stories, the beauty and tragedy of nature, lessons from their hearts and souls, the wisdom contained in literature and the arts, hunches from intuition, and the insights that come from experience and the wisdom of the ages.

Great leaders all have this deep storehouse to draw from, so they are able to create rich metaphors from the stuff of everyday life, ennobling and lending integrity to their decisions even when there are no scientific benchmarks against which to measure those choices. The greatest leaders build their leadership from universal stories that cross not only continents but also space and time. They benchmark not only against other organizations but also against the legends of King Arthur, the paintings of Eugène Delacroix, and the parables from the Bible.

Leadership is not something that stops at the company door. People who are driven to lead are hungry for the kind of stories that inspire them to think ahead about their own future decisions. In even the most everyday circumstances—a Little League game, a movie, a family disagreement, a tennis match—they can find substance that inspires their thoughts about leadership. They are always pondering the stuff of everyday life and making decisions about it that will inform their future choices and help them hold the high ground when they have to think quickly. In this sense their leadership ability is a continually developing skill that is honed and improved consciously and deliberately by study and observation. The result is aesthetic in that it doesn't merely conform with natural and universal laws but is also elegant and of high quality. This continually developing proficiency and production of elegant results is what makes leadership an art.

Summary Chart

HOW TO WRITE AN ARGUMENTATIVE SYNTHESIS

---

1. **Analyze the assignment.**
   - *Determine whether you are being asked to write an informative or argumentative synthesis.*
   - *Determine the number and types of readings you are expected to use in your paper.*

---

2. **Review and annotate the readings.**
   - *Review the readings with your assignment in mind, looking for and marking information related to the topic of your paper.*
   - *Briefly summarize and critique each reading.*

---

3. **Formulate a thesis.**
   - *Determine what stance you will assume in your essay.*
   - *Determine whether you will use an open or closed thesis statement.*

---

4. **Choose an organizational plan.**
   - *Decide how you will order the ideas you will develop in your essay.*
   - *Decide whether you will present your ideas using a block or alternating format.*

---

5. **Write your rough draft.**
   - *Follow the organization plan implied or stated by your thesis.*
   - *Combine your insights, ideas, arguments, and findings with material in the source texts to develop and support your thesis.*
   - *Both paraphrase and quote material as necessary.*
   - *Add transitions, elaborations, clarifications, and connections where needed.*
   - *Include a concluding paragraph.*

6. Revise your draft.

Revise to improve the content of your essay.
- *Have you clearly indicated the point you want to prove?*
- *Have you clearly indicated the reasons you believe others should accept your position?*
- *Have you supported each of those reasons with expert testimony, statistics, or some other means of support as well as with clear explanations?*
- *Have you acknowledged opposing views in your paper when necessary? Have you found ways of refuting, accommodating, or conceding to them?*

Revise to improve the organization of your essay.
- *Is the thesis statement clearly worded and does it control the structure of the essay?*
- *Have you provided clear transitions between the major sections of your essay?*
- *Are there clear connections between the material drawn from the readings and your own elaborations and explanations?*

Revise to improve the accuracy and clarity of your essay.
- *Have you chosen words that are clear and contribute to the effect you want to elicit from your readers?*
- *Are your sentences clearly structured with adequate variety?*
- *Have you defined all the terms you need to define?*
- *Have you proofread for spelling, punctuation, or usage errors?*

7. Check your quotations and documentation.
- *Have you quoted and paraphrased material properly, accurately, and fairly?*
- *When incorporating quoted or paraphrased material in your synthesis, have you supplied enough background information on the source text so that the material makes sense to your readers?*
- *Have you documented all the material that needs to be documented?*
- *Have you documented material employing the proper format?*

ARGUMENTATIVE SYNTHESIS REVISION CHECKLIST

	Yes	No
1. Have you checked your assignment to be sure you have written the proper kind of synthesis essay: informative or argumentative?	___	___
2. Have you carefully read, annotated, and critiqued all of the source texts you will use in your essay?	___	___
3. Examine the wording of your thesis statement. Does it clearly state the stance you will assume in your essay?	___	___
4. Check the opening section of your essay. Does it:		
• introduce the topic of your paper?	___	___
• capture reader interest?	___	___
• include your thesis statement?	___	___
5. Examine each section in the body of your essay. Do you:		
• focus on just one issue at a time?	___	___
• make clear assertions?	___	___
• support your assertions with evidence?	___	___
• explain the link between each assertion and its supporting evidence?	___	___
6. Check the organization of your essay. Do you:		
• follow the organizational plan indicated by your thesis?	___	___
• provide transitions to help guide your reader through your essay?	___	___
7. Have you supported your assertions with some combination of quoted, summarized, and paraphrased source material?	___	___
8. Have you documented all the material that needs to be documented?	___	___

	Yes	No
9. Have you checked the content of your essay to be sure it accurately communicates your position and intention?	____	____
10. Have you reviewed your sentences for accuracy and variety?	____	____
11. Have you reviewed your word choice for clarity and accuracy?	____	____
12. Is your works cited or reference list correct?	____	____

Chapter 12

PLAGIARISM

In this chapter you will learn how to

1. Define plagiarism

2. Recognize common forms of plagiarism

3. Avoid plagiarism in your own writing

DEFINITION

Plagiarism occurs when writers take credit for work that is not really theirs. Because it encompasses a wide range of errors in academic writing, from improper citation to calculated fraud, plagiarism is an especially common problem for writers unfamiliar with the conventions of source-based writing. These writers often do not realize that any material they quote or paraphrase from a reading must be documented to avoid plagiarism.

Penalties for plagiarism vary from school to school, department to department, even instructor to instructor. They can range from a warning, to a failing grade on a paper, to a failing grade for a course, to expulsion from school. The academic community takes plagiarism seriously, but with care and honesty you can avoid problems and give the authors of the readings you use the credit they deserve for their work.

FORMS OF PLAGIARISM

Plagiarism is a difficult problem to address because it can assume so many different forms and involves so many different types of errors, some more serious than others. Understanding the various forms that plagiarism can assume will help you avoid problems.

PURCHASING A PAPER

Sometimes students will decide to purchase a paper rather than write one themselves. Whether you buy one from a fellow student or from a commercial vendor, purchasing a paper and turning it in as if it were your own is clearly a form of plagiarism. You are purposely taking credit for work that is not truly yours. Your teachers expect you to do your own work. Sometimes they may ask you to work with other students to write an essay, but even then you will be expected to do your own work in the group. Purchasing a paper—or even part of a paper—from someone and turning it in as if were your own is never acceptable.

TURNING IN A PAPER SOMEONE ELSE HAS WRITTEN FOR YOU

This form of plagiarism, related to the first, occurs when two students decide to let one take credit for work the other has actually completed—a student may ask his roommate to write a paper for him, then turn it in for a grade. If caught, both students may face some sort of penalty for plagiarism. In other cases, roommates taking different sections of the same class may hand in the same paper to their instructors without permission. In this case, both students have committed plagiarism. Finally there are instances in which a student retrieves a paper from the "fraternity" or "sorority" file, collections of papers written for various courses kept for students to copy and turn in (high-tech versions of this file are the collections of student papers kept on university computer systems). These papers may have been written by people the student has never known; however, if the student represents it as her own work, that student is guilty of plagiarism.

TURNING IN ANOTHER STUDENT'S WORK WITHOUT THAT STUDENT'S KNOWLEDGE

This form of plagiarism has increased over the past few years as more and more students write their papers on computers. Here a student searches another student's computer files for a paper, copies the paper, and then turns it in as if it were his own work. This is clearly a form of plagiarism.

IMPROPER COLLABORATION

More and more teachers are asking students to work together on class projects. If a teacher asks you to collaborate with others on a project, be sure to clarify exactly what she expects you to do individually when preparing the final essay. Sometimes a teacher will want a group of students to produce a single paper. The members of the group decide among themselves how they will divide the labor, and all group members get equal credit for the final essay. Though the group members should help each other complete the essay, if you are asked to complete a certain task as part of the larger project, make sure you give credit to others, when appropriate, for any material that was not originally your own. Other times a teacher will want the members of the group to work individually on their own papers; the other group members serve as each other's consultants and peer editors rather than as coauthors. In this case, you should acknowledge at the beginning of your essay or through documentation in the body of your paper any ideas or material that you did not develop yourself.

COPYING A PAPER FROM A SOURCE TEXT WITHOUT PROPER ACKNOWLEDGMENT

This form of plagiarism occurs when a student consults a website, an encyclopedia, book, or journal article, copies the information directly from the reading into his paper, puts his name on the essay, and turns it in for a grade. Sometimes a student will compose an entire essay this way; sometimes he will copy only part of his paper directly from a source. In either case, copying from a reading without proper quotation and documentation is a form of plagiarism. So is copying material directly from a computerized encyclopedia. Even though your computer may come with a subscription to a well-respected online encyclopedia, you cannot copy material from it and turn it in as your own work without proper documentation and acknowledgment.

CUTTING AND PASTING MATERIAL FROM SOURCES

Instead of copying all of the material for a paper from a single source text and passing the work off as their own, students increasingly lift material from several source texts and weave it together to construct a paper. This form of plagiarism is especially common when students gather information from the Web. Copying chunks of text from several websites into an essay and passing it off as your own work is unacceptable. All of the material drawn from websites must be properly documented.

LIFTING IMAGES FROM THE WEB OR OTHER SOURCES

If you copy photographs, pictures, charts, artwork, cartoons, or any other type of visual image from the Web or any other source, you need to document its source and give proper credit to its creator. Normally you would cite its source in a caption below the image or include the information as a way of introducing the image in your essay. Include a works cited or reference list entry for it at the end of your essay.

COPYING STATISTICS

Properly cite and document any statistics you use in your paper. If they come from a source text, including a website, they need to be documented. The same holds true if you include statistics from your own research in an essay you write. Indicate in your essay the source of these statistics and include a proper works cited or reference entry for them.

COPYING MATERIAL FROM A SOURCE TEXT, SUPPLYING PROPER DOCUMENTATION, BUT LEAVING OUT QUOTATION MARKS

Many students have a hard time understanding this form of plagiarism. The student has copied material directly from a source and has supplied proper documentation. However, if the student does not properly quote the passage, the student is guilty of plagiarism. The documentation a student provides acknowledges the writer's debt to another for the ideas she has used in the paper, but by failing to supply quotation marks, the writer is claiming credit for the language of the passage, language originally employed by the author of the source text. To properly credit the author for both the ideas and the language of the source text, the student needs to supply both proper quotation marks and proper documentation.

PARAPHRASING MATERIAL FROM A READING WITHOUT PROPER DOCUMENTATION

Suppose a student takes material from a source, paraphrases it, and includes it in his paper. Has this student committed an act of plagiarism? The student has if he fails to document the passage properly. The language is the student's own, but the original ideas were not. Adding proper documentation ensures that the author of the source text will receive proper credit for his ideas.

SELF-PLAGIARISM

The concept of self-plagiarism is difficult for many students to grasp: How is it possible to plagiarize or "copy" my own work? Self-plagiarism is considered an act of academic dishonesty for one primary reason: when teachers give students a writing assignment, they expect the student will turn in original work. If a student simply "recycles" an earlier paper—turns in a paper she or he had written in the past or for another class—the teacher is not receiving original work. Plagiarism also occurs if a student uses parts of an earlier paper in a current assignment without acknowledging the source of the recycled material. Keep in mind that unless otherwise indicated, teachers expect original work in the papers they assign—properly acknowledge and document material that comes from any outside source, including your own prior writing.

WHY STUDENTS PLAGIARIZE WORK

Students plagiarize work for many reasons—to boost their course grade, to meet an impending deadline, or to avoid the hard work of writing. It's easier for them to have a friend write the paper, to "borrow" a roommate's essay, or to purchase a paper from an online paper mill. Clearly these are all instances of fraud—the students are intentionally passing off someone else's work as their own.

Other times, though, plagiarism can be unintentional. For example, students may plagiarize work because they do not fully understand the rules and conventions governing citation practices in academic writing. They may not know what material needs to be cited. Plagiarism can also result from weak paraphrasing skills—though students provide in-text documentation for a paraphrased passage, its language and/or syntax is still too close to the original and parts of it should have been placed in quotation marks as well. It can even result from faulty note taking. Students may copy passages from source texts in their notes but not place quotation marks around them. When they write their essay, they copy the passage from their notes into their paper, and though they might document the passage correctly, they still commit plagiarism because the passage is not also placed in quotation marks. Understanding why students plagiarize work can help both instructors and students avoid the problem. However, whether committed intentionally or unintentionally, plagiarism is never acceptable.

HOW TO AVOID PLAGIARISM

DO YOUR OWN WORK

Obviously, the first way to avoid plagiarism is to do your own work when composing papers—do your own research and write your own essay. This suggestion does not mean, however, that collaborating with others when you write or getting needed help from your teacher, tutor, or classmates is wrong. Many instructors will suggest or even require you to work with others on some writing projects—classmates, writing center tutors, friends. Just be sure the paper you turn in fairly and accurately represents, acknowledges, and documents the efforts you and others have put into the essay. If you get help on a paper you are writing, make sure that you can honestly take credit for the unacknowledged ideas and language it contains. If important or substantial ideas or words in the paper came from someone else, be sure to document those contributions properly. When you turn in a paper with your name on the title page, you are taking credit for the material in the essay. You are also, though, taking responsibility for that material—you are, in effect, telling your reader that you compiled this information, developed these arguments, or produced these findings and will stand behind what you have written. Taking that responsibility seriously, doing the hard work of writing yourself and composing papers that represent your best efforts, can help you avoid problems with plagiarism.

TAKE GOOD NOTES

One common source of unintentional plagiarism is poor note taking. Here is what can happen: a student goes to the library and looks up an article she thinks will help her write her paper. She reads the piece and, taking notes, copies down information and passages she thinks she might use in her essay.

However, if she is not careful to put quotation marks around passages she takes word for word from the source, she can be in trouble when she writes her essay. If she later consults her notes when drafting her paper, she may not remember that the passage in her notes should be quoted in her paper—she may believe she paraphrased the material when taking notes. If she copies the passage exactly as she has it written in her notes and fails to place it in quotation marks in her paper, she has plagiarized the material, even if she documents it. Remember, to avoid plagiarism, passages taken word for word from a source must be quoted *and* documented. Therefore, be very careful when taking notes to place quotation marks around material you are copying directly from a reading. If you later incorporate that material in your essay, you will know to place the passage in quotation marks and document it.

To avoid problems, consider developing a consistent system for taking notes. In many high schools, students are required to write their notes on index cards with the source text's full bibliographic information on each card. If you find this system of note taking helpful, you can continue it in college. If you found this method too repetitive and time consuming, you can make a few alterations. For example, you can take notes on lined paper, citing the bibliographic information at the top and the source text's page numbers along the left margin. Consider writing on only one side of the paper, though, so you're not flipping sheets around when you write your essay. You might consider using a research journal as a place to keep all of your notes for an assignment. One common practice among academics is to keep content notes from source texts on the left-hand side of the journal and their own responses, insights, and questions on the right-hand side so as not to confuse the two (these are frequently referred to as "dual entry" journals). Whatever system you use, employ it consistently and be sure to indicate in your notes what material is copied verbatim from a source and what is paraphrased.

PARAPHRASE PROPERLY

Another source of unintentional plagiarism is improper paraphrasing. When you paraphrase material, you have to be sure to change substantially the language of the source passage (see Chapter 3 for guidelines on paraphrasing material). If you do not do a good job paraphrasing a passage, you can be guilty of plagiarism even if you document the material. If in your paraphrase there are phrases or clauses that should be quoted (because they appear in your paper exactly as they appear in the source), you will be guilty of plagiarism if you do not place quotation marks around them, even if the whole passage is properly documented.

SUPPLY PROPER DOCUMENTATION

When you proofread a source-based essay, set aside time to look for problems involving documentation before you turn it in. Problems like these can be hard to detect; you need to pay close attention to finding them as you review your work. Make sure everything that should be documented is properly cited. If you ever have any questions about whether to document a particular passage or word, see your instructor. Because instructors know the documentation conventions of their particular fields of study, they can often give you the best advice. If you have a question about whether to document a passage and you cannot reach your teacher for advice, you should probably err on the side of documentation. When responding to your work, your teacher can indicate whether the documentation was absolutely necessary.

Remember, whenever you quote *or* paraphrase material, you need to supply proper documentation, indicating the source of those words or ideas. Most students remember to document quotations. Remembering to document paraphrased material can be more problematic, especially if you have been told *not* to document "common knowledge." Though this may appear to be a fairly simple guideline, in practice it can be confusing and vague. What is **common knowledge**? What qualifies as common knowledge varies from discipline to discipline in college, as well as from audience to audience. Information that does not need to be documented in a history research paper may need to be documented in a philosophy research paper—the information is common knowledge for readers in history but not for readers in philosophy. Among one group of readers, certain facts, references, statistics, claims, or interpretations may be well known and generally accepted; among other readers, the same material may be new or controversial. For the first group of readers, documentation may not be necessary; for the second, it probably is. Again, if you ever have a question concerning whether something should or should not be documented, ask your instructor, who has expert knowledge about the discipline.

Many students express dismay over this guideline because it means that if they are writing a paper on a topic relatively new to them, they will have to document almost everything. When you are writing certain kinds of papers in certain classes, there may be no way to avoid having documented material in almost every paragraph. However, this situation is not "bad"; in fact, it is to be expected when you are writing on a subject new to you. There are ways to consolidate your documentation so the citations do not take up too much space in your essay (see the two "Consolidating References" sections in Chapter 13).

ONLINE PLAGIARISM CHECK

Many professors employ online plagiarism detection services like TurnItIn.com. These services search electronic versions of your paper to detect strings of words that match strings in the vast collection of source texts and prior student papers the company maintains on its server. At many schools, professors ask students to turn in the final drafts of their papers electronically so they can use a service like this. Other professors ask students to run rough drafts of their papers through the service in order to detect and fix passages that might be plagiarized. Check with your instructor or school librarian to see if you can take advantage of a service like this as you draft your essay.

CLARIFY COLLABORATION GUIDELINES

If you are asked to collaborate with others on a project, be sure to clarify the guidelines your teacher wants you to follow. You want to be sure you know what your teacher expects of each student in the group. Are the individual members of the group supposed to work together to produce a single essay? Are the group members supposed to help each individual member of the group write his or her own paper? How much help is acceptable? Can another student supply you with the material or arguments you will use in your essay? Can others help you with the organization, perhaps suggesting how you should structure your work? Can other students write part of your paper for you? Can others revise your paper for you, changing the language when needed? Be sure you know what your teacher expects before you begin work on a collaborative project, and be sure to ask your teacher to clarify how she expects you to acknowledge and document the help you receive from others.

Summary Chart

PLAGIARISM

1. **Forms of plagiarism**

   Purchasing a paper

   Turning in a paper someone else has written for you

   Turning in another student's work without that student's knowledge

   Improper collaboration

   Copying a paper from a source text without proper acknowledgment

   Cutting and pasting material from multiple sources

   Lifting images from the Web or other sources

   Copying statistics

   Copying material from a source text and supplying proper documentation, but leaving out quotation marks

   Paraphrasing material from a reading without proper documentation

   Self-plagiarism

2. **How to avoid plagiarism**

   Do your own work.

   Take good notes.

   Paraphrase properly.

   Supply proper documentation.

   Use an online plagiarism check.

   Clarify collaboration guidelines.

PLAGIARISM CHECKLIST

	Yes	No
1. Are all of your quotations properly documented?	____	____
2. Is all paraphrased material properly documented?	____	____
3. Have you acknowledged or documented the help you have received in writing your paper?	____	____
4. If this is a group project, have you checked the original assignment to be sure your work conforms to the teacher's guidelines?	____	____
5. Does the paper truly represent your own original work and effort?	____	____

Chapter 13

DOCUMENTATION

In this chapter you will learn how to

1. Recognize when you need to document material in your writing

2. Apply APA documentation guidelines

3. Apply MLA documentation guidelines

DEFINITION AND PURPOSE

Proper documentation for your papers serves several functions. First, it allows your readers to know exactly where to find specific information if they want to check the accuracy of what you have written or if they want to learn more about the subject. When combined with a reference list or bibliography, proper documentation enables readers to locate information easily and efficiently. Second, documentation gives credit to others for their ideas, arguments, findings, or language. When you write from readings, you are joining an ongoing conversation—people have likely written on the topic before you began your research and will likely write on it after you have finished your essay. With documentation, you acknowledge the work of those previous authors and locate your work clearly in that conversation. Finally, as a practical matter, proper documentation helps you avoid plagiarism. Many instances of unintentional plagiarism result from improper documentation. You can avoid these problems if you take a few minutes to check the accuracy of your documentation before you turn your papers in for a grade.

TYPES OF DOCUMENTATION

In college, you will encounter two primary methods of documentation: (1) in-text parenthetical documentation and (2) footnotes or endnotes. When you use in-text parenthetical documentation, you indicate where that information can be found in the original source by placing a citation in parentheses right after the quoted or paraphrased material. With footnotes or endnotes, you place a raised (superscript) number after the quoted or paraphrased material and then indicate where in the source text that information can be found.

Your citation will be placed either at the bottom of your page (in a footnote) or at the end of your paper (in an endnote). Over the past few years, parenthetical methods of documentation have largely replaced footnotes and endnotes. You may still find professors, though, who prefer those older forms of documentation. Always check with your teacher if you have any questions about the type of documentation you should be using in a class.

PRIMARY ACADEMIC STYLE MANUALS

The biggest problem you will face when documenting papers in college is lack of uniform practice, as styles of documentation will vary from class to class. When you write papers in college, your teacher will expect you to follow the guidelines set out in the style manual commonly used in that field of study— a set of directions that writers in that discipline follow when composing and documenting papers.

Teachers in humanities classes (English, history, philosophy, art) often follow the guidelines established by the Modern Language Association (MLA), as published in the *MLA Handbook for Writers of Research Papers* (7th ed., New York: Modern Language Association, 2009). Teachers in the social sciences (sociology, anthropology, psychology, criminal justice) tend to follow the rules set by the American Psychological Association (APA), which appear in *Publication Manual of the American Psychological Association* (6th ed., Washington, DC: American Psychological Association, 2010). However, you may have a class with a sociology teacher who prefers that you follow MLA rules or a philosophy teacher who wants you to use APA style. Also, teachers within a given field may want their students to follow different style manuals. During the same term, for example, you may be taking two communication courses, with one teacher asking you to use MLA documentation and the other wanting you to follow APA guidelines. If teachers do not specify the format they want you to follow, always ask them which style manual they want you to use when writing your paper. If a teacher voices no preference, then choose one format and follow it consistently.

The APA and MLA style manuals agree that writers should employ in-text parenthetical documentation and explanatory footnotes; however, they disagree over the exact form this documentation should assume. Though differences between the formats dictated by these style manuals may seem minor, knowing how to properly document your work helps mark you as a member of a particular academic or research community. Not knowing how may mark you as a novice or outsider.

The following are guidelines for using APA and MLA styles of documentation. The examples offered are not comprehensive. They may be sufficient for some of the papers you write, but you may have to use types of source texts not covered here. If you do, you can find each of the major style manuals in your college library; consult them if the following examples do not answer your questions.

APA GUIDELINES

In-Text Documentation

The APA recommends an author-date-page method of in-text documentation. When you quote material, note parenthetically the last name of the author whose work you are using, the year that work was published, and the page number in the reading where that material can be found. When you paraphrase material, you need to note the last name of the author whose work you are using and the year that work was published, but you do not need to include a specific page number in the documentation. What you include in a parenthetical citation can change, however, depending on the information you have already included in your text. For example, if the author's name has already been used to introduce the material, you do not repeat the name in the parenthetical citation.

Source with One Author

When you quote a passage from a source that has only one author, place the author's last name in parentheses, followed by the year the work was published and the page number where the passage can be found in the source text, all separated by commas. Precede the page reference with "p." if the passage is located on one page in the source text ("p. 12") and with "pp." if the passage runs on more than one page ("pp. 12–13"):

Example 1

> "Drug-using women may be in a position to capitalize most on the advantages of women-inspired prevention methods, and be hindered the least by the disadvantages, as compared with other groups of at-risk women" (Gollub, 2008, p. 108).

If you were to paraphrase that passage, following APA guidelines, you would not include a specific page number in the documentation, only the author and year of publication:

Example 2 Paraphrase

> Prevention methods designed and inspired by women may offer more help to drug-using women than to other similar at-risk groups (Gollub, 2008).

Note the space between the end of the paraphrased passage and the parenthetical citation. Also, the period for the sentence follows the documentation (which is not the case with block quotations). Remember not to repeat information in your parenthetical citation that is included in the body of your essay. For example, if you mention the author's name to introduce a quotation or paraphrase, that information does not need to be repeated in the parenthetical citation. The year of publication should be in parentheses (preferably right after the author's name), and the page number, also in parentheses, should be after any quoted source material:

Example 3

> According to Erica L. Gollub (2008), "Drug-using women may be in a position to capitalize most on the advantages of women-inspired prevention methods, and be hindered the least by the disadvantages, as compared with other groups of at-risk women" (p. 108).

Source with Two Authors

If a work has two authors, cite the last names of both authors when you refer to their work. Separate the names with an ampersand (&) if you are citing them parenthetically, but use "and" if they appear in the body of your text:

Example 4

> "At the beginning of the AIDS epidemic, the large size of high-risk groups, and their lack of organization around public health issues virtually guaranteed that high levels of collective action to combat AIDS would be extremely low" (Broadhead & Heckathorn, 1994, p. 475).

Example 5 Paraphrase

> According to Broadhead and Heckathorn (1994), because the group of people most likely to be affected by AIDS was so large and tended not to focus on health issues, a poor response to the epidemic was almost certain.

Source with Three to Five Authors

The first time you refer to work from a source with three to five authors, list the last names of all the authors in the order in which they appear in the source. Again, use an ampersand before the last name when citing the authors parenthetically. In subsequent references to the work, cite the last name of the first author followed by "et al." (which means "and others"):

Example 6

> A recent study has shown that people who are infected with the HIV virus live longer and healthier lives when they receive various combinations of antiretroviral treatments (Kalichman, Eaton, Cain, Cherry, & Pope, 2006).

Example 7

> A recent study by Kalichman, Eaton, Cain, Cherry, and Pope (2006) has shown that people who are infected with the HIV virus live longer and healthier lives when they receive various combinations of antiretroviral treatments.

Example 8

> Kalichman et al. (2006) found that . . .

If shortening a citation through the use of "et al." will cause any confusion (that is, if two or more citations become identical when shortened), include as many names as necessary to distinguish the works.

Source with Six or More Authors

If a work has six or more authors, cite only the last name of the first author followed by "et al." and the year of publication:

Example 9

> A recent study in Africa confirms that among sexually active people, regular condom use helps prevent the spread of HIV and AIDS (Laga et al., 1994).

Example 10

> A recent study in Africa by Laga et al. (1994) confirms that among sexually active people, regular condom use helps prevent the spread of HIV and AIDS.

As in the previous examples, if shortening a citation through the use of "et al." will cause any confusion, list as many authors' last names as needed to differentiate the works, and then replace the remaining names with "et al."

Source with No Author

When a work has no author, cite the first word or two of the title and the year of publication. If the source text is a journal article or book chapter, the shortened title will appear in quotation marks; if the work is a pamphlet or a book, the shortened title should be italicized:

Example 11

> "The world has recognized that an adult with AIDS in Zambia has as much right to treatment as one in Norway. Children should not be left to die simply because they cannot pay" ("Children," 2005, p. 16).

Example 12

> In "Children and AIDS" (2005), the editors of the *New York Times* argue, "The world has recognized that an adult with AIDS in Zambia has as much right to treatment as one in Norway. Children should not be left to die simply because they cannot pay" (p. 16).

Because the title of the article is used to introduce the quotation in Example 12, it is not repeated in the parenthetical citation.

Sources Whose Authors Have the Same Last Name

If two authors have the same last name, differentiate them by their first initials:

Example 13

> Surveys have found that many people avoid discussing AIDS because they feel they know too little about the topic (J. Brown, 1991); consequently, a number of companies are beginning to develop programs to educate their workers (L. Brown, 1991).

Two or More Sources by the Same Author

If you are referring to two or more works by the same author, differentiate them by date of publication separated by commas. If both are included in the same parenthetical citation, order them by year of publication:

Example 14

> Because AZT has proved to be ineffective in controlling the effects of AIDS (Brown, 1993), scientists have been working hard to develop a vaccine against the virus, especially in developing countries where the epidemic is spreading quickly (Brown, 1994).

Example 15

> A series of articles in *New Scientist* by Phillida Brown (1993, 1994) traces efforts to develop adequate treatments to combat AIDS.

Two or More Sources by the Same Author Published the Same Year

If you are referring to two or more works by the same author published in the same year, differentiate them by adding lowercase letters after the dates:

Example 16

> Two recent articles (Brown, 1994a, 1994b) trace the efforts to improve AIDS treatment in developing countries.

The "a" article is the reference that appears first in the reference list, the "b" second, and so on.

Electronic Sources of Information

If you refer to the work as a whole, include the author's last name and the year of publication. If, instead, you are citing specific information in the source text, include the author's last name, the year of publication, and the page number. If the pages are not numbered, include the paragraph or section number in the source text where the material can be found, preceded by "para.":

Example 17

> According to one expert, AIDS has killed 14 million people over the past 20 years (Underwood, 1999, para. 1).

As always, do not repeat information in the citation that is already present in your essay.

Consolidating APA-Style References

If you want to include references to two or more sources in one parenthetical citation, arrange them alphabetically by the last name of the authors and separate them with semicolons:

Example 18

> Many recent studies have examined the best treatment options for women who suffer from HIV infection (Gollub, 2008; Kalichman et al., 2006; Wanjama, Kimani, & Lodiaga, 2007).

FOOTNOTES AND ENDNOTES

Some style manuals still advocate using footnotes or endnotes as the primary means of documenting source-based essays, but the APA suggests they be used sparingly, only to supply commentary or information you do not want to include in the body of your paper. These notes are numbered consecutively in the text with superscript numerals.

Example 19

> A survey of recent articles published on AIDS shows a growing interest in developing reliable research methods to test high-risk groups, such as drug abusers and prostitutes.[1]

The notes may be placed at the bottom of the page on which they appear or on a separate page at the end of the paper with the word "Footnotes" centered at the top. The footnotes are double-spaced in numerical order, preceded by superscript numerals. The first line of every note is indented five to seven spaces.

MLA GUIDELINES

IN-TEXT DOCUMENTATION

MLA style uses an author-page system of in-text documentation. When you quote or paraphrase material, you tell your reader parenthetically the name of the author whose work you are using and where in that reading the passage or information can be found. If your reader wants more information on this source text (for instance, whether it is a book or an article, when it was published, or what journal it appeared in), she will refer to the works cited list at the end of your paper, where you provide this information.

The exact form of the parenthetical documentation—what information goes into the parentheses and in what order—varies depending on the type of source you are referring to and what you have already mentioned about the source in the body of your essay.

Source with One Author

When you quote or paraphrase information from a reading that has just one author, place the author's last name in parentheses, leave a space, and then indicate the page number or numbers in the source where the passage or information can be found. Whether you are quoting or paraphrasing material, the period follows the parentheses. In the following examples, pay particular attention to spacing and the proper placement of quotation marks:

Example 20

> "Drug-using women may be in a position to capitalize most on the advantages of women-inspired prevention methods, and be hindered the least by the disadvantages, as compared with other groups of at-risk women" (Gollub 108).

Example 21 Paraphrase

> Prevention methods designed and inspired by women may offer more help to drug-using women than to other similar at-risk groups (Gollub 108).

When using the MLA format, do *not* include "p." or "pp." before the page number or numbers. Again, notice that the final period is placed *after* the documentation. The only exception to this punctuation rule occurs when you block quote information, in which case the period comes before the parenthetical documentation.

Do not repeat in the parentheses information that is already included in the text itself. For example, if you mention the author's name leading up to the quotation or believe your reader will know who the author is from the context of the quotation, you do not need to repeat the author's name in parentheses:

Example 22

> According to Erica L. Gollub, "Drug-using women may be in a position to capitalize most on the advantages of women-inspired prevention methods, and be hindered the least by the disadvantages, as compared with other groups of at-risk women" (108).

MLA style requires you to record specific page references for material directly quoted or paraphrased. If you are quoting or paraphrasing a passage that runs longer than one page in a reading, indicate all the page numbers where that information can be found:

Example 23

> According to Gollub, many recent studies have investigated the sexual practices of drug users who are infected with the HIV virus (107-8).

Source with Two Authors

If a work has two authors, list the last names of the authors in the order they appear in the source, joined by "and." If you mention the authors in the body of your essay, include only the page number or numbers in parentheses:

Example 24

> "At the beginning of the AIDS epidemic, the large size of high-risk groups, and their lack of organization around public health issues virtually guaranteed that high levels of collective action to combat AIDS would be extremely low" (Broadhead and Heckathorn 475).

Example 25 Paraphrase

> According to Broadhead and Heckathorn, because the group of people most likely to be affected by AIDS was so large and tended not to focus on health issues, a poor response to the epidemic was almost certain (475).

Source with Three Authors

If a work has three authors, list the last names of the authors in the order they appear in the source, separated by commas, with "and" before the last name:

Example 26

> Recently, researchers have begun to examine the AIDS epidemic by combining a wide range of scientific and social perspectives and methodologies (Fan, Conner, and Villarreal).

Since this citation refers to the entire work, no specific page reference is provided.

Source with More Than Three Authors

If a source has more than three authors, include the last name of the first author followed by "et al.":

Example 27

> A recent study has shown that people who are infected with the HIV virus live longer and healthier lives when they receive various combinations of antiretroviral treatments (Kalichman et al. 401).

Source with No Author

If a work has no author, parenthetically cite the first word or two of the title. If the work is a journal article or book chapter, the shortened title will appear in quotation marks. If the work is longer, the shortened title should be italicized. If you mention the title of the work in the body of your essay, you will need to include only the page number or numbers in parentheses:

Example 28

> "The world has recognized that an adult with AIDS in Zambia has as much right to treatment as one in Norway. Children should not be left to die simply because they cannot pay" ("Children" 16).

Example 29

> In "Children and AIDS," the editors of the *New York Times* argue, "The world has recognized that an adult with AIDS in Zambia has as much right to treatment as one in Norway. Children should not be left to die simply because they cannot pay" (16).

Sources Whose Authors Have the Same Last Name

If two different authors have the same last name, differentiate them in your documentation by including their first initials:

Example 30

> Surveys have found that many people avoid discussing AIDS because they feel they know too little about the topic (J. Brown 675); consequently, a number of companies are beginning to develop programs to educate their workers (L. Brown 64).

Two or More Sources by the Same Author

If you are referring to two or more works by the same author, differentiate them in your documentation by putting a comma after the last name of the author and adding a shortened version of the title before citing the specific page reference:

Example 31

> Because AZT has proved to be ineffective in controlling the effects of AIDS (Brown, "Drug" 4), scientists have been working hard to develop a vaccine against the virus, especially in developing countries where the epidemic is spreading quickly (Brown, "AIDS" 10).

Again, the shortened title of an article or chapter is placed in quotation marks; the shortened title of a longer work would be italicized.

Electronic Sources of Information

If the pages in the electronic source text are numbered, include the author's last name and the page number. If, instead, the paragraphs or sections in the source text are numbered, include the author's last name and the paragraph or section number or numbers (use "par." for one paragraph, "pars." for more than one paragraph). *Separate the author's last name and the paragraph numbers with a comma.* If the source text does not number pages, paragraphs, or sections, include only the author's last name.

Consolidating MLA-Style References

Many times in papers, you will include in one paragraph information you gathered from several different sources. When you document this passage, arrange the references alphabetically by the last names of the authors and separate them with semicolons:

Example 32

> Many recent studies have examined the best treatment options for women who suffer from HIV infection (Gollub; Kalichman et al.; Wanjama, Kimani, and Lodiaga).

No page numbers are included here because the passage refers to the general topic of the articles, not to specific information in them.

FOOTNOTES AND ENDNOTES

The MLA suggests that footnotes or endnotes be used only to supply commentary or information you do not want to include in the body of your paper. Whether you are adding content notes (explanations of or elaborations on ideas you have discussed in the body of your paper) or bibliographic notes (a list of sources your readers might want to consult if they are interested in learning more about the topic you are discussing), try to keep them to a minimum because they can be distracting.

Number footnotes and endnotes consecutively in the body of your essay with superscript numerals:

> A survey of recent articles published on AIDS shows a growing interest in developing reliable research methods to test high-risk groups, such as drug abusers and prostitutes.[1]

If you are using footnotes, the citation appears at the bottom of the page on which the corresponding number appears. If you are using endnotes, all the citations appear in numerical order at the end of your paper on a separate page with the heading "Notes" centered one inch from the top margin. Double-space after typing this heading and then begin the citations. All the citations are double-spaced and begin with the corresponding full-size number followed by a space. Indent the first line of each note five spaces or one-half inch from the left margin.

Chapter 14

··

REFERENCE LISTS AND WORKS CITED ENTRIES

In this chapter you will learn how to

1. Explain the role reference lists and works cited play in academic writing

2. Apply APA reference list guidelines

3. Apply MLA works cited guidelines

DEFINITION AND PURPOSE

A reference or works cited list comes at the end of your paper. In it you provide all of the bibliographic information for the sources you used when writing your essay. You have one entry for every source you refer to in the body of your paper, an entry that lists for your readers the information they would need to locate the source and read it themselves.

With in-text documentation you indicate where you found the specific information or language you used in your paper, usually including only the last name of the author and the page number on which the material is located. In your reference list you will give your reader much more information concerning this reading: the author's full name, the full title of the piece, and the place and year of publication. Also, while in-text documentation indicates a specific page where the material can be found, a reference list citation indicates all the page numbers of the source.

A works cited or reference list is sometimes also called a *bibliography*, but the two may not be the same, depending on the style you are following. While the entry format for each is the same, in a bibliography you might include an entry for every source you *consulted* when researching your paper; in a works cited list you include an entry only for the sources you actually *included* in your paper. Suppose you consulted ten books or articles when researching a topic for a paper but used only seven of them in your final draft. If your teacher asked you to put together an APA bibliography for your essay, you would have ten entries. If she asked you for a works cited or reference list, you would have only seven entries. If you are unsure what to include in your list of references, consult with your teacher.

Putting together a works cited or reference list can be tedious and time-consuming because there are specific forms you have to follow. These forms are dictated by the type of source you are using and the style manual you are following. Your job is to follow these forms exactly. There is an important reason for this uniformity. When you put together a works cited list in the proper form, you are providing a valuable service for your readers: when writers in a discipline agree to follow the same format for reference lists, readers can easily determine where to locate the sources that interest them because they know how to read the entries.

Complicating your efforts to put together a proper reference list is the fact that each field of study has its preferred ways of structuring entries. Although the information in the entries generally stays the same across the disciplines, the order in which you present that information varies widely. As explained in the previous chapter, teachers in the humanities tend to follow the guidelines established by the Modern Language Association (MLA) and those in the social sciences typically employ the guidelines established by the American Psychological Association (APA). When putting together a works cited or reference list, your best approach is to follow the guidelines and sample entries as closely as you can, placing the information from your source exactly where it appears in the model. Pay very close attention to capitalization, spacing, and punctuation.

The samples provided in this chapter follow the guidelines of the major style manuals, but they are not comprehensive. As you write a paper, you may use types of readings not covered in these examples. If this occurs, you can obtain a copy of each style manual at your library and follow the sample entry it contains for the type of text you are employing.

APA FORMAT

SAMPLE REFERENCE LIST ENTRIES

In an APA reference list, you include the name of the author, the publication date, the title, and the publishing information for all of the readings you use in the body of your essay. You include each author's last name, followed by a comma and the initials of the first and middle names. If a source has more than one author, list their last names first, followed by their initials and a comma, then use an ampersand (&) to introduce the final name. The date of publication appears in parentheses, followed by a period. Book and journal titles are italicized; article titles are not (neither are they placed in quotation marks). In the titles of books and articles, you capitalize only the first word of the title and subtitle (if any) and any proper nouns and proper adjectives. The format for listing the publishing information varies by the type of source, so follow the sample entries precisely. The first line of every entry is flush with the left margin; all other lines are indented, and all entries end with a period except where they end with a DOI or a URL.

Journal Article, One Author

Gollub, E. L. (2008). A neglected population: Drug-using women and women's methods of HIV/STI prevention. *AIDS Education & Prevention, 20*(2), 107–120.

- Note how the author's first and middle initials are used.
- Note where the year of publication is listed.
- Note how the title of the article is not placed in quotation marks.
- Note which words are capitalized and which are not in the title of the article.
- Note how the journal title and volume numbers are italicized.

Journal Article, Two Authors

Broadhead, R. S., & Heckathorn, D. D. (1994). AIDS prevention outreach among injection drug users: Agency problems and new approaches. *Social Problems, 41*(3), 473–495.

- Note the order of the names: last name first followed by initials. The names are separated by a comma and the second name is introduced by an ampersand.
- The year of publication comes next, noted parenthetically.
- Note that the "A" in "Agency" is capitalized because it is the first word in the subtitle.
- Note that the volume number follows the title of the journal; it is also italicized.

Journal Article, Three to Seven Authors

Kalichman, S., Eaton, L., Cain, D., Cherry, C., Pope, H., & Kalichman, M. (2006). HIV treatment beliefs and sexual transmission risk behaviors among HIV positive men and women. *Journal of Behavioral Medicine, 29*(5), 401–410.

- When there are three to seven authors, list all of their names.

Journal Article, More Than Seven Authors

Laga, M., Alary, M., Nzila, N., Manoka, A. T., Tuliza, M., Behets, F., . . . Pilot, P. (1994). Condom promotion, sexually transmitted diseases treatment, and declining incidence of HIV-1 infection in female Zairian sex workers. *The Lancet, 344*, 246–248.

- When there are eight or more authors, list the first six, then include an ellipsis and the last author's name.
- When you cite an article like this in the body of your essay, you will use the first author's surname followed by "et al." (Laga et al., 1994).

Article from a Monthly Periodical

Minkel, J. R. (2006, July). Dangling a carrot for vaccines. *Scientific American, 295*, 39–40.

- For a monthly periodical, indicate the month of publication after the year, separating the two with a comma.
- Be sure to include the volume number as well, after the journal title.

Article from a Weekly Periodical

Clinton, B. (2006, May 15). My quest to improve care. *Newsweek, 147*, 50–52.

- Indicate the month and day of publication after the year, separating the year and month with a comma.
- Include the volume number after the journal title.

Newspaper Article

Chase, M. (2005, April 20). Panel suggests a "Peace Corps" to fight AIDS. *The Wall Street Journal*, pp. B1, B5.

Dugger, C. W. (2008, March 9). Rift over AIDS treatment lingers in South Africa. *The New York Times*, p. 8.

- Note the placement of the date: year followed by month and day, with a comma separating the year and month.
- The title of the newspaper is capitalized and italicized.
- Precede the page number with "p." if the article is on one page, and with "pp." if it runs longer than one page.
- If the newspaper is divided into sections, indicate the section along with the page number.

Newspaper Article, No Author

Children and AIDS. (2005, February 16). *The New York Times*, p. 16.

- When there is no author, begin the citation with the title.

Book with One Author

Hinds, M. J. (2008). *Fighting the AIDS and HIV epidemic: A global battle.* Berkeley Heights, NJ: Enslow.

- Note that the order of information for citing a book parallels the order of information for citing an article.
- Book titles are italicized. The first word in the title is capitalized and so are all proper nouns and proper adjectives and the first word in the subtitle.
- Following the title, indicate the city of publication and the publisher.

Books with Multiple Authors

Douglas, P. H., & Pinsky, L. (1991). *The essential AIDS fact book.* New York: Pocket Books.

Wanjama, L. N., Kimani, E. N., & Lodiaga, M. L. (2007). *HIV and AIDS: The pandemic.* Nairobi: Jomo Kenyatta Foundation.

- List multiple authors by their last names and initials, separating them with commas, and using an ampersand to introduce the final author.
- If a book has up to seven authors, list all of their names in your reference citation. For more than seven authors, see the previous guideline for periodicals. In the body of your paper, when you parenthetically cite a source with six or more authors, use only the first author's name followed by "et al." and the year of publication.

Two or More Works by the Same Person

Squire, C. (1997). *AIDS panic.* New York: Routledge.

Squire, C. (2007). *HIV in South Africa: Talking about the big thing.* London: Routledge.

- Arrange the citations in chronological order, with the earliest first.

Book, Corporate Author

National Gay and Lesbian Task Force. (1987). *Anti-gay violence: Victimization and defamation in 1986.* New York: Author.

- If the publisher is the same as the corporate author, simply write "Author" after the city where the work was published.

Book, Later Edition

Fan, H. Y., Conner, R. F., & Villarreal, L. (2007). *AIDS: Science and society* (5th ed.). Sudbury, MA: Jones and Bartlett.

- If you are using a later edition of a book, list the edition number parenthetically after the title.

Edited Book

Cohen, A., & Gorman, J. M. (Eds.). (2008). *Comprehensive textbook of AIDS psychiatry.* New York: Oxford University Press.

- If one person edited the book, place "(Ed.)." after his name. If more than one person edited the work, place "(Eds.)." after their names.
- Pay particular attention to the periods in this citation. It is easy to leave some of them out.

Book, No Author or Editor

Corporate responses to HIV/AIDS: Case studies from India. (2007). Washington, DC: World Bank.

- When the title page of a book lists no author, begin your citation with the title.
- Note that in this type of entry, an edition number would precede the year of publication.

Multivolume Book

Daintith, J., Mitchell, S., & Tootill, E. (Eds.). (1981). *A biographical encyclopedia of scientists* (Vols. 1–2). New York: Facts on File.

- Indicate for your reader how many volumes comprise the work. This information follows the title.

One Volume of a Multivolume Book

Daintith, J., Mitchell, S., & Tootill, E. (Eds.). (1981). *A biographical encyclopedia of scientists* (Vol. 1). New York: Facts on File.

- When you use just one volume of a multivolume work, indicate the volume number parenthetically after the title.

English Translation of a Book

Jager, H. (Ed.). (1988). *AIDS phobia: Disease pattern and possibilities of treatment* (J. Welch, Trans.). New York: Halsted Press.

- Open the citation with the name of the author or editor.
- Following the title, give the translator's name followed by a comma and "Trans."
- Note that in giving the translator's name, you begin with her initials, followed by the last name.
- Again, pay attention to all the periods included in this citation.

Article or Chapter from an Anthology

Many times in writing a source-based paper you will use a work contained in an anthology of readings. When this is the case, follow this format in your reference list:

Bethell, T. (2006). The African AIDS epidemic is exaggerated. In D. A. Leone (Ed.), *Responding to the AIDS epidemic* (pp. 18–22). Detroit: Greenhaven Press.

Patton, C. (1993). "With champagne and roses": Women at risk from/in AIDS discourse. In C. Squire (Ed.), *Women and AIDS* (pp. 165–187). London: Sage.

- Open your citation with the name of the author whose ideas or language you included in your paper.
- Next, give the title of the specific reading you referred to in the body of your essay.
- Next, give the name of the author or editor of the anthology and the larger work's title (the title of the book is italicized). Precede this information with the word "In" (note capitalization).
- Follow the title with the specific page numbers on which the article can be found. In this case, Patton's article can be found on pages 165–187 of Squire's book; Bethell's article can be found on pages 18–22 of Leone's book.
- Close the entry with the publishing information.

Article in a Reference Work

Acquired immune deficiency syndrome. (1990). In *The New Encyclopaedia Britannica* (Vol. 1, p. 67). Chicago: Encyclopaedia Britannica.

Haseltine, W. A. (1992). AIDS. In *Encyclopedia Americana* (Vol. 1, pp. 365–366). Danbury, CT: Grolier.

- When the entry in the reference work is signed, begin the citation with the author's name; when it is not signed, begin the citation with the title of the entry.
- Include the year the reference work was published, the title of the work (italicized), the volume number and inclusive page numbers of the entry (noted parenthetically), followed by the publishing information.

Personal Interview

Under APA guidelines, all personal communications are to be cited in the text only. Include the name of the person you interviewed (first and middle initials, full last name), the words "personal communication," and the date of the interview (month, day, year), all separated by commas:

(F. Smith, personal communication, June 24, 1995)

Electronic Sources of Information

The latest set of guidelines published by the American Psychological Association (www.apa.org) stipulates that writers include in their reference list entries specific information concerning where the material can be found online. The APA requires writers to include either the document's digital object identifier (DOI) number or to write "Retrieved from" followed by the Uniform Resource Locator (URL). Include the URL for a site's home page, not for the source text itself. If the source text cannot be reached from the site's home page, then include the source text's URL. Give preference to the DOI—include that number if available and not the URL.

Entire Website

APA recommends incorporating bibliographic information for an entire website parenthetically in the body of the text, not as a separate reference list entry:

One source of current information on the worldwide threats posed by AIDS is the United Nations' website UNAIDS (http://www.unaids.org/en/).

- The APA recommends that writers check the links they include in their work to ensure they function.
- To avoid mistakes in typing, copy and paste the URL from the website itself.

Page on a Website

Bonsor, K. (n.d.). How AIDS works. howstuffworks. Retrieved from http://www.howstuffworks.com

- This particular website had no date of publication, indicated by "n.d."
- The URL is for the website itself, not for the particular page on that website.
- Do not include a period at the end of the entry—readers may believe it is part of the URL.

Article in an Online Publication

If the text exists only electronically, use this format:

Ambinder, M. (2007, December 8). Huck and AIDS. Retrieved from http://theatlantic.com

- Note how the date of publication is listed.

Article in a Scholarly Journal

Honer, P., & Nassir, R. (2013). Social cultural stressors in Dominican Republic HIV/AIDS prevention and treatment. *Journal of AIDS & Clinical Research 4*(10). doi:10.4172/2155-6113.1000242

- Note that "doi" is followed by a colon with no space after it.
- Note that you do not add a period at the end of the DOI.

Jacobson, S. (2011). HIV/AIDS interventions in an aging population. *Health & Social Work 36*(2), 149–156. Retrieved from http://www.naswpress.org/publications/journals/hsw.html

- This article does not have a DOI number, so "Retrieved from" is used instead.

Baligh, Y., & Frank, I. (2011). Battling AIDS in America: An evaluation of the national HIV/AIDS strategy. *American Journal of Public Health 10*(9), 4–8. doi:10.2105/AJPH.2011.300259

- If you need to break a DOI number or a URL at the end of your line, do so in front of a punctuation mark (a slash or a period).

Article from an Online Database

Harris, A. (2013). Framing AIDS facts. *Black Theology: An International Journal 11*(3), 305–322. Retrieved from Academic Search Complete database.

Book on the Web

Fan, H. Y., Connor, R. F., & Villarreal, L. P. (2011). *AIDS: Science and society.* Retrieved from http://books.google.com/books/about/AIDS .html?id=wyfWRd6k2lAC

Pepin, J. (2011). *The origin of AIDS.* Retrieved from http://ebooks .cambridge.org/ebook.jsf?bid=CBO9781139005234

- Publication information for the print edition of the book is not required.

Newspaper on the Web

Holland, J. (2001, December 15). Delivering hope by another route: H.I.V. activists collect drugs for the needy outside the U.S. *The New York Times.* Retrieved from http://www.nytimes.com

Movers and shakers in the AIDS community. (2006, August 13). *The Toronto Star.* Retrieved from http://www.thestar.com

- If the newspaper article is unsigned, begin the entry with the title.

An Image

Dillon, T. (2012, February 13). AIDS quilt [Photograph]. Retrieved from http://www.huffingtonpost.com/012/02/13/aids-memorial -quilt-san-francisco_n_1274035.html

- Note how the type of image (in this case a photograph) is listed in brackets.
- Provide the URL for the image.

Video

Swoope, T. (2013, May 7). Famous people who have died from Aids [Video file]. Retrieved from http://www.youtube.com/watch?v=BTYP03DuVH4

- Note how to format the date the video was posted: year, month day.
- The type of file is included in brackets.

E-mail

APA considers e-mails to be a form of personal communication that should not be included on your reference page. Instead, include the reference information parenthetically in the text: author of the e-mail, nature of the communication, and date it was received:

(J. Edwards, personal communication, July 31, 2011)

Blog Entry

Gordon, N. (2013, December 11). New Senate bill would help end HIV discrimination [Blog post]. Retrieved from http://www.hrc.org /blog

- Begin the entry with the name of the author.
- Note how the date of the blog post is provided: year, month day.
- In brackets indicate the nature of the entry.
- Provide the URL for the blog, not for the specific blog entry.

Online Reference Work

AIDS. (2011). In *Encyclopaedia Brittannica*. Retrieved from http://www .britannica.com

- If the source text is signed, begin the entry with the author's name.
- If the text is unsigned, begin the entry with the title.

SAMPLE APA-STYLE REFERENCE LIST

List all of your references at the end of your paper, beginning the list on a new page. At the top of the page, center the word "References." After the heading, double-space and list your citations in alphabetical order according to the last name of the author or first key word in the title if there is no author. The first line of every citation should be set flush left. Indent subsequent lines.

References

AIDS. (2011). In *Encyclopaedia Britannica*. Retrieved from http://www

.britannica.com

Bethell, T. (2006). The African AIDS epidemic is exaggerated. In D.

    A. Leone (Ed.), *Responding to the AIDS epidemic* (pp. 18–22).

    Detroit: Greenhaven Press.

Chase, M. (2005, April 20). Panel suggests a "Peace Corps" to fight

    AIDS. *The Wall Street Journal*, pp. B1, B5.

Children and AIDS. (2005, February 16). *The New York Times*, p. 16.

Clinton, B. (2006, May 15). My quest to improve care. *Newsweek, 147*,

    50–52.

Cohen, A., & Gorman, J. M. (Eds.). (2008). *Comprehensive textbook of

    AIDS psychiatry*. New York: Oxford University Press.

Corporate responses to HIV/AIDS: Case studies from India. (2007).

    Washington, DC: World Bank.

Douglas, P. H., & Pinsky, L. (1991). *The essential AIDS fact book*. New

    York: Pocket Books.

Dugger, C. W. (2008, March 9). Rift over AIDS treatment lingers in

    South Africa. *The New York Times*, p. 8.

Fan, H. Y., Conner, R. F., & Villarreal, L. (2007). *AIDS: Science and

    society* (5th ed.). Sudbury, MA: Jones and Bartlett.

Gollub, E. L. (2008). A neglected population: Drug-using women and

    women's methods of HIV/STI prevention. *AIDS Education &

    Prevention, 20*(2), 107–120.

Hinds, M. J. (2008). *Fighting the AIDS and HIV epidemic: A global

    battle*. Berkeley Heights, NJ: Enslow.

Honer, P., & Nassir, R. (2013). Social cultural stressors in Dominican

    Republic HIV/AIDS prevention and treatment. *Journal of AIDS*

    & Clinical Research 4(10). doi:10.4172/2155-6113.1000242

Laga, M., Alary, M., Nzila, N., Manoka, A. T., Tuliza, M., Behets, F.,

    . . . Pilot P. (1994). Condom promotion, sexually transmitted

    diseases treatment, and declining incidence of HIV-1 infection in

    female Zairian sex workers. *The Lancet, 344,* 246–248.

Minkel, J. R. (2006, July). Dangling a carrot for vaccines. *Scientific*

    American, 295, 39–40.

Squire, C. (1997). *AIDS panic.* New York: Routledge.

Squire, C. (2007). *HIV in South Africa: Talking about the big thing.*

    London: Routledge.

Wanjama, L. N., Kimani, E. N., & Lodiaga, M. L. (2007). *HIV and AIDS:*

    The pandemic. Nairobi: Jomo Kenyatta Foundation.

MLA FORMAT

SAMPLE WORKS CITED ENTRIES

In a works cited list following MLA style, include the name of the author and full title of the works you cited in the body of your essay, along with relevant publication information. When listing the authors, include their full names, last name first. Titles of articles are placed in quotation marks; titles of books are italicized. All words in titles are capitalized in MLA style except prepositions and conjunctions. Journal titles are italicized, and you should list all the pages you read in the source text. Do not precede page numbers with "p." or "pp."; simply list inclusive page numbers. Finally, MLA style employs hanging indentation: begin the first line of each entry at the left margin and indent all subsequent lines one-half inch.

Journal Article, One Author

Gollub, Erica L. "A Neglected Population: Drug-Using Women and Women's
    Methods of HIV/STI Prevention." *AIDS Education and Prevention*
    20.2 (2008): 107-20. Print.

- Give the full name of the author as it is printed with the article, last name first. Place a period after the name.
- The title of the article is placed in quotation marks. Note how the first and last word of the title are capitalized, as are all key words in between. Also note that the period at the end of the article title goes inside the closing quotation mark.
- The title of the journal is italicized.
- Indicate the inclusive page numbers of the article.
- Indicate the medium of publication.

Journal Article, Two or Three Authors

Broadhead, Robert S., and Douglas D. Heckathorn. "AIDS Prevention Outreach among Injection Drug Users: Agency Problems and New Approaches." *Social Problems* 41.3 (1994): 473-95. Print.

Mitchell, Roger E., Paul Florin, and John F. Stevenson. "Supporting Community-based Prevention and Health Promotion Initiatives: Developing Effective Technical Assistance Systems." *Health Education and Behavior* 29.5 (2002): 620-39. Print.

- When there are two or three authors, list all of them in the order they appear in the article. Give the first author's last name, then his first name. Give the other authors' names first name first. Separate the names with commas and introduce the last name with "and."

Journal Article, More Than Three Authors

Kalichman, Seth, et al. "HIV Treatment Beliefs and Sexual Transmission Risk Behaviors among HIV Positive Men and Women." *Journal of Behavioral Medicine* 29.5 (2006): 401-10. Print.

- When there are more than three authors, list only the first author, last name first. Follow that name with the expression "et al." (which means "and others").

Article from a Monthly Periodical

Minkel, J. R. "Dangling a Carrot for Vaccines." *Scientific American* July 2006: 39-40. Print.

- Note the month of publication after the title. Months are abbreviated, except for May, June, and July.
- Note that there is *no* comma between the month and year.
- Note that you do *not* include the volume number of the work, only the month and year.

Article from a Weekly Periodical

Clinton, Bill. "My Quest to Improve Care." *Newsweek* 15 May 2006: 50-52. Print.

- After giving the title of the periodical, list the day, month, and year of its publication in that order, without any punctuation between them.

Newspaper Article

Chase, Marilyn. "Panel Suggests a 'Peace Corps' to Fight AIDS." *Wall Street Journal* 20 Apr. 2005: B1+. Print.

Dugger, Celia W. "Rift over AIDS Treatment Lingers in South Africa." *New York Times* 9 Mar. 2008, natl. ed.: 8. Print.

- If the newspaper article is signed, give the writer's name, last name first.
- After the title of the piece, give the name of the newspaper, italicized.
- Next, give the date of publication: day, month, then year, without any intervening punctuation.
- Give the page number, indicating the section number or letter when applicable.
- Use a plus sign (+) to indicate interrupted pagination.

Newspaper Article, No Author

"Children and AIDS." *New York Times* 22 Feb. 2005, natl. ed.: 16. Print.

- If the article is unsigned, begin the entry with the title.

Book with One Author

Hinds, Maurene J. *Fighting the AIDS and HIV Epidemic: A Global Battle.* Berkeley Heights: Enslow, 2008. Print.

- Again, note how the entry begins with the author's last name.
- Note how the title is italicized and how the first, last, and all other key words are capitalized.

Book with Multiple Authors

Douglas, Paul Harding, and Laura Pinsky. *The Essential AIDS Fact Book.* New York: Pocket Books, 1991. Print.

Wanjama, Leah Niambi, et al. *HIV and AIDS: The Pandemic.* Nairobi: Jomo Kenyatta Foundation, 2007. Print.

- When a book has two or three authors, list all their names. Begin with the last name of the first author; the names of the other authors are listed first name first. Separate the names with commas and use "and" before the last name.
- If there are more than three authors, list only the first author and follow it with "et al."

Two or More Books by the Same Person

Squire, Corinne. *AIDS Panic.* New York: Routledge, 1997. Print.

---. *HIV in South Africa: Talking about the Big Thing.* London: Routledge, 2007. Print.

- When you have two or more books by the same author or authors, list them on your works cited list in alphabetical order by the first key word in the title.

- For the first work by the author, give his or her full name, last name first. For subsequent entries by the author, instead of repeating the name, type three hyphens followed by a period. Then list the title of the work and the relevant publishing information.

Book, Corporate Author

National Gay and Lesbian Task Force. *Anti-gay Violence: Victimization and Defamation in 1986.* New York: National Gay and Lesbian Task Force, 1987. Print.

- Treat a corporate author just as you would an individual author.

Book, Later Edition

Fan, Hung Y., Ross F. Conner, and Luis Villarreal. *AIDS: Science and Society.* 5th ed. Sudbury: Jones and Bartlett, 2007. Print.

- Indicate the edition number after the title.

Edited Book

Cohen, Ann, and Jack M. Gorman, eds. *Comprehensive Textbook of AIDS Psychiatry.* New York: Oxford UP, 2008. Print.

Squire, Corinne, ed. *Women and AIDS: Psychological Perspectives.* London: Sage, 1993. Print.

- If one person edited the work, place "ed." after his name. If there is more than one editor, use "eds."

Book, No Author or Editor

Corporate Responses to HIV/AIDS: Case Studies from India. Washington: World Bank, 2007. Print.

- When there is no author, begin the entry with the title.

Multivolume Book

Daintith, John, Sarah Mitchell, and Elizabeth Tootill, eds. *A Biographical Encyclopedia of Scientists.* 2 vols. New York: Facts on File, 1981. Print.

- Indicate the number of volumes in a multivolume work after the title.

One Volume of a Multivolume Book

Daintith, John, Sarah Mitchell, and Elizabeth Tootill, eds. *A Biographical Encyclopedia of Scientists.* Vol. 1. New York: Facts on File, 1981. Print.

- If you use only one volume of a multivolume work, indicate the volume number after the title.

English Translation of a Book

Jager, Hans, ed. *AIDS Phobia: Disease Pattern and Possibilities of Treatment.* Trans. Jacquie Welch. New York: Halsted, 1988. Print.

- Begin the entry with the name of the author or editor whose work has been translated, followed by the title of the work.
- Next, write "Trans." followed by the name of the translator, first name first.

Article or Chapter from an Anthology

Bethell, Tom. "The African AIDS Epidemic Is Exaggerated." *Responding to the AIDS Epidemic.* Ed. Daniel A. Leone. Detroit: Greenhaven, 2006. 18-22. Print.

Patton, Cindy. "'With Champagne and Roses': Women at Risk from/in AIDS Discourse." *Women and AIDS.* Ed. Corinne Squire. London: Sage, 1993. 165-87. Print.

- First, list the name of the author whose article or chapter you are using.
- Next, give the title of the article or chapter in quotation marks. If the title of an entry already contains quotation marks, the original quotation marks are shifted to single quotation marks in the citation.
- Next, give the title of the work that contained the article and the name of the editor or editors, preceded by "Ed." (for "Edited by").
- Finally, list the publication information and the page numbers in the larger work where the article or chapter can be found.

Article in a Reference Work

"Acquired Immune Deficiency Syndrome." *Encyclopaedia Britannica: Micropaedia.* 1990 ed. Print.

- If the author of the entry in the reference work is listed, begin with that. If it is not, begin with the heading of the entry, in quotation marks.
- After indicating the heading of the entry, list the name of the reference work and the edition.

Personal Interview

Alexander, Jane. Telephone interview. 16 June 2008.

Smith, John. Personal interview. 16 June 2008.

- List the name of the person interviewed, the nature of the interview (whether done in person, over the telephone, etc.), and the date of the interview: day, month, and year. Personal interviews are included on your Works Cited list.

Electronic Sources of Information

Increasingly, writers are citing material they gathered by searching the World Wide Web. Many of the works cited entries for material found on the Internet resemble closely entries for the same material found in print but with some additional information. Material found only on the Internet (for example, websites) has specific works cited formats to follow as well.

You will need to identify in your entries where you located the material, for example through a search of the Web, via e-mail, or on YouTube. If the material has no date of publication or posting, include "n.d." where the date should be ("n.d." means "no date"). Indicate a lack of page numbers with "n. pag." Use "n.p." if the name of the publisher is unknown. Since information on websites can change quickly, you will also need to include the date you accessed it yourself. When doing so, list the day, then the month, then the year, abbreviating all months except for May, June, and July. Finally, you do not need to include the URL for the site unless you believe your readers will not be able to find the information without having the URL. If you think you need to include it, after the date you accessed the information, place the URL in between greater-than and less-than signs with a period at the end: <URL>.

Entire Website

UNAIDS. United Nations, n.d. Web. 11 Jan. 2014.

- Begin the entry with the name of the author (last name, first name) if there is one. Otherwise begin with the name of the website in italics.
- Include the sponsor or publisher of the website (in this case, the United Nations).
- Use "n.d." when the website's date of creation is not available.
- "Web" indicates the publication medium.

Page on a Website

Bonsor, Kevin. "How AIDS Works." *howstuffworks*. HowStuffWorks, n.d.
     Web. 1 Feb. 2014.

- Include the name of author, the title of the page, the title of the website, the sponsor or publisher of the site, the date the site was created, the medium of publication, and the date you accessed the page.
- You do not need to include the URL if readers could easily locate the page without it.

Article in an Online Periodical

Ambinder, Marc. "Huck and AIDS." *TheAtlantic.com*. Atlantic Monthly,
     8 Dec. 2007. Web. 2 July 2013.

Underwood, Anne. "How the Plague Began." *Newsweek.com*. Newsweek,
     8 Feb. 1999. Web. 3 July 2013.

- Indicate the title of the work, in quotation marks.
- Include the title of the online site, in italics.
- Include the name of the sponsoring institution or organization and the date of posting.

Article in an Online Scholarly Journal

Horner, Pilar, and Reza Nassir. "Social Cultural Stressors in Dominican
     Republic HIV/AIDS Prevention and Treatment." *Journal of AIDS and
     Clinical Research* 4.10 (2013): n. pag. Web. 22 Mar. 2014.

- The online version of this article did not include page numbers, which is indicated by "n. pag."
- Adding the medium of publication and access date indicates that this is an online source.

Article in an Online Scholarly Journal also Appearing in Print

Baligh, Yehia, and Ian Frank. "Battling AIDS in America: An Evaluation of
     the National HIV/AIDS Strategy." *American Journal of Public Health*
     10.9 (2011): 4-8. Web. 2 Mar. 2014.

Jacobson, Stephanie. "HIV/AIDS Interventions in an Aging Population."
     Health Social Work 36.2 (2011): 149-56. Web. 19 Jan. 2014.

- If you used the online version of the article, you need to include the publication medium ("Web") and the date of access.
- If the piece lists no author, begin your entry with the title and alphabetize it on the works cited page using the first key word.

Article from an Online Database

Dhamane, Vijay F. "Knowledge and Attitude of Student Teachers' towards HIV/AIDS and Life Skills Education." *Golden Research Thoughts* 3.5 (2014): 1-4. *Academic Search Complete*. Web. 22 Jan. 2014.

- If you use an online database to find the source text (like Academic Search Complete or Lexis-Nexis), specify which one before the medium of publication. The name of the database should be italicized.
- If you did not use an online database—for example, if you went directly to and searched a journal's website—you do not include a database name in your works cited entry.

Book on Web/Electronic Book

Pepin, Jacaques. *The Origin of AIDS*. New York: Cambridge UP, 2011. Web. 14 Feb. 2014.

Fan, Hung Y., Ross F. Connor, and Luis P. Villarreal. *AIDS: Science and Society*. 6th ed. Sudbury: Jones and Bartlett, 2011. *Google Books*. Web. 24 Jan. 2014.

- Include the medium of publication and access date following the information you would include for a print book.

Newspaper on the Web

Holland, Jenny. "Delivering Hope by Another Route: H.I.V. Activists Collect Drugs for the Needy outside the U.S." *New York Times*. New York Times, 15 Dec. 2001. Web. 2 May 2014.

"Movers and Shakers in the AIDS Community." *Toronto Star*. Toronto Star, 13 Aug. 2006. Web. *Lexis-Nexis*. 25 Feb. 2014.

- If no author is given, begin the entry with the title.
- Include both the name of the newspaper and the name of the newspaper's publisher.
- If you used an online database to locate the newspaper article, include the name of the database in italics.

An Image

Dilon, Tommy. "AIDS Quilt." Photograph. *Huffington Post*. Huffington Post, 13 Feb. 2012. Web. 22 Jan. 2014.

- Begin your entry with the name of the image's creator and the image's title.
- Next indicate what type of image it is, for example "photograph" or "painting," followed by the name of the website in italics.

Video

Swoope, Terry. "Famous People Who Died from Aids." *YouTube*. YouTube, 7 May 2013. Web. 7 May 2014.

- Begin the entry with the creator of the video and the video's title.
- Next include the name of the website where you found the video, the website publisher, the date the video was posted, the medium of publication, and the date you accessed the video.

E-mail

Edwards, John. "AIDS Resources." Message to author. 31 July 2011. E-mail.

- Begin with the name of the person sending the e-mail and the e-mail's subject line (placed in quotation marks).
- Next indicate who received the e-mail and the date it was sent.
- Finally, indicate the medium of publication ("E-mail").

Blog Entry

Gordon, Noël. "New Senate Bill Would Help End HIV Discrimination." *HRC Blog*. Human Rights Campaign, 11 Dec. 2013. Web. 19 Jan. 2014.

- Include the person who wrote the blog entry, the title of the blog entry, the name of blog itself, the blog's sponsor or publisher, the date the blog was posted, the medium of publication, and the date you accessed the blog.
- If the person writing the blog uses a screen name, begin the entry with that.
- If the person uses a screen name and his or her actual name, open the entry with the screen name followed by the person's real name in brackets.

Online Reference Work

"AIDS." *Encyclopaedia Britannica Online*. Encyclopaedia Britannica, 2011. Web. 16 Jan. 2014.

- Begin the entry with the name of the author.
- If the name is not given, begin with the title of the entry in the reference work.
- Include the name of the reference work (in italics), the publisher's name, and the date of publication (use "n.d." if the date of publication is unknown).

Sample MLA-Style Works Cited List

Begin the works cited list on a separate sheet of paper at the end of your essay. Centered at the top, write "Works Cited" and then double-space before you begin listing your entries. Entries are alphabetized by the author's last name or by the first key word in the title if there is no author. The first line of each entry begins on the left margin, and all subsequent lines of each entry are indented one-half inch. The entire list is double-spaced.

Works Cited

"AIDS." *Encyclopaedia Britannica Online*. Encyclopaedia Britannica, 2011. Web. 16 Jan. 2014.

"AIDS: Education Cuts the Toll." *Business Week* 5 Dec. 2005: 112. *Academic Search Premier*. Web. 1 July 2014.

Alexander, Jane. Telephone interview. 16 June 2014.

Bethell, Tom. "The African AIDS Epidemic Is Exaggerated." *Responding to the AIDS Epidemic*. Ed. Daniel A. Leone. Detroit: Greenhaven P, 2006. 18-22. Print.

Broadhead, Robert S., and Douglas D. Heckathorn. "AIDS Prevention Outreach among Injection Drug Users: Agency Problems and New Approaches." *Social Problems* 41.3 (1994): 473-95. Print.

Chase, Marilyn. "Panel Suggests a 'Peace Corps' to Fight AIDS." *Wall Street Journal* 20 Apr. 2005: B1+. Print.

"Children and AIDS." *New York Times* 22 Feb. 2005, natl. ed.: 16. Print.

Cohen, Ann, and Jack M. Gorman, eds. *Comprehensive Textbook of AIDS Psychiatry*. New York: Oxford UP, 2008. Print.

Edwards, John. "Re: AIDS Sources." Message to author. 31 July 2013.

    E-mail.

Fan, Hung Y., Ross F. Conner, and Luis Villarreal. *AIDS: Science and*

    Society. 5th ed. Sudbury: Jones and Bartlett, 2007. Print.

Kalichman, Seth, et al. "HIV Treatment Beliefs and Sexual Transmission

    Risk Behaviors among HIV Positive Men and Women." *Journal of*

    Behavioral Medicine 29.5 (2006): 401-10. Print.

Patton, Cindy. "'With Champagne and Roses': Women at Risk from/in

    AIDS Discourse." *Women and AIDS*. Ed. Corinne Squire. London:

    Sage, 1993. 165-87. Print.

Shadlen, Kenneth C. "The Political Economy of AIDS Treatment:

    Intellectual Property and the Transformation of Generic Supply."

    International Studies Quarterly 51.3 (2007): 559-81. *Academic*

    Search Complete. Web. 5 July 2013.

Squire, Corinne. *AIDS Panic*. New York: Routledge, 1997. Print.

---. *HIV in South Africa: Talking about the Big Thing*. London:

    Routledge, 2007. Print.

CREDITS

Bauerlein, Mark. "Generation Text." Reprinted with permission of America Press, Inc., © 2009. All rights reserved. For subscription information, call 1.800.627.9533 or visit www.americamagazine.com.

Chan, Sarah. "Humanity 2.0? Enhancement, Evolution and the Possible Futures of Humanity." Published by EMBO, July 2008. Copyright © 2008 by European Molecular Biology Organization. Reprinted by permission.

Chesbrough, Ron. "From *Animal House* to *Big Brother:* Student Privacy and Campus Safety in an Age of Accountability." Copyright © 2008. Reprinted with authorization from Magna Publications. www.magnapubs.com.

Ellis, Lee. "Understanding Your Leadership Balance." Reprinted by permission of Leadership Freedom LLC®. Lee Ellis is president of Leadership Freedom LLC®, a leadership and team development company.

Klann, Gene, and Cartwright, Talula. "A Question of Leadership: Is Leadership More an Art or More a Science?" from *Leadership in Action*, Vol. 24, Issue 1, pp. 12–13. Copyright © 2004. Used by permission.

Kom, Sandra Y. L. "Academic Freedom vs. Academic Justice." © 2014 The Harvard Crimson, Inc. All rights reserved. Reprinted with permission.

Krimsky, Sheldon. "On Designer Babies." Reprinted by permission from Sheldon Krimsky, Tufts Medicine. Published by Tufts University School of Medicine. Copyright © 2013.

LaBossiere, Michael. "Academic Freedom vs. Academic Justice" in *A Philosopher's Blog*. Reprinted by permission from Michael LaBossiere. Copyright © 2014 by Michael LaBossiere.

Misner, Josh. "A New Definition of Leadership." Originally published by TheHuffingtonPost.com, Inc., March 21, 2014. Copyright © 2014 by Josh Misner. Reprinted by permission from Josh Misner.

Moore, Patrick. "Hard Choices." Reprinted by permission from Patrick Moore, Hard Choices. Copyright © 1995 by Patrick Moore.

Selgelid, Michael. "A Moderate Approach to Enhancement" originally appeared in *Philosophy Now*, 91. © Michael Selgelid, 2012. Used with permission of Michael Selgelid.

Wechsler, Henry. "Getting Serious about Binge Drinking." Reprinted by permission from Henry Wechsler, *The Chronicle of Higher Education*. Copyright © 1998 by Henry Wechsler.

INDEX